PEACE, IN DEED
Essays in Honor of Harry James Cargas

SOUTH FLORIDA STUDIES IN THE HISTORY OF JUDAISM

Edited by
Jacob Neusner
Bruce D. Chilton, Darrell J. Fasching, William Scott Green,
Sara Mandell, James F. Strange

Number 162
PEACE, IN DEED
Essays in Honor of Harry James Cargas

edited by
Zev Garber and Richard Libowitz

PEACE, IN DEED

Essays in Honor of Harry James Cargas

edited by

Zev Garber and Richard Libowitz

Scholars Press
Atlanta, Georgia

PEACE, IN DEED
Essays in Honor of Harry James Cargas
edited by
Zev Garber and Richard Libowitz

Publication of this book was made possible by a grant from the Tisch Family Foundation, New York City. The University of South Florida acknowledges with thanks this important support for its scholarly projects.

Library of Congress Cataloging in Publication Data
Peace, in deed : essays in honor of Harry James Cargas / edited by Zev
    Garber and Richard Libowitz.
              p.   cm. — (South Florida studies in the history of Judaism ;
    no. 162)
        Includes index.
        ISBN 0-7885-0497-5 (alk. paper)
        1. Holocaust, Jewish (1929–1945)—Moral and ethical aspects.
    2. Ethics in the Bible. 3. Judaism—Relations—Christianity—1945–
    4. Christianity and other religions—Judaism—1945– 5. Cargas,
    Harry J.   I. Cargas, Harry J.   II. Garber, Zev, 1941–
    III. Libowitz, Richard, 1948–   . IV. Series.
    D804.3.P39   1998
    940.53'18—dc21   98-41123
                                                      CIP

Printed in the United States of America
on acid-free paper

∞

"[H]eaven and earth (is called) to witness that whether it be Gentile or Israelite, man or woman, slave or handmaid, according to the deeds which one does, so will the Holy Spirit rest on him/her."

Tanna De Vei Eliyahu

Our beloved friend and colleague, Harry James Cargas, died suddenly and unexpectedly on August 18, 1998. Harry was a man of uncompromising decency and catholic interests, counting friends in the worlds of academe, literature and sports. Informed of the completion of this text just three weeks before his passing, Harry was excited by the list of authors and was looking forward to reading their contributions. Intended as a tribute, *Peace, In Deed* must now also serve as a memorial to a true *mensch*, a devout post-Auschwitz Catholic about whom the words of the traditional Jewish *Siddur* hold true:

"Mark the innocent man and behold the upright; for the latter end of that man is peace. In the way of righteousness is life and in the pathway thereof there is no death. The Lord sets free the soul of his servants; and none that take refuge in Him shall be condemned. And the dust returns to the earth as it was, but the spirit returns to God, who gave it."

May his memory be for a blessing.

TABLE OF CONTENTS

Aftermath

Reflections for Harry

Foreword

Harry James Cargas is a person of historical importance for having taken into his very bones, as a Christian, the horrifying mystery of how persons could profess love of Jesus Christ, as did most Nazis, whose symbol was a cross, and yet commit a crime as merciless as the extermination of Europe's Jews. Every word he writes or speaks is somehow atonement, which he knows cannot help at all, for the deafness of so many others to the Sermon on the Mount.

When we met some twenty years ago, at a Congress in Vienna of PEN, the international writers' organization founded after World War One, he reminded me of yet another Roman Catholic writer who suffered painful remorse for the inhumanity of others, who was Heinrich Böll, a winner of the Nobel Prize for Literature.

While in Vienna, Harry and I, an hereditary atheist, and the Southern novelist Borden Deal, an apostate Baptist now regrettably dead, formed what proved to be a most durable and amusing and rewarding friendship. There was never any doubt as to which of us was the most virtuous. "Father Cargas," as we were quick to name him, is the most morally graceful man I ever knew.

Kurt Vonnegut

Preface

Rabbi Simeon said there are three crowns, the crown of Torah, the crown of priesthood, and the crown of kingship, but the crown of a good name excels them all (*Avot* 4:13). Harry James Cargas has long borne the crown of a good name with his unique admixture of leadership, perception, sensitivity and wit, in recognition of which we, his friends and colleagues, offer this *Festschrift* in his honor. It is published in his 66th year, which also marks the occasion of his retirement as Professor of Literature and Language at Webster University in St. Louis (Summer 1998).

Harry James Cargas was born in Detroit, Michigan, on June 18, 1932. His formal education includes B.A. and M.A. degrees from the University of Michigan and a Ph.D. from St. Louis University. In his distinguished professional and scholarly career, he has given lectures at more than 200 colleges and universities in the United States and abroad. He has served as a host, commentator and producer of television and radio talk shows, including the commentaries he has broadcast for 24 years on KWMU, Missouri Public Radio. He has written more than 2600 articles on a truly catholic range of topics, for the *National Catholic Reporter*, *Negro American Literary Forum*, *Commonweal*, *Christian Century*, *Jewish Spectator*, *Cross Currents*, *LA Times*, *New York Times* and a host of other publications. He is a columnist for *Limelight* (a St. Louis Black newspaper) and *Catholic Messenger* (Belleville, IL), while his editorial positions include associate and founding editor of *Holocaust and Genocide Studies*. He is also the only Catholic ever appointed to the International Advisory Board at Yad Vashem, the Holocaust Memorial Center in Jerusalem.

Professor Cargas has written numerous scholarly essays and has authored and edited more than 34 books, including *Conversations with Elie Wiesel*, *Exploring Your Inner Self*, *Religious Experience and Process Theology*, *When God and Man Failed: Non-Jewish Views of the Holocaust*, *Contemporary Christian Meditations*, *Voices of the Holocaust*, *Shadows of Auschwitz*, *The Holocaust: An Annotated Bibliography*, *English as a Second Language*, *Encountering Myself*, *and U.S. Holocaust Scholars Write to the Vatican*. His repertory includes a balanced criticism on the Church and the Shoah, as contained in his *Reflections of a Post-Auschwitz Christian* (1989), within which he explores the failure of Christianity in the mid-twentieth century. A personal, moral statement addressing critical issues for Christians, particularly Roman Catholics, *Reflections* dares non-Jews to make the Holocaust a watershed event in their thinking about Judaism and their relations with Jews. Cargas poses painful questions and draws difficult conclusions, proposing specific actions both for individuals and the institutional church. In seventeen essays, he evokes a rare honesty and immediacy, shedding light on the Shoah from a Christian perspective while defining Christian-Jewish relations.

As we ponder the role played by classical Christian "teaching of contempt" towards the Jews and Judaism and its theological contribution to the murder of European Jewry, we become increasingly certain that Cargas' challenge sets the right agenda for Church-Jewish relations today. At the close of the century of the Shoah, the Roman Catholic Church—and a number of Protestant denominations, large and small—have begun to take the necessary steps to recognize that Christianity is neither superior to nor a replacement of Judaism. Converting the "teaching of contempt" to the "teaching of reconciliation" is the reality of *Peace, In Deed*—Harry James Cargas' signatory statement. It is with the guidance of that spirit that the contributors to this volume reflect and write. For all the right reasons, we come to honor this man for all seasons.

To the contributors, we offer a hearty *todah rabbah*; their diverse talents and scholarship, as filtered through their own particular specialties, are greatly appreciated. Their contributions have been kept intact, despite the emendations necessary to ensure editorial conformity. We wish to thank Susan Garber for her help in drawing up the index and Sue Libowitz for her patience during many late evenings at the computer. Finally, we are indebted to Professor Jacob Neusner, Editor of the South Florida Studies in the History of Judaism, for his support in the publication of this book.

Zev Garber   Richard Libowitz
June 1998   Tammuz 5758

ANOTHER TIME, ANOTHER PLACE
Nechama Tec

Harry James Cargas, through his intellectual and spiritual integrity, has helped to keep the field of Holocaust Studies on a high moral plane. I would like to pay tribute to Harry James Cargas, a valuable scholar, highly principled individual and loyal friend, by sharing a moral, and previously untold, Holocaust story.

It happened at another place and another time. The place was western Belorussia, previously a part of eastern Poland and now a part of the country known as Belarus. Much of this region is covered by huge forests, some of which are jungle-like, swampy, partly inaccessible to humans, and even less accessible to man-made vehicles. During the German occupation, western Belorussia became the center of Soviet partisan activities and an important refuge for thousands of prospective Nazi victims, especially Jewish ghetto escapees.

The time was September, 1943; the liquidation of the Lida ghetto was taking place. As Hannah was being forcefully separated from her husband, she heard him whisper: "You and the baby must live. Save yourself, run!"

Not quite sure how it came about, with an infant daughter in her arms, Hannah found herself on a deserted country road heading toward a farm owned by a Belorussian friend. She walked for hours, cautiously avoiding people, hardly stopping for rest. Only when the day was coming to an end did she dare to knock at the familiar hut. Though glad to see the mother and child, the Belorussian woman was scared. Dusk might not have concealed the fugitives' arrival. Did anyone see them enter the hut? If neighbors caught sight of the uninvited guests, denouncement and death could follow. Such punishment would not only involve the Jewish fugitives but also the entire host family. This was the German law.

Indeed, early the next morning, a kind neighbor sounded the alarm. There was talk among the villagers that ghetto runaways were hiding on the farm. Someone was likely to report to the authorities. Hannah and the baby had to go.

On leaving the village, Hannah stayed close to the edge of the woods. From time to time, she would enter a peasant hut to ask for food and shelter. Some people fed her and let her rest a while. Others gave her food but refused to let her in. Still others angrily chased her away. None wanted to keep her. Those who had shown some compassion advised Hannah to go deep into the forest and search for the Bielski partisans, a Jewish group that was known for accepting all fugitives regardless of age, sex or health. But no one could tell her where the Bielski partisans were.

As the refusals to aid continued to multiply, Hannah followed the suggestion of the well-wishers. Now, inside the forest, she continued to walk, her destination unknown. At night, the branches offered only a semblance of warmth. Cold prevented sleep from coming and deprived her of much needed rest. Soon, the little food she had was gone. Unaccustomed to the woods, Hannah had a hard time finding the nourishment which was a natural part of the surroundings. Neither the berries and mushrooms she had managed to collect, nor the dew from the leaves satisfied her hunger and thirst. The baby was quiet. Perhaps she was too weak to cry, as she sucked on her mother's dry breasts?

Hannah lost track of time, distinguishing only between night and day. Her early resolve to stay alive was deserting her. Death, she began to feel, might be the only solution. But to die painlessly, she needed help. There was no one around and she did not know how to get out of the forest.

Exhausted, dejected, she spent more and more time leaning against a tree, listening, hoping and dreading at the same time. During one of these rests, her ears registered the breaking of branches, followed by a rustling of leaves and a voice: "Who is there? Don't move. If you do I will shoot!" Spoken in Russian, the words had a familiar tinge. Could the man be Jewish? Without bothering to answer her own question, Hannah heard herself say in Yiddish: "I am Hannah Rabinowicz from Lida. I escaped during an 'Aktion' with my baby." A reassuring answer came in Yiddish. "I am here to help you, don't be afraid." Then Hannah faced a man, an acquaintance from Lida. Next to him appeared another man, a stranger. Both carried rifles. They introduced themselves as Bielski partisan scouts, on a mission to find Jews who were in need of protection.

Bewildered, Hannah had a hard time grasping what it all meant. Even the bread and water they gave her, she took without any show of enthusiasm. She let the men lead her to the Bielski encampment. There, following the custom, Hannah was introduced to the commander of the partisan unit, the charismatic Tuvia Bielski. He looked like God to her. For many, many years, the images from this first meeting stayed with her. Hannah delighted in retelling how Tuvia greeted her with tears in his eyes. He wanted to know all that had happened to her. He listened closely and, when she had finished, with a deep sigh he said to no one in particular: "Such a pity that so few can come."

Accepted into the Bielski partisan unit, Hannah and her baby survived the war. These two cases can be multiplied by hundreds. Whoever reached this Jewish partisan unit, and by whatever means, was automatically admitted. All those who came were entitled to food and shelter. At first, the Bielski partisan unit led a nomadic existence, moving from place to place. Later on, the people built a stable camp, a "shtetl", deep in the Nalibocka forest. Suspended in a hostile environment, under the command of Tuvia Bielski, the group continued to expand as it cooperated with different Soviet partisan groups.

By 1944, when the Bielski detachment was liberated by the Red Army, it had grown to over 1200 individuals. Most of them were older people, women and children, precisely the kind of fugitives whom hardly any other partisan group was likely to accept and who therefore had the least chance to make it in the forest. Assuming the dual role of rescuers and fighters, with time the Bielski partisan unit became the largest armed rescuer of Jews by Jews during World War II.

AMERICANS WHO CARED
Pierre Sauvage

Do the righteous Gentiles of the Holocaust have spiritual descendants? I am sometimes asked about the children of the rescuers: What is left? What, if anything, has been passed on?

It is a wonderful question, to which I do not know the answer. I have an *impression*, and that is that yes, something was passed on. To begin with, this makes sense. A characteristic of many of the rescuers I've known is the respect they had for parental figures, who had set some sort of a moral example. How could their children not feel the same and not similarly be shaped by the values their parents put into action?

And what has any of this to do with my friend Harry James Cargas? Simply this: if the righteous Gentiles of the Holocaust have spiritual descendants they are Christians like Harry James.

I have to admit that I'm not entirely comfortable making this affirmation. I'm not sure Harry James has ever really been put to the test. I know that I certainly don't have to go into hiding again for the foreseeable future, at least not for any reason connected to my being Jewish.

But should that day happen in America, I might well find my way to St. Louis and get in line outside Harry James' house. Moreover, should he have by then moved on to the greener pastures of immortality, I trust that he will feel compelled to resurrect once again and do what needs to be done.

My confidence about him has little to do with his revolutionary theological stances—although this is fertile ground for the future, and I do not minimize its importance. My feelings have even less to do with his scholarship about the Holocaust. I have absolutely no confidence whatever that Holocaust scholars would act any better in *that* sort of a pinch than anybody else. Indeed, to the extent that they are academics, the odds are that they would act worse. "It takes a great deal of elevation of thought to produce a tiny elevation of life," said my other friend Ralph Waldo Emerson, who said much about these things that needs to be said.

Harry James, the reasons I'm going to be knocking on your door should the need arise is: a) the somewhat public pressure that I am putting on you now increases the chances that you'll open up; b) as a further inducement, I promise to introduce you to Elie Wiesel; and c) my judgment of such things is based above all on my sense of people's character. And on that limb, I'm willing to venture, at least rhetorically.

But you are too self-effacing a presence for me to go on much longer about you. Instead it seems highly relevant to share some further thoughts about somebody I know you find interesting, the only American recognized as a righteous Gentile by Yad Vashem: Varian Fry.

An anecdote. Because my *decadial* documentary—I've just coined the word, there is no familiar English word covering the span between annual and centennial—will be *And Crown Thy Good: Varian Fry and the Emergency Rescue Committee*, I have a vested interest in the statement that Fry is the only American to have been honored thus far by Yad Vashem. In fact, I have even repeated it, knowing full well when I did so that the wife of the assistant pastor of Le Chambon-sur-Lignon, Mildred Theis, who was honored by Yad Vashem along with the remarkable Edouard Theis, hailed from Ohio...

Last summer, during a visit to Le Chambon for the services in honor of the late Magda Trocmé, I ran into one of the Theis' eight daughters, and admitted my verbal slovenliness. "You know what," she said—quite literally, as she is American—"my mother had given up her American citizenship when she was honored by Yad Vashem." So there is a sense in which it can continue to be stated that Varian Fry is the only American to have been formally recognized as a righteous Gentile...

Every time I speak on *Yom Hashoah*, I begin with the same words: I am a Jew born in Nazi-occupied Europe in 1944. And that that means that much of my family was humiliated, tortured and murdered—while the world watched.

Nobody's ever challenged me on those words. Nobody wants to nit-pick in such a context. But when I say "the world," I don't exclude America. Indeed, there was an *American* experience of the Holocaust too, although we either don't know it or pretend otherwise.

And yes, of course, there were some Americans who cared. Like good people everywhere and at any time, *they* are the ultimate challenge to us. If they knew what was going on, why didn't we? If they understood what was going on, why didn't we? If they tried to do something about what was going on, why didn't we?

As it happens, the story I am now addressing is, in a sense, yet another chapter in my own life, although my life before I was born, the life of my parents after they left Paris ahead of the Nazis and fled, like so many others, to

France's second city, the bustling port of Marseilles in the still unoccupied Southern zone of France.

Marseilles in 1940-1941 was, to make a movie reference that many of us resonate to, the real "Casablanca." As you and your fellow scholars know, Harry, as Europe had fallen, many Jews and anti-Nazis made their way to France; when France fell, many Jews and anti-Nazis made their way to Marseilles, the port, feeling, as one of them put it, like rats on a sinking ship.

If my parents also felt that way when they were in Marseilles they never admitted it to me. Since my parents went so far as not even to tell me they were Jewish, that I was Jewish, until I reached the age of 18, everything that concerns my parents' life has always had and probably always will have an air of mystery to it.

Thus, when I was doing research for my documentary "Weapons of the Spirit" years ago and stumbled on a book, a memoir, called *Crossroads Marseilles 1940*, I was absolutely fascinated by it. It told an incredible story, which I'd never, heard before, by an obviously remarkable woman, and touched on aspects of my parents' life about which I knew next to nothing.

The author of the memoir was a woman named Mary Jayne Gold, who became a close friend and who died in October 1997. A sloppy AP obituary stated that Varian Fry had helped *her* start the rescue effort in Marseilles, which would have given her no end of amusement...

Mary Jayne was not Jewish, despite her last name. In fact, she was an American blueblood. Not long before she died, she told me with delight that she had been asked to join the Colonial Dames or some such organization whose ancestors have to have set foot in the colonies practically the second after Columbus did. And she qualified.

In the summer of 1940, after years of living it up in Europe in the 30s— not a difficult feat considering the fact that she was beautiful, an heiress, and flew her own plane from capital to capital—Mary Jayne found her way to the American Consulate in Marseilles not long after France fell to the Nazis, in order to proceed with the formalities of going home.

Waving what then seemed an incredible document—an American passport—Mary Jayne self-consciously made her way through people who had been standing forlornly for hours and hours and hours outside of what was, as it happens, a pretty little castle in a park. The world had become small for these refugees, but America still seemed big.

Mary Jayne Gold soon learned that there was something to do in Marseilles, and she stayed on for a year, her path having crossed that of two men, one of them the aforementioned fellow American, who had himself just arrived from New York on his singular mission. Mary Jayne would come to view that year in Marseilles as the only important one in her life. She wrote the following in *Crossroads Marseilles 1940*:

> I was not there to witness the worst, only the beginning, and even then I was sometimes embarrassed into a sort of racialism—like being ashamed of belonging to the human race. Fortunately, at the time of which I speak, not one of us could know what was coming. In our ignorance of the limits of human depravity there was time for fun and laughter. That is why when I try to recapture and write about what happened and what I saw, it turns out to be a series of double exposures, and I have to take them apart and fit them together again to make sense. One series is snapped through my 1940-41 lens, pictures that often stand out in photographic clarity of incident and detail. In the other series, the negatives are superimposed on original ones, colored by the stark statistics, the newsreels of atrocities then yet to come, and all the history of those dark years just ahead.

What sort of a man was Varian Fry? Well, in 1943, long after he'd returned to the United States, Fry for some reason attended a church service (he was not a religious man) and tore out and kept a quotation from the program. The quotation happened to be from the inescapable Ralph Waldo: "There are men who rise refreshed on hearing a threat; men to whom a crisis which intimidates and paralyzes the majority—demanding not the faculties of prudence and thrift, but comprehension, immovableness, the readiness of sacrifices—comes graceful and beloved as a bride." I have abridged this quote to give it wider circulation: "There are men to whom a crisis comes graceful and beloved as a bride."

In 1940, our bridegroom was a dapper, prep school and Harvard educated young intellectual of 32, then working as an editor. Not Jewish.

He and some people in New York had realized—as had the pastors of my birthplace of Le Chambon incidentally—that when France had signed the armistice with Germany it had agreed to turn over refugees to the Nazis. Most of these stranded refugees were anonymous, but some were not, and Fry and his friends, lovers of the arts, also realized that there were many prominent artists, intellectuals and anti-Nazi political figures who might indeed be especially vulnerable because of their relative prominence. They created an outfit which they called the Emergency Rescue Committee, which was a totally private, shoestring, volunteer effort.

Now these New Yorkers had some good contacts, including Eleanor Roosevelt, and it seemed like some special visas could be obtained despite the State Department's determined and remarkably successful efforts to block refugee immigration to the U.S. Still, somebody had to go over to Marseilles and track down the people who could be helped, do whatever was necessary—legal or illegal—in order to get them out of Vichy's clutches before it was too late, and help them in the meantime. Varian Fry, with no experience in cloak-and-dagger work whatever, volunteered to take a month's leave of absence from his job, and go to France to be the Scarlet Pimpernel that the situation required.

When Mary Jayne Gold offered to work with him, Fry was initially skeptical about this rich dilettante, but soon he found himself relying on her for some delicate missions. She also helped to subsidize the operation, allowing his A-list to expand to a B-list, or as it was dubbed, the Gold list.

As it happens, she also had an affair with a young French gangster, which created some problems. But that's a story for another time—for the movies, if I am ever able to make the necessary compromises.

There were other Americans involved in what was locally called the *Centre Américain de Secours*—the American Relief Center: Mary Jayne's buddy, the witty and intellectual Miriam Davenport Ebel; the ladies' man and adventurer Charlie Fawcett, from Virginia; the mysterious Leon Ball who disappeared in 1941. There were also French people importantly involved, and a few others from all over Europe, some of whom, such as the great economist Albert Hirschman, long ago became Americans.

The documentary will recount the extraordinary adventure that they all participated in until, after a tumultuous year, Varian's disciples lined up at the railway station to say goodbye. Fry, having finally been arrested by the Vichy authorities, was kicked out of France in August of 1941 with the complicity of the U.S. Government that had never looked upon him as anything other than a troublemaker.

In fact, in the Marseilles archives there is a still classified document which I was allowed to look at but neither copy nor even make any notes about, and that document may be the smoking gun in regard to what happened. A Marseilles police official reports the American consul had asked him to "get rid" of Fry.

What gives this whole story an additional resonance is that it was during this same period of 1940-1941 that the Nazis decided on that major change in policy. When I bring this up with audiences I sometimes ask how many of them know what I'm about to say, as I suspect that few of them do. For some reason, this change of policy doesn't get much attention. Could it be that it's because *we* have something to do with it?

After all, until that time, for all of Hitler's rantings and threats, the Nazis had never quite been able to imagine something on the grand scale of a Final Solution. As scholars know but much of the public doesn't, until that time, the policy with regard to the Jews had been one of persecution, expulsion, and theft. But not murder. I'm surprised how little significance is attributed to the fact that in October of 1940, Eichmann loaded several thousand German Jews on trains and deported them to the *west*, dumping them in Vichy France, to the consternation of the French authorities, who first protested to the Germans, then begged the United States to help out by taking in a fair share of these refugees.

Comparatively obscure as well is the fact that Assistant Secretary of State Sumner Welles prepared a response to the French Ambassador, which he submitted to Roosevelt for the President's approval. The response basically told the collaborationist French regime, with which we had good relations, to get lost, that the U.S. could not do anything more than it was doing. Welles explained to the President, who approved the response, that if the U.S. gave in to the French we would never hear the end of it, that the Germans would, in effect, be in a position to keep shoving these poor refugees down our throats. Which was true.

Perhaps my historian friends will squirm that I oversimplify, but just how wrong am I that the Nazis ultimately set in motion the Final Solution of the Jewish Question when they concluded that there weren't any viable middle-ground, temporary solutions, that the U.S. and the Western World didn't want these Jews either, that in fact, the Western world probably wouldn't care all that much?

It is with this shift in policy occurring in the background, unbeknownst to Varian Fry, Mary Jayne Gold and their friends, that this tiny group succeeded in helping to save some 2,000 people, among them, many of the artistic and intellectual luminaries of our age. Artists Marc Chagall and Max Ernst, poet André Breton, sculptor Jacques Lipchitz, harpsichordist Wanda Landowska, writers Heinrich Mann and Franz Werfel, the legendary muse Alma Mahler Werfel, philosopher Hannah Arendt, the list, Fry's list, goes on and on. Many of the names on it are obscure to most of us today, but this was the intelligentsia of Europe at the time.

The list was not quite big enough to include my parents. Although my father never told me and I'll never know precisely what happened, I have learned that he applied for help from the Committee and it would appear that my parents didn't receive it. In any event, they didn't leave. Before finding their way to Le Chambon after the Germans occupied southern France and my mother became pregnant with me, my father founded a traveling theatrical troupe which staged French medieval farces not always devoid of contemporary relevance.

Back in the States, Fry spent the war years trying to sensitize American public opinion to what was happening in Europe. In December 1942, The New Republic magazine published an extraordinary cover story: *The Massacre of the Jews*, by Varian Fry.

Earlier in 1942, Fry wrote some words he intended for his memoir of the year in Marseilles. Among his papers in a binder marked "Suppressed Material," they are the words of a caring American in 1942.

I have tried—God knows I have tried—to get back again into the mood of American life since I left France for the last time. But it doesn't work. There is only one way left to try, and that is the way I am going to try now. If I can get it all out, put it all down just as it happened, if I can make others see it and feel it as I did, then maybe I can sleep again at night, the way I used to before I took the Clipper to Lisbon. Maybe I can even become a normal human being again—exorcise the ghosts which haunt me, stop living in another world, come back to the world of America. But I know that I can't do that until I have told the story—all of it.

Those ghosts won't stop haunting me until I have done their bidding. They are the ghosts of the living who do not want to die. Go, they said, go back and make America understand, make Americans understand and help before it is too late.

I have tried to do their bidding in other and easier ways. By lecturing, writing articles, talking to friends. But it doesn't work. People don't understand. Because they don't see the whole thing, or because what they see they see distantly, impersonally. It doesn't touch them, any more than a table of statistics (...). When I think of all this, it seems incredible, macabre, even, that I should have spent some of my last few hours in New York worrying about not having a new dress shirt, and actually going over to Brooks Brothers and buying one.

Varian died alone and forgotten in 1967, a failed businessman, a failed husband, a rather lonely teacher of Latin and Greek in a preppy Connecticut high school. A few months before his death, his old comrade Mary Jayne Gold had sent Varian some cheerful greetings on a postcard. Her last words: "Well, we shared our finest hours, my friend."

Peace indeed.

LIVING THE LIVING GOOD
David Patterson

As I pondered the question of an appropriate topic for this volume honoring Harry James Cargas, a statement once made by Martin Buber came to mind: in my youth I would seek out smart people, but as I matured I searched for good people. Had the aging Buber come across Harry James Cargas, he would not have been disappointed. Harry James Cargas is many things—a brilliant scholar, a dedicated teacher, a generous friend—but of all the things that might be said of him, the most accurate is the most simply stated: he is a *good* man. While many of us may find it difficult to define exactly what a good man is or what makes a person good, those who know Harry James Cargas know something more about goodness. And so when we consider this good man, we are led to consider something more: what is the "good" that a good person exemplifies?

There is perhaps no word so ambiguous as the word *good*. We speak of a good deed, a good dog, a good time, or a good book; there is good sense, good taste, good news, and good food. Most of us want to feel good and look good; some of us even want to do good, which is often confused with doing well. Doing well generally means being successful, which in turn means *having* something: power, possessions, prestige. To be sure, in the confusion between being and having lies much of the general confusion in our thinking about the Good. While doing well may imply having something, doing good entails *being* something. And being good entails *doing* something. One point to be clarified in the remarks that follow, then, concerns the relation between being and having with respect to the Good.

A second point requiring some clarification concerns the matter of how we are to understand "the Good," with a capital **G**. Capitalizing the letter and thus elevating the word, we impart a dimension of height to our thinking about the Good. What opens up in this dimension of height is not only the Most High but also the Most Dear, in a word: the Holy. Understood as the Holy, the Good is something other than what Socrates sought through philosophical contemplation. What reveals itself here is not the Good of Greek philosophy but something that has defined a very different tradition, the tradition of Jewish

13

monotheism. It is the Good that we invoke in our prayers as *HaTov*. It is the Good that we choose when we choose life.

Our concern, then, lies not with an abstract concept but with the essence and origin of life. And so we shall finally discuss the question of how the good person exemplifies the Good that is the living Presence known as life. Is this life within us or above us? Or could it be between us? As we respond to these questions, we shall discover that the Good is not something we have or something we are; it is not even some particular deed that we do. The Good, rather, is something we live. And only where the Good is lived is there a life that is lived.

Having, Being, and Doing Good

When we die, as it is told in an old Jewish legend, we lie in the grave and wait for the Angel of Death to come to us, so that he might bring us into the presence of the Holy One, blessed be He. There is, of course, a catch: in order to draw nigh unto the Divine Presence, we must correctly answer a certain question. The question is the same for all, but for each the answer is different. And so, with his thousand eyes gazing upon us to see what we shall say, the Angel poses the fearsome question:

"What is your name?"

It seems so simple at first glance; who, after all, does not know his own name? But how, indeed, do we determine our name, the utterance that articulates the essence of who we are? It will be of no avail to explain to the Angel, "I am the one who owns this company, who bears that title, and who has made these conquests." No, to know our name is to know the names of those who name us, the names of our mother and father. It means knowing a tradition borne by those who have borne our names before; it means knowing a teaching that opens up a future and a mission. Asking our name, the Angel tries to establish something about our being that is intimately tied to our doing: knowing our name means knowing what must be done. Which is to say: our *doing* lies at the heart of our *being*. In order to come into the presence of the One who is the Good, we must decide what being good has to do with being who we are.

One key, then, to understanding the ways in which having, being, and doing are interconnected—and frequently confused—lies in the issue of how we understand who we are. Very often we identify ourselves in terms of what we have, as if to say, "The more I have, the more I am." Yes, a person may be associated with an old sweater, a favorite armchair, or a watch inherited from his grandfather. But such associations are not the same as the false sense of substance that we derive from owning expensive clothing, fancy cars, and big houses. This false sense of substance is akin to a sense of satisfaction or satiety, as though the more I consume, the more I am. Indeed, the appetite increases with the eating, so that human identity soon becomes a matter of material obesity. A wealthy man, in fact, is a man "of substance," one who "carries a lot of weight."

The pull of gravity, then, underlies much of the talk about those for whom more is better but never enough. This "more," however, is not more life; no, it is an empty mirage for which we trade our lives. Locked into the longing to have more, we never live but only hope to live. Why? Because we are trapped in the illusion that having the Good means having *it* good, which amounts to simply having the inanimate It. Possessing and being possessed by the inanimate, we seek life in lifeless matter; but this seeking, this seizing, loses what it grabs and drains the soul of life. Wherever having is confused with being, having It amounts to being It, dead and indifferent to all except the vanity of self-satisfaction. Laboring to surround ourselves with "the finer things," we strive to have it good by seizing the Good. But it always slips through our fingers; there is no having the Good. For the Good will not be had.

Clothing, cars, and houses, of course, are not the only things that we would possess. Instead of seeking such material objects, many of us are more interested in having power and prestige than in having things. Indeed, we look down our noses at those who succumb to such vulgar materialism. Like one who has donned a virtual reality helmet—and just as blind—we relish the illusion of importance that comes with the ascent to those artificial heights where we assume the smug air of pseudo-spirituality. Here the interest lies not so much in having it good as in being in a position to define and dictate the Good, one of the "higher-ups" who would displace the Most High.

The longing to be in possession of such power rests on the premise that there is no good other than what the powerful say is good. Hence there is no common humanity, no equality of human beings. Rather, every so-called human relation is reduced to a master/slave relation characterized by a constant power struggle, not only between individuals but between races, cultures, classes, and genders. To be sure, the (false) idea here is that we are utterly defined by a combination of our race, culture, class, and gender, and not by something so superstitious or unsophisticated as a spiritual good that we embrace or shun. No, according to this thinking, being good means being powerful; only the weak are in error. It is not the perpetrator or the oppressor who is in the wrong but his victim, who suffers for the sin of being weak.

When power becomes intertwined with prestige, being good means being recognized, so that, like the weak, those who fail either to win acclaim or to pay homage are in error. When someone commits the latter transgression, we indignantly declare, "Do you know who I am?" And yet as soon as this thought creeps through our minds, we are reduced to nothing and no one. This longing to have the recognition of others is a longing to be looked up to and admired, a longing to be set on high. It is a longing to be better, not in the eyes of God but in the eyes of others—not better than we are but better than others. And it manifests itself in the wish to be adored not only for our wealth or our power, but for our intelligence, our righteousness, our beauty, even our humility.

In such instances being good amounts to looking good in the eyes of as many others as possible, so that any presence that we might have had *here* is scattered like dust among the eyes out *there*. Set adrift amidst those admiring eyes, we frantically search for our own reflection. But soon we tumble into the abyss of that mirror and fade into an unreal image. In that instant the first question put to the first human being, the question emblematic of all human being, struggles to make itself heard: Where are you? And it reverberates in the two questions put to Cain: Where is your brother? And: What have you done? Blinded by our own reflection, we are blind to our brother. Blind to our brother, we have a hand in his death.

Being there for another means doing something for another. And only in the midst of doing something for another is our identity established. For only in such doing can a person establish himself as one who is irreplaceable: only I can open this door, offer this word of kindness, give this pint of blood here and now. In the contexts of this doing, the other person is not to be possessed, dominated, or won over. He is to be helped: to be my brother's keeper is to be my brother's servant. And so in *this* moment of *this* helping we leave off with the project of seizing power and possessions, of setting ourselves on high, to situate the other person in a position above our own, more dear than our own.

This "more dear" opens up something more than human within the human. For it opens up a Most Dear, One who is infinitely dear, within human finitude. It is a trace of the divine, a dimension of the Holy. Once the Holy is added to the Good, being good becomes a matter of being *for the other*. Only in this way do we take on significance: by becoming a sign of the depth and the dearness of the other human being. Only by thus situating the other human being in a position of height can we catch a glimpse of the Most High. Only when that dimension of height opens up can we create an opening in the fabric of indifferent being through which the Good might find its way into the world.

The Height of the Holy

In the beginning God created the heavens and the earth—the heavens first and then the earth, as if to say, "Let there be height," before He declared, "Let there be light." Turning to the Torah for His blueprint, God began His creation with the dimension of height; for this dimension confers significance upon the light that comes into being prior to the creation of the luminaries of the heavens.

Signifying the sense that belongs to truth, meaning, and direction, the height of the Holy is what might be termed "the signifyingness of signifi-cation." It makes possible the utterance of the *ki tov*, the "it is good," that sanctifies creation. The tale of Creation does not begin with the fabrication of matter out of nothing; contrary to the *ex nihilo* thinking, the Creation recounted in the Scripture begins with a creation of the Good not out of nothing but out of God's very Being, out of the Being of *HaTov*. It begins with the creation of height from within the Most High. Without the revelation of this height that belongs to the Most High, everything below is indeed reduced to a struggle for power, possession, and prestige.

This dimension of height is revealed to us through God's commandments, the *mitzvot*, which are not only commandments but are good *deeds*. And they are *good* deeds not because we have chosen the Good but because the Good has chosen us prior to all our choosing. When the Angel of Death asks us our name, he does not ask who we have chosen to be; he asks whether we have become who we were chosen to become. This having been chosen beforehand is precisely what makes the choice between good and evil *matter*. Our freedom, then, does not lie in the freedom to choose between good and evil—which would wrongly suggest that even in choosing evil we remain free. No, it lies in our having been already chosen by the Good, chosen from a time immemorial, that is, from the womb. For this having been chosen is what lends meaning and direction to our choosing, thus making our freedom meaningful, something other than mere caprice, a play for power, or a cultural curiosity.

By whom are we chosen, and for what? We are chosen by the Good for the Good, chosen by God for the child of God, for the widow, the orphan, and the stranger. Which means: we are chosen to declare in word and in deed the chosenness of all, to affirm with gratitude and rejoicing a life not of empty success and vain pleasure but of sacred truth and profound meaning. Only a life laden with meaning is one in which we may rejoice and for which we can be grateful. When we lose sight of the Most High, we are left to grabbing our enjoyment whenever we can and counting what lucky stars we have. Enjoyment, however, no more resembles rejoicing than being lucky resembles being blessed. We sit back and enjoy, but we rise up to rejoice; we grin and nod at being lucky, but we sing songs of praise and thanksgiving at being blessed.

If being chosen means being blessed, being blessed means being commanded. That is why in our prayers we declare that God has not only commanded us but has sanctified us with His commandments. And that makes the *mitzvot* far more than rules to follow: a *mitzvah* is a portal through which the Most Dear enters our lives, so that we do not live in the shadows, like Plato's cave dwellers, but in the light of the Holy. A *mitzvah* is a prayer in the form of a deed, a prayer through which we are commanded ever more profoundly by our very action, in a calling of deep unto deep. Greek philosophy knew nothing of this calling. And there is no deeper difference between Athens and Jerusalem in their concern for the Good than the difference in their concern for prayer. Indeed, whereas the Greeks produced no major treatise on prayer, the Talmud begins with the question of when one may say the *Shema*.

Further, while Athens places its accent on a contemplation of the Good that removes us from the world, Jerusalem emphasizes the good deed that sanctifies the world. This sanctification is what makes the deed into a form of prayer. To be sure, the deed is the first form of prayer, the first attempt to hear the summons from on high. Here we catch a glimpse of the mystery behind the assertion, "We shall do and we shall hear" (Exodus 24:7). Because our doing is a response to the Holy, it arises from the Holy One; because it is sanctified from on high, it enables us to hear the injunction of the Holy One. Our realization of the dearness of the other person, then, arises not prior to but in the midst of the act of loving kindness performed for him. As realization breeds realization, we soon discover that the other is not only dear but is infinitely dear, which, in turn leads to the realization of an infinite responsibility. The infinite scope of that responsibility cannot be thought in a moment of contemplation. But it can be acted upon. The question put to Cain is not "What have you contemplated?" but "What have you done?"

Recall in this connection that powerful scene near the end of "Schindler's List" when, surrounded by the hundreds of Jews he has saved, Schindler gazes upon his car and cries, "The car! Why did I keep the car? It would have bought ten more lives!" Through eyes informed by his actions Schindler sees what is signified by the two scenes in color that frame the film, at the beginning and near the end: the scenes of the Sabbath observances. He sees what he saw when he saw the child in red, in *adom*: he sees the *adam*, the human being, through whom the Holy shows itself.

Like Schindler, as we offer help, we see what is at stake in helping. Seeing what is at stake, we see that we have not yet offered enough. Where the height of the Holy opens up, the debt increases in the measure that it is paid. Where doing good is concerned, we are never quits with our neighbor. So we are overwhelmed by a "not yet" that accompanies the Good. But without this "not yet" we are truly nothing more than dust and ashes scattered to the winds.

This "not yet" is a definitive feature of the height that belongs to the Holy. Just as our being derives its sense from the dimension of height, so do our lives take on meaning in the contexts of the yet-to-be. To have meaning is to have direction, and to have direction is to move toward a horizon where we have yet to arrive. Memory, then, becomes not only a memory *for* the future but, in a sense, a memory *of* the future. It is a mindfulness of the task that we have yet to engage; of the truth beyond us that calls us by name; of who we shall have been, in the light of what we are in the process of becoming. The height of the Holy, therefore, has a bearing on the identity issues discussed above. If the Holy can show itself as an infinite responsibility, it can also resound in an eternal question, whose secret is couched in the silence of the future: What is your name?

By now we can see that the dimension of height belonging to the Holy is not physical but metaphysical, not spatial but spiritual. Therefore the "above" that characterizes this height is also a "within." And yet, because it turns on a doing that is the basis of our relation to another, it is a "beyond" that is also a "between," that space into which we move when we draw nigh unto the Holy by way of the human. Determining who we are *already*, this movement toward the other is a movement of return, a *teshuvah*, which means not only "return" but also "response" and "redemption." It is a kind of *aliyah*, a movement of ascent, in which we answer with our lives for all there is to hold dear in life. That accountability to the One who is above me is what imparts meaning to my response to one who stands before me.

But where, one may ask, does love fit in? Does it not make the relation to the other meaningful? Love does not fit in, nor can it impart meaning to human relation, if it is understood to be nothing more than a feeling or an emotion. Christians declare that God is love, but surely they do not mean to suggest that God is a feeling. Feelings abide within us, but we dwell within our love; feelings float around inside an individual, but love arises between two. If love is holy, then it comes from the Holy One; if it comes from the Holy One, then it is commanded. Indeed, perhaps God is better understood not as love but as the commandment to love. If God is the commandment to love, then the Holy lies in doing, and not in feeling. Hence God does not ask Cain, "What do you feel?" but, again, "What have you done?"

So understood, love is not something present in us but something or someone into whose presence we must enter. How? Through the *mitzvah*. The good deed is a portal not only through which the Holy becomes present in the world but through which we become present before the Holy, where we answer with our lives for our lives. Here the Holy manifests itself not as an idea or a category but as a living presence, whose life inheres in the life of the Good.

The Life of the Good

In the Torah we are taught that God places before us good and evil, life and death, and that He enjoins us to choose life (Deuteronomy 30:19). Choosing life, we do not choose merely to be alive—we choose to affirm the holiness of a life that has its origin in the Holy One, in the One who is called Torah, in the Torah that is called Life. Making this choice does not mean that we no longer pass away from the earth. Rather, it means that in choosing life we understand death to be part of the process of sanctifying life, the testimonial outcome of a life steeped in the Good. For a human being, then, death is not a natural phenomenon that befalls him after three score and ten years but part of a task that he is summoned to engaged from the moment he is called into being.

We have an important teaching from the Midrash in this connection. During the first five days of the Creation (with the exception of the second day) God pronounced His labor to be good; but on the sixth day He declared it to be **very** good. Commenting on the difference, Rabbi Meir maintains that this "very" signifies death, a category belonging to life alone (*Bereshit Rabbah* 9:5). To choose life is to choose this "very good" that distinguishes the animate from the inanimate, a living Good from a conceptual good. Choosing this "very good" means realizing that the basis of our relation to another human being—underlying the commandment to love our neighbor—is our fear for his death. Only others lie in the cemeteries.

Choosing life over death, then, does not mean choosing to stay alive at all costs. On the contrary, it means choosing a martyrdom that attests to a good that is higher than our own survival. Left with nothing but ourselves to live for, we have nothing left to die for; with nothing to die for, we have nothing to live for. When we choose the life that is *very* good, death is situated within the contexts of the Good, as a culmination and not a negation of life. Murder is evil; in itself death is not. Standing by while people die is evil; in itself, dying is not. Thus taking death to be part of life, we begin the *Kaddish*, the prayer for the dead, with a magnification and sanctification of the Holy Name, in which all life has its origin. And we end by declaring, "Amen."

Jews do not gather to pray without saying this prayer. To be sure, the life of prayer is an essential feature in the life of the Good. We have already spoken of the *mitzvah* as a prayer in the form of a deed; there too, as in all prayer, we see the life of the Good made manifest. Why? Because it is not we alone who utter the prayer or choose the deed. No, we are *moved* to speak or to act, often in spite of ourselves. The life of the Good is revealed through the disturbance of the witness, of the one in prayer, in word and in deed. We think we pray to God, but this is not precisely the case: for the prayer itself is divine. That is why we cry out for God to open our lips each time we pray the *Amidah*. And when we pray the *Shema*, the "Hear, O Israel," who is speaking and who is being asked to heed the voice that speaks? It is God addressing us through our own mouths, pleading with us to hear His Word.

The character of Schindler from Spielberg's film once more provides us with an illustration. The measures that he takes to save lives do not arise from personal inclination or self-satisfaction. He does not *choose* to realize the sanctity of the human being—he is overwhelmed by it. Thus the saving of lives is summoned from him, in such a way that he cannot do otherwise. Something alive takes hold of Schindler; he is like a man possessed by another entity. What is it? It is life itself, which is the life of the Good: and so he comes alive by doing good. We do not decide whether this life is at work within us and beyond us any more than we decide whether our heart shall beat. That is why we are healed by the help we offer, saved by the salvation we bring.

Does this movement of the living Good mean that we have no responsibility, that it is out of our hands? No. Just the opposite: it means that every-thing is in our hands, that our responsibility is neither of our own making nor of our own choosing, and that a world rests on our every action. Because we are not free of responsibility, we are not free to choose between good and evil; we *must* choose good. That does not make it impossible to choose evil; it makes it wrong. Therefore the prayer we utter in word must be articulated in deed. If our prayers are more precious than all the sacrifices offered up by Solomon, our deeds of loving kindness are more precious than our prayers. And every bit as mysterious. For in doing good we participate in the life of the Good, in the life of the Infinite, so that the finite becomes a vessel of the Infinite, where the Infinite is manifested not as the infinitely vast but as the infinitely precious, the infinitely urgent.

Here the life of the Good unfolds in a process of transformation that may be characterized as the transformation of matter into spirit. And it is as mundane as it is mysterious. Water, dirt, and light, for example, get transformed into a stalk of wheat, which in turn gets made into a piece of bread. We take the bread, say a *motzi*, and place it in our mouths, where yet another transformation is set into motion: what had assumed the form of light, dirt, and water now takes on the form of blood, muscle, and bone. And more: it is transformed into laughter and tears, into a word or a thought, into an embrace of another being, into an act of loving kindness. That is why we pray when we eat: the act of eating is a sacred act in the life of the Good.

Or better: the act of eating *together* is a sacred manifestation of the life of the Good. Partaking of a single bread is an affirmation of a single humanity, a single divinity, a single sanctity. When we eat together, this oneness that lives in the living Good is most profoundly revealed not by our own eating but by our offering the other something to eat. The cliche "you are what you eat" does not apply to those who would join their lives to the life of the Good; rather, you are what you snatch from your own mouth and offer the other to eat. And so we realize that, if being good is tied to doing good, then the link is established in a being-for-the-other that is a doing-for-the-other. With this *for-the-other*, there opens up between two people a space in which a Third appears. And that third Presence is the living Good.

What I refer to here as "the living Good" goes by many names: Divine Presence, *Shekhinah*, Holy Ghost, and so on. The Christian Scripture declares that this Presence abides where two are gathered in its name (Matthew 18:20). The Talmud tells us that it manifests itself where two are gathered to study Torah (*Avot* 3:2). But what does it mean to be gathered in the name of the Holy One or to come together to study Torah? Here too the Talmud can help. For it teaches us that the service of Torah is greater than Torah (*Berakhot* 7b), that the deed is greater than the study (*Avot* 1:17). Which means: to study Torah is to live Torah. The *Etz Chaim*—the Tree of Life, as the Torah is called—grows in the soil of loving kindness. It lives in the doing good that constitutes being good. It lives only inasmuch as we live it, not just in this deed or that, but in our every word, thought, and gesture. Only in this living of the living Good do we have any life. To choose life is to choose the Good that has chosen us; to choose the Good is to choose the life—to live the life—that summons us.

What, then, is the Good that the good person exemplifies? It is a life lived in accordance with the first utterance of Creation—"Let there be light!"— a life lived in such a way that it transforms darkness into light. How? Through deeds of loving kindness. *Chesed*, the sages teach us, lies at the root of Creation (*Avot d'Rabbi Natan* 20a). And the essence of *chesed* lies in *doing good*. What God offers to Moses we receive not from the mouth of our Teacher, but *b'yad Moshe*, by the hand of Moses. Which means: we hear by doing. We receive the Good by living the Good, which is not a principle, an idea, or a rule to follow but is a living Presence that enables us to become present. And it manifests itself as such a Presence each time we declare, "*Hinehni!*—Here I am!" as we stand face to face with another.

This "Here I am" does not mean "Here I am in this spot" but rather "Here I am for you." Presence *here* is a movement *toward*. Thus being there means being there for another. The living Good is the being that is a being there for another; and being there for another is how we live the living Good. That is what Martin Buber was looking for when he left off with searching for smart people and began seeking out good people. And that is what those who are blessed enough to know Harry James Cargas have found.

REFLECTIONS
Shadows of the Holocaust
Leon Wells

Our past experiences cast shadows on all the happenings of our present lives. As Sigmund Freud said, "Everything new must have its roots in what was before."[1] My experiences are the shadows of the Holocaust years. John Richardson writes about Picasso, "He could never depict anything without some degree identifying with it."[2] And so it is with those of us who experienced the Holocaust.

I met Harry James Cargas when both of us were members of the U.S. Commission of the Memorial Council in Washington, D.C. It was a commission, appointed by President Carter and headed by Elie Wiesel, whose goal was the establishment of the Holocaust Museum. In 1981 I left the commission when the Presidency of the United States changed from Democrat to Republican. The newly elected President Reagan appointed his own people to the commission. A while later, when we were both speakers at a Holocaust conference, Professor Cargas told me that he had resigned from the commission and that his place was filled by the Wall Street speculator, Ivan Boesky.

I was drawn to Dr. Cargas from the first day I met him, maybe because I associated him with Joseph Kalwinski, whose family saved me during the Nazi time.[3] The Kalwinski family risked their lives to hide me, in spite of the fact that they did not know me, nor had any connection with my family.

When I escaped from the "Death Brigade," I met another escapee on the road. Koczanos was his nickname because he had a nose like a duck. His real name was Mojshe Korn, but nobody called him by this name. He took me with him to the home of Joseph Kalwinski's son, with whom he had business dealings in horses prior to the war. Koczanos assumed that because I had been an orderly in the "Death Brigade" I had a stash of valuables on me—gold teeth sifted from the ashes after the bodies were burned, or other treasures that could be found there. The S.S. came to pick up these "treasures" every evening and Koczanos was sure that I must have stolen some and concealed them—that I had escaped with a fortune. But, in truth, I had nothing; I carried no fortune on me. My only concern in the Death Brigade was the day-to-day life, I did not care if the S.S. got these valuables or not. I never considered having the need for any valuables. Even my own survival was not of paramount importance to me. I was concerned with suffering.

We all spoke of the corpses which we burned as, "they will not suffer any more," and "they are lucky to be out of it." When Koczanos found out that I had nothing and could not support myself in the hiding place (not to speak of supporting him), he wanted to be rid of me. Joseph Kalwinski took us to his own house, because we were not safe in his son's home.

During the transfer in the dark of night, Kaczanos suggested that I could easily be lost, since I did not know the neighborhood. Mr. Kalwinski, looking at me said in a low, sad voice, "How can I lose him, he looks like a baby." While everything was said in Polish, he used the English word for "baby." When we arrived at the hiding place in the basement, Mr. Kalwinski introduced us to the other twenty-one Jews hiding there, as Kaczanos and "baby." From that day on my name became Baby, even for the members of the Kalwinski family, who did not know the English meaning of the word. When one of the sons, Kazik, who was two years younger than me, came to visit me after the liberation at an apartment house in Lwow, he asked the superintendent where Baby lived, and was told that no one by that name lived there. Luckily I appeared on the scene as he was walking away.

In 1970, when Kazik visited our home in the U.S., he repeatedly told my family about the layout of the basement where we were hidden and about my reading my memoirs to him, which I had written there. He also spoke dejectedly of one of his "shadows," an incident that took place while we were all in hiding.

Kazik and a childhood friend were walking in neighboring fields when they were approached by two youngsters, a boy and a girl, emerging from the surrounding woods, begging to be hidden, obviously running away from the Nazis. He could not offer them any help, shouting to them, "get away dirty Jews." Kazik was afraid that his friend might talk about this incident, possibly casting suspicion, which could endanger the lives of all of us hiding in the basement, as well as those of his own family. Nearly thirty years later this still bothered him. The two children lay heavily on his conscience.

At the same time as this incident, Kazik's younger brother, Staszek, was eight years old. One day, German officers came to see if the farm would be suitable to house German Headquarters when they retreated from the Russian front. When Staszek made the observation that the electric clock was running during the day, his mother became frightened. She knew that we, in the hiding place, were using the electricity. The Germans did not pay any attention to the child, but Mrs. Kalwinski was very upset. During that time a twelve year old girl, being scolded by her father at the Jozefek house, ran out of the house screaming, "You are hiding Jews and I must suffer."[4] Jozefek, his wife and the twelve Jews in hiding were immediately rounded up. While the Jews were sent to the crematorium, Jozefek and his wife were hanged publicly in the center of town to show others what happens to Poles who hid Jews. They hung in the town square for 48 hours.

With this picture in mind, little Staszek, the beloved youngest child, was sent away from home. The neighbors, as well as friends, were told that Staszek was sent away because his parents feared that the area would be bombed. Staszek later told me that he had a very hard time at his new home, a few hundred miles away. The child was overworked and went hungry.

Years later, when he lived in New York, having been brought to the U.S. on scholarship and being supported by us survivors of the hiding place, he very often mentioned that he could not understand how his beloved parents could send him away and sacrifice him...a shadow that continued to color his life. In many ways Harry James Cargas reminded me of Joseph Kalwinski—not only physically, but more in kindness and humanity and his love of mankind.

A while ago I visited the Statue of Liberty with my grandchildren. In the museum, I read a plaque with the poem written by Emma Lazarus in 1883: "...Give me your tired and poor, your huddled masses yearning to be free..." As I read this noble poem which is so humane and gives such pride to Americans, I could not help recalling another shadow from my past during the Holocaust. During World War II, the people of Poland could not physically escape to the U.S. When the war started, the Jews from Nazi-occupied Poland could only escape to the East, the part occupied by Russia. Russia was the country that, in the beginning of the war, opened its borders to anyone who wanted to come in, without question. There was no interrogation about one's past, heart conditions, spots on lungs; no sponsors were needed.

One who escaped to Russia was Menachem Begin, who before the war was the head of Poland's right-wing Zionist party, "*Betar*," a strong anti-communist organization.[5] After having settled with his young wife near Vilna, Russian Lithuania, he was arrested for being a leader of an anti-communist party and put into jail with many Polish Army officers. His wife was not bothered and was able to get out of Russia and, from there, go to Palestine.

Begin was released in 1942, joined the Polish Army in Russia, and went to Palestine too. Within twelve to eighteen months after the start of the war, other escapees from Nazi-occupied territories were rounded up and shipped to the Asian part of Russia. This was right before Nazi Germany attacked Russia and occupied the rest of Poland. Dr. Yisrael Gutman and Shmuel Krakowski, both research directors of *Yad Vashem* in Jerusalem, write that the refugees from Warsaw and Lodz (Nazi-occupied territories) who reached Minsk and Moscow at the beginning of World War II, "were welcomed with music and meals. About 1,000 of such refugees returned from Russia to Nazi-occupied Poland where they were immediately arrested by the Nazis."[6] Because of the hard life in Russia and with no inkling of the fate that awaited them under Nazi occupation, very few Jews living in the Russian-occupied territories in 1941 escaped along with the Russian Army when Germany attacked Russia.

By far the majority of Polish Jews who survived the war were the Jews who returned from Russia after the war. If it were not for Russia, almost 100 percent of Polish Jewry would have perished. We, in Poland, could not have escaped to any other place. We had no choice. It was too late. After the war, there were 380,000 survivors out of the 3,300,000 Jews in Poland. Over 200,000 were returnees from Russia.[7] Another 180,000 either stayed in Russia, mostly because of intermarriage, or left with the Polish Army to fight the Nazis and thus got out to England, Palestine, Italy, etc. To have a life of opportunity, one has to live—to survive. Russia gave them that opportunity. The shadows of Russia during the war live in many of us.

After the liberation of Lvov by the Russian Army, I met Vladimir Belayev, an important journalist of the leading Russian newspaper, *Izvestia*, and a member of the Communist Politburo. He spoke to me about the concentration camps, and advised me to move to the American Zone of Germany to try to get to the U.S. He explained that while he believed in Communism and would stay in Communist Russia, it would take many years of hardship to achieve the Communist goal and, as I had already suffered enough, I should look to the future. He even gave me a pass to the border police to help me get out of Russia. I did not need his letter because I got out as a Polish citizen under the agreement of the resettlement. In 1963 he sent me his newly published book.[8]

It seems that during the von Ribbentrop-Molotov meeting there was an understanding that, when Poland was divided between Germany and Russia, certain military personnel and others who escaped to the Russian part of Poland would be returned to the German authorities. Some prisoners who were Jewish applied to the Russian NKVD (the Russian secret police) that as Jews, they should not be handed over to the Germans. From one report found after 1982, there were six camps in Russia where there were 13,891 civilian prisoners, 303 of whom were Jewish. It was less than .2 percent. Among the young officers, below the rank of Major, out of the 2,140 of whom the Germans demanded, there were 22 Jews. Did Russia send back the Jewish prisoners?

The late Dr. Philip Friedman told me about his meeting with Louis Segal, the representative of the American Zionist Jewish Labor Party. As a part of his visit, Mr. Segal met with surviving Jewish leaders, and among them Dr. Friedman, who was at that time Director of the Jewish Historical Commission of Poland. Dr. Friedman wanted to tell Mr. Segal about the Holocaust since Mr. Segal was the first Jewish representative from America that Friedman had met. Segal was not interested in Holocaust stories, he only wanted to know one thing: "Why didn't they fight?" a constant question and shadow that passes over Holocaust survivors.

I am reminded that when I was liberated by the Russian Army in 1944, I met Russian soldiers and wanted to tell them about my tragedy. I wanted to share with them, but they were not interested. They only wanted to know why I was not with the Partisans fighting the enemy. They did not care that I was only

16 years old when the Germans occupied our part of Poland. For a nineteen or twenty-year-old soldier, I was a grown person. Actually, I never knew anyone in the Partisans and was even unaware that such a group existed. But they were soldiers and their thoughts were on "fighting."

My shadows include images of post-liberation events. I am often reminded about a speech given by Joseph Rosensaft at his yearly conference of the concentration camp survivors from Bergen-Belsen. He was one of the main leaders of this group after the war. He constantly told the story of how, after the war, thousands of survivors of this camp were dying and no medical help was available to them because there was a lack of volunteer doctors. Bergen-Belsen was in the English-occupied zone of Germany. It took an excess of two weeks after liberation before approximately three hundred volunteer doctors arrived from England. There were no Jewish doctors from the U.S. or Israel. He always finished in a sad, low voice asking, "where were the Jewish doctors?" There wasn't a shortage of them. This is a painful memory of the liberation for him and also for us—the survivors listening to his speech.

I frequently read manuscripts of children who survived the Holocaust, how they were the only survivors and as such stayed with those who had hidden them—the only families that some of them knew. Some religious Jewish organizations, as well as some Zionists groups, tried to kidnap these children from the gentile families who had suffered and risked their lives to hide them. These families did not want to give the children up. No effort was made to approach this painful matter in a humane manner, to ease the pain of both children and adoptive parents. I recall reading a speech given by Rabbi Stephen Wise, head of the Jewish Congress of the Rehabilitation of European Children, September 24, 1945. More than four months after the end of the war, he announced that the World Jewish Congress was now managing a home in Switzerland for fifty children...it was estimated that there were thousands of Jewish children survivors.[9] In 1942 there was a conference about how much *Wiedergutmachung* (restitution money) to ask from the German government after the war. In this matter, planning ahead was important.

All of these thoughts came to mind after I received a letter from a nun in a monastery near Warsaw.[10] She wrote, "When I returned from the concentration camp in Poland, there was no one left and I was alone." She was not a child, but a nineteen-year-old girl. There was no home for Jewish girls, it had not been planned for. "The sisters in the monastery, four years after the war in 1949, became my family." When I sent this letter, with an introduction, to a publication which was a division of B'nai B'rith, the Board of Directors over-ruled the editor's decision to publish it. It was not considered to be positive about Judaism that a survivor became a nun. They did not express their sorrow, at least not to me, that they, too, might have been at fault for not having planned aid to survivors after the war.

Another vignette from my past was triggered by a performance of Rigoletto my wife and I attended at the Metropolitan Opera House. I knew an opera singer in the Death Brigade, where I was an inmate for five months. I never knew his real name; for us prisoners he was the "Opera Singer." I could not judge his voice since this kind of singing was strange to me. I was used to folk singing or to emotional praying. As a child I had very seldom even heard cantorial singing, so, I did not know if he had a good voice or a bad one. His most frequent arias were from Rigoletto: *"La Donna Mobile," "Qua Piu-Mail Vento Muta," "D'accento"* and Tosca's *"Svani Per Sempre Il Sogno Mio D'Amore"* and *"L'ora e fuggita e Muoio Disperato."* He was not a strong looking man, not a person to be selected for the hard work in the Death Brigade. The Nazis, being music lovers, must have selected him for his singing.

There were a variety of tasks assigned to us in the Death Brigade. The youngest of our group was the *Zahler*, the one who kept tally of the number of bodies that were exhumed from the graves to be burned. The Nazis kept an exact count in their documents of how many were buried in each grave. The *Zahler*'s count had to match the original number. The Firemaster, nicknamed *"Meshugener* (crazy) *Avrum,"* was dressed like a devil with horns, and always carried a three-pronged fork which, when not in use, rested upright in his right hand. His job was to keep up the fire on the Pyre, which burned the cadavers. He escaped with us and lived after the war in Israel.

There was also an *"Asch Kolone,"* the easiest job in the Brigade. About twenty inmates sat on low wooden tree stubs and sifted through the ashes, picking out valuables like gold teeth, rings, etc. that had not been burned with the bodies. Near the place of the *Asch Kolone* there was a large cemented area where the bones that had not burned to ashes were crushed. All ashes were afterwards scattered in the nearby fields. The Opera Singer worked in the *Asch Kolone*. He looked like a court jester and he behaved like one. He spoke to me about his daughter, saying she was in hiding and he offered her to me after the war. He spoke about her in beautiful words, "believe me you will adore her..." I never did meet her after the war. I had no real relationship with the Opera Singer and he must have spoken to others about her too. I do not know whether he even had a daughter or whether this was part of his operatic imagination. Was she Gilda to his Rigoletto? I did not ask any questions because, at that time, the less one knew the better. Information could not be tortured out of you if you didn't know it. The Opera Singer, in his early 40's, was one of the older people in our group. His singing did not ultimately save him, but it helped him evade some tortures.

Writing about the Opera Singer makes me recall the second in command of the Janowska Camp, SS man Rokita.[11] By profession he was a musician and he particularly loved Beethoven's Ninth Symphony. A leading Conservative Rabbi from Westchester once told me that he considers Beethoven to be one of the Western World's greatest humanitarians. Who could put more meaningful words to such glorious music? "Brothers of the world unite," written by Schiller, a German. At the end he added, "The greatest prophet couldn't have said more beautiful words." Rokita never killed anyone standing in front of him. He used to give his victim a piece of bread and while he ate it with full gusto, Rokita went in back of him and shot him. He never tortured his victims. Was it the music that was "ennobling?"

More than fifty years have passed since the war ended, and I still cannot make any sense of the havoc and the destruction. I can only find solace in remembering the many people who had not lost their souls, who risked their lives to help others with no material gain for themselves. They carried a sense of righteousness. Their shadows live with me too. Our hope today is that this small minority of just people continues to grow. "Let the epic of heroic deeds of love, as opposed to destruction, bear equal witness to unborn generations."[12]

1. David Balkan, *Sigmund Freud and the Jewish Mystical Tradition* (New York: Schocken Books, 1965), Introduction.
2. John Richardson, *A Life of Picasso, Vol. 2, 1907-1917* (New York: Random House, 1996).
3. Leon Weliczker Wells, *Janowska Road* (New York: Macmillan, 1963), p. 227.
4. Philip Friedman, *Their Brothers' Keepers* (New York: Crown Publishers, 1957), p. 18.
5. Yisrael Gutman and Shmuel Krakowski, *Unequal Victims: Poles and Jews During World War II* (New York: Holocaust Library, 1986), p. 310.
6. Ibid., p. 363.
7. Ibid.
8. Vladimir Belayev, *Granica w Ogniu* [Border in Fire] (Moscow, 1962).
9. Leon Weliczker Wells, *Who Speaks for the Vanquished?* (Bern/New York: Peter Lang, 1987), p. 235.
10. Leon Weliczker Wells, *Commonweal*, 1997.
11. Leon Weliczker Wells, "Living Ghosts of Concentration Camps," *New York Times Magazine*, January 26, 1964.
12. Philip Friedman, *Their Brothers' Keepers*, p. 14.

HOLOCAUST DENIAL
Tempest in a Teapot, or Storm on the Horizon?[1]
Alan L. Berger

> The very immensity of their crimes guarantees that the murderers who proclaim their innocence with all manner of lies will be more readily believed than the victims who tell the truth. Hannah Arendt[2]

In April of 1993, along with seven thousand other rain-drenched souls, I attended the dedication ceremony for the United States Holocaust Memorial Museum in Washington, D.C. The day fit the mood: somber and overcast, the low-hanging clouds ultimately burst forth in a torrent of rain. It was as if heaven itself was weeping at the memory of the Shoah. The speakers that day were eloquent; their words, heartfelt and moving, captured the pathos of the moment. Perhaps the victims' desire to bear witness to the world would, after all, come to fruition. Their warning to humanity would be heeded. Yet there were other, discordant and highly disturbing, presences that fateful day in Washington. Protestors, who were kept away from the ceremony itself, chanted slogans including "We don't buy the Holocaust lie." Others held signs reading "Germany is the real victim of World War Two."

I had been teaching the Holocaust for nearly twenty years and discussed the perverse phenomenon of denial with my students. Furthermore, I had seen these contemporary antisemites at academic conferences. However, encountering the deniers on that particular day was both chilling and enraging. In a macabre way, their presence was a ghastly perversion of the American belief—which may yet prove our undoing—that there are two sides to every issue.

Beyond the purely personal disgust at what is called in Yiddish *schmutz* (dirt or garbage), I was struck by two things. The first was the truth of Arendt's observation. Secondly, I understood, in a way that had eluded me before, three ominous facts: so-called Holocaust revisionism, which in fact is Holocaust denial, is an unrelenting attack on the very idea of reason itself;[3] next, the tactics of the deniers mercilessly reveal the moral poverty of much of moral culture; and, finally, the fact that many allegedly respectable institutions of higher education accepted denier "advertisements" in their campus newspapers reveals how much further universities must travel before their emphasis on values is on a par with their teaching of skills.

My discussion begins with a prolegomenon of sorts; discriminating types of Holocaust denial. I then address the issues of the attack on reason, the infantilization of culture, and the obtuseness of the academy in dealing with this newest incarnation of antisemitism. Hovering above yet interwoven with this, I offer some observations on what popular culture does to history. I conclude by suggesting a possible path for Holocaust educators to follow as we move inexorably into the twenty-first century.

Types of Holocaust Denial

There are two broad types of Holocaust denial; that which emerges from within the Jewish community, and that which comes from the non-Jewish world. Moreover, denial exists in a crude and sophisticated form among both Jews and antisemites. It is the sophisticated form that we should most fear. Most American Jews react strongly *against* the assertion that the Holocaust never happened. Even those with minimal knowledge understand that events during the years 1933-1945 fundamentally altered our understanding of deity, humanity, and modernity. The old certainties were no longer so certain. World War II was, after all, a clear-cut example of a "Just War." Morally, Nazism was and is an unmistakable embodiment of evil for all who have eyes to see and ears to hear. There was *then* none of the ambiguity which was subsequently to surround American efforts, two decades later, in Vietnam. Yet, denial of the Holocaust is itself undeniable.

Jewish Holocaust Denial

Within the Jewish community denial assumes one of two forms. The first is espoused by the position that claims something like, "Enough with the Holocaust! We are tired of hearing about it. And so are our friends." The not so subtle subtext of this position is, our friends may not be our friends if we make them uncomfortable with what they perceive to be our "Holocaust complex." Perhaps this is a contemporary rendition of the Jewish preoccupation with the question "What will the *goyim* think?" The second type of "in-house" denial is found in statements of rabbis and others who go to the death camps and declare that their faith and Jewish commitment are renewed by the experience.

About the first point of view, several things can be said. While the Holocaust is indeed the most written about and massively documented event in Jewish history, it is hardly an exhausted theme. For example, think of the furor over the revelations concerning the wartime roles of Switzerland and France, and the post-war records of Canada and the United States; stealing Jewish assets on the one hand, and sheltering the murderers on the other. Further, the public interest in Secretary of State Madeleine Albright's alleged ignorance of her Jewish heritage is only comprehensible against the background of the legacy of the Holocaust. On the scholarly level, it is important to note the large amount of previously unknown documents that have come to light in the wake of the collapse of the Soviet Union. This data indicates that the numbers of victims may far exceed previous estimates. Second, new interpretations are being posited that help clarify both the nature of human behavior and the distinctiveness of the *Endlosung*. For instance, Christopher Browning's book, *Ordinary Men: Reserve Police Battalion 101 and the Final Solution in Poland*, represents a significant advance over Hannah Arendt's questionable "banality of evil" thesis in seeking to understand the nature of moral—and evil— decisions. Additionally, Steven Katz's magisterial *The Holocaust in Historical Context: The Holocaust and Mass Death Before the Modern Age* reveals the unparalleled nature of the project to rid the world of its Jewish presence by noting the demographics, ideology, and *intentions* of earlier state sanctioned genocidal events.

Speaking of books, *note well* the widespread, and continuing, attention attending the publication of Daniel J. Goldhagen's *Hitler's Willing Executioners: Ordinary Germans and the Holocaust*. Regardless of what one thinks of the book's scholarship and thesis, and putting aside the historiographical debate between "intentionalists" and "functionalists," how can one account for the intensity of reaction, both pro and con, more than a half century after the event? Media hype aside, if the Shoah were an exhausted theme, who would care? Imagine, if a book appeared with the title "Attila the Hun's Willing Executioners," would we notice?

Emil Fackenheim, the distinguished philosopher whose work has significantly influenced scholarly discussion of the Shoah for nearly three decades, reported at a Jerusalem conference being accused of having a Holocaust complex. His response? Those making such accusations have a non-Holocaust complex.[4] Perhaps Elie Wiesel has said it best in observing that one Jew died two thousand years ago in Jerusalem and millions of people all over the world are still talking about it. Shall the Jewish people stop talking about the murder of six million Jews only a half-century ago?

There is also the curious phenomenon of contending that one feels a sense of Jewish renewal when visiting the death camps. The literary critic Lawrence Langer comments on the preposterousness of this position. It is itself, he attests, a form of denial. The intention of the Shoah was murder, not renewal. In Langer's phrase, the Jews were doomed. There is no renewal from doom. To speak otherwise is implicitly to deny the reality of the Holocaust. Of course, one should make pilgrimages to the sites of the death camps. The Shoah happened. We need to study the event, learn its possible lessons, and seek to move the world away from genocidal modes of thought and behavior. Yet, as far as feeling renewal at these places of agony, dehumanization and death, that is blasphemous.

Non-Jewish Holocaust Denial: The Attack on Reason

I turn now to non-Jewish denial. This is the denial of neo-Nazis and other antisemites that is a characteristic feature of our age. Jeffrey Mehlman, reflecting on the Argentinean poet E. S. Discepolo's "Cambalache," describes the end of the twentieth-century as the time of the "leveling of all values in the 'moral and intellectual junkshop' [this century] has become."[5] Holocaust denial presents the clearest example of this junkshop mentality.

It is fitting at the outset to note the central paradox of the denial phenomenon; the people who today denied the Holocaust happened, or minimize what it was, would have been the first to applaud its successful conclusion. Once they, or, rather, their Nazi progenitors argued that they were doing the world a favor. Now they contend nothing happened. Primo Levi's *The Drowned and the Saved* reports an observation made by an SS guard to a Jewish victim: "Even if some proofs should remain," says the guard, "we will be the ones to dictate the history of the *lagers*" [camps]. Holocaust deniers are the heirs of the guard's words. By denying any facts that do not fit their theories, by seizing on any discrepancies that occur as a result of legitimate scholarly discussion, and by asserting theories that are epic in their falseness, such as Germany was the real victim of the Holocaust which was, after all, a lie invented by the Jews, deniers now seek to sow seeds of doubt while in the process de-constructing World War II, de-legitimizing Israel, and liquidating memory of the victims. Assaulting real history, deniers attempt to replace it with what historian Deborah Lipstadt rightly terms disinformation.

Denial masquerades under the name of revisionism and began in Europe shortly after the end of the Second World War. The history of the movement, and its assault on truth and democratic values has been well and insightfully told by Lipstadt and others.[6] Although I shall not repeat it here, it is important to emphasize several points. Deniers are against the very idea of reason itself. This heightens the intensity of their attacks on reason which are carried out on university campuses, the presumptive location of rational enquiry. I shall return to this point later. Second, the deniers' attack on Jewish history and the legitimacy of Israel is simultaneously an assault on the underpinnings of democratic society. Furthermore, deniers view the world through the lens of conspiracy. Far from searching for the truth, Holocaust deniers seek its suppression and distortion. Yet what makes them so pernicious is that they have mastered both the rhetoric and dress of respectability. The leap from crude pamphlets to professionally bound books replete with footnotes and bibliographies, a journal (*The Journal of Historical Review*), and now a web site means that deniers cloak their antisemitism, racism, and conspiracy theories in a mantle of academic respectability. Footnoted lies, however, remain lies.

Two Examples

Two examples of the attack on reason are provided by the cases of Robert Faurisson and Arthur Butz. The Frenchman Faurisson, who has a Ph.D. and served as associate professor of 20th century French literature at the University of Lyons-2, contends that the alleged gassings of Jews is in fact a "gigantic politico-financial swindle whose beneficiaries are the state of Israel and International Zionism." The university catalogue identifies Faurisson as a specialist in "criticism of texts and documents, investigation of meaning and counter-meaning, of the true and the false."[7] In other words, as Nadine Fresco observes: "Faurisson—the master of deceit—will be the one to determine what is true and what is false."[8] Faurisson, moving with the technological times, now is on the Internet with items such as "A Prominent False Witness: Elie Wiesel." After "debunking" Wiesel's testimony, the item concludes by inviting readers to purchase the Institute for Historical Review catalogue for two dollars. Mark Weber, editor of *The Journal of Historical Review*, lists Faurisson as a "respected scholar"—along with Arthur Butz and David Irving—who challenges the "widely accepted extermination story" (page 1 of internet report titled "Different Views of the Holocaust," 1/12/97).

Rushing to demonstrate that the political left is as dense, disingenuous, fundamentally flawed, and dangerous to democracy as their counterpart on the ultraright, Noam Chomsky wrote a preface to Faurisson's book, *A Memoir in Defense*. On Chomsky's behalf, it needs to be stated that he mistakenly believed that Faurisson had been forbidden to teach, barred from public libraries and archives, and his books censored.[9] Yet, Chomsky, himself a hater of the State of Israel, declared himself insufficiently competent to determine the accuracy of Faurisson's comments about the Holocaust. One wonders what Chomsky, and others on the ultraleft, would consider suitable evidence.

The second example is that of Arthur Butz, associate professor of Electrical Engineering and Computer Science at Northwestern University. Author of *The Hoax of the Twentieth Century* (1976), Butz asserts that the "hoax" in question is what he terms the "Holocaust legend." Hoping to persuade readers of his sincerity, Butz confides that once he, like millions of other Americans, used to believe that the Holocaust happened. Now, however, after exhaustive research, he has come upon the truth of the matter.[10] Unlike earlier deniers, Butz's work has a veneer of scholarship. It is replete with footnotes, bibliography and a modest critique of the work of his predecessors. Butz' own work criticizes what he terms "leading exterminationist mythologists" such as Gerald Reitlinger, Raul Hilberg (referred to by the denier Serge Thion as a "railroad addict"), and Lucy Dawidowicz. Arthur Butz, with footnotes, is still ethically offensive, historically wrong, and morally pernicious. Antisemitism and racism have no rightful place either in or out of the academy. Willful misuse of scholarly documents, e.g. citing out of context sentences, coupled with propagandistic lies, have nothing to do with reputable scholarship. The fact that Northwestern's faculty supported the principle of academic freedom and right of tenure in the Butz case underscores the importance of recognizing that Holocaust denial is clearly more than a tempest in a teapot.

Butz, like his French counterpart, has discovered the usefulness of technology. He has a Home Web Page with three stated aims: To present his article on Holocaust revisionism, initially published in the campus newspaper, "with supplementing commentary and documentation;" To occasionally present *new material* "likely to be appreciated only be advanced students of Holocaust revisionism," and To present *news items* "of particular interest to Holocaust revisionists."[11] Butz may be pernicious but he is no fool. For instance, he prefaces his Home Web page with the follower disclaimer: "This Web site exists for the purpose of expressing views that are outside the purview of my role as an Electrical Engineering faculty member."

Arguments and Methods of Revisionism

One may legitimately enquire on what grounds are these lies built, and why is there an audience for them among those who are not hard-core antisemites? Professor Pierre Vidal-Naquet summarizes the revisionists' "arguments."[12] There are two central contentions; there was no genocide, and, gas chambers never existed. The alleged genocide was in reality Allied propaganda fueled by Jewish and Zionist pressure. The main enemy of the human race in the decades of the 1930s and 1940s was Stalin. Furthermore, the number of victims in the genocide that did not happen was far less than claimed. Adding to the moral outrage is the claim that Hitler's Germany bears either co-responsibility [with the Jews], or no responsibility for what happened during the years 1939-1945.

The methods for supporting these claims are quite clear. Direct testimony by a Jew is, observes Vidal-Naquet, either a lie or a fantasy. Any testimony or document dating from before the end of the war is a forgery, unacknowledged, or treated as rumor. Any first-hand information concerning Nazi methods is either a forgery or has been altered. Nazi use of camouflaged language is treated as revealing rather than concealing the truth. All post-war Nazi testimony is, by definition, coerced. Revisionist/deniers also employ a pseudo-technical arsenal of data to demonstrate that gassings were impossible. Those endorsing this perverted line of reasoning range from the discredited Fred Leuchter, a self-styled engineer without an engineering degree, to the populist and nativist Patrick Buchanan.

History Revisited, Revised, and Denied

The notion of history itself is, notes Lipstadt, up for grabs. Frequently history deteriorates into ethnic cheerleading, rhetoric, or spin control. In the process, the notion of truth itself is the first casualty. Furthermore, historical naivete and ignorance is found even among otherwise sophisticated people. To cite but one example, it is instructive to turn to the world of computers. Computer software is constantly being upgraded, i.e., new versions of "truth" regularly appear. Moreover, ours is an age of quantum leaps in scientific advancement ranging from the age of earth itself to genetic engineering, from space exploration to cloning. Modifications of long-held theories about the nature of reality yield the feeling that truths are, at best, temporary. This, in turn, creates a certain climate in which, as the ancient Greek philosopher Heraclitus stated, one cannot step into the same river twice. We live in a time of transition and impermanence.

History emerges as a form of fiction that can and should be written whimsically and according to different ethnic standards. Hollywood exemplifies this phenomenon while simultaneously revealing the complexity of the situation. For instance, two examples of history as fiction come from recent films. Oliver Stone's picture "Nixon," and Milos Foreman's "The People Versus Larry Flynt," provide evidence of clear distortion, highly selective portions of evidence, and clearly manipulative cinematic techniques. Playing fast and loose with data is nothing new, but the directors should have at least recognized a moral obligation to shed light on, rather than impede, relevant constitutional issues. Further, it is unlikely that audiences for these two films will pursue further research. More likely is the possibility that the versions of reality presented by these works will enter culture as a type of oral history that provides subconscious markers for "reality."

Yet it is important to resist the temptation of facilely dismissing motion pictures; viewing them as simplistic attempts to tell a story without regard for historical accuracy. For instance, Mark C. Carnes remarks on "Hollywood's often heroic efforts at reproducing historical costumes, interiors, and settings."[13] Further, Oliver Stone himself expressed outrage when the Warner Studio attempted to suppress portions of *Past Imperfect: History According to the Movies*, a book that Carnes edited. Stone chastised Warner executives, writing: "I make films like "JFK" and "Nixon" to stimulate discussion of the past. I expect and even welcome criticism...Please, in the future, do not justify censorship out of some imagined concern for my feelings."[14]

What then is the problem? Simply stated, it is the duration of visual memory. Camera angles, lighting techniques, and other technical devices are powerful instruments for conveying a sense of "reality," especially in the post-literate age. But the power of film to manipulate reality is not new. For example, Leni Riefenstahl's "Triumph of the Will" purports to be a "documentary" but is in fact a massive celluloid lie that filmmakers still consider the standard against which all propaganda films are judged. Further, people remember films in greater detail and with greater conviction of their truth than they recall the contents of essays or the written word. Robert Zemeckis' film "Forrest Gump" frequently cited by critics as part of the "dumbing" of America, provides a case in point of how a technique such as digital computing can be employed to create a "reality" that never existed. For example, juxtaposing Forrest Gump and images of Presidents Kennedy and Johnson, the director is able present a "conversation" between an actor portraying a fictional character and two deceased presidents of the United States who lived three decades before the movie appeared.

Zemeckis' more recent film, "Contact," takes this process a step further. Here, scientists from this planet attempt intergalactic communication. In order to lend an air of authenticity to the film, the director utilizes clips from a 1996 presidential press conference to make it appear as if President Clinton himself is in the film, actually reassuring the American public in the face of this dangerous experiment. Clinton was, in fact, speaking about the relationship of outer space and earth; a meteorite from Mars had struck earth. What, one wonders, will deniers be able to do with films of the camps? Or images of the Nuremberg Trials? Cinematic manipulation and corporate production of "truth" adds to the landscape of impermanence.

Culture Infantilized

I referred earlier to Mehlman's characterization of the twentieth century as an "oral and intellectual junkshop." His phrase indicates the erosion of standards and a relativizing of truth in both the academy and in popular culture. An arena in which all that is "given" is suspect provides fertile ground for the emergence of Holocaust denial. Concerning academia, there is the curious phenomenon of deconstruction. Ostensibly a Hermeneutics of Suspicion in the wake of Auschwitz, the deconstructive enterprise seems an end in itself. Unlike those who assert the epoch making nature of Auschwitz, and the consequent need for reevaluating all human activity with the aim of achieving a *tikkun* of the world, deconstructionism frequently ends in nihilism. For example, texts have no intrinsic meaning; a laundry list, newspaper articles, Shakespeare and the Bible all have the same valence. Texts are, as it were, problematized to the point of meaninglessness. Meaning is supplied by the reader. Multiple meanings indicate no fixed point. Furthermore, our age is characterized as one of postmodernity, a time of the reassertion of tribal as opposed to universal affiliation. Competing ethnic truths, rather than careful research carried out according to acceptable standards, rule the day.

The situation is exacerbated when one turns to the arena of popular culture. Reading is becoming a lost art. Or, rather, a decreasing number of people seriously read important works. Television is the main purveyor of [mis]information. Alvin Rosenfeld notes the disturbing tendency of both radio and television talk shows to encourage "debate" whether or not the Holocaust happened. Tellingly, Rosenfeld argues that by giving airtime to antisemitic Holocaust deniers who argue against Jewish survivors, these programs "recapitulate the fundamental aggression of the Holocaust itself."[15] Furthermore, he astutely notes that this becomes a "continuation of the war against the Jews by other means."[16] This is hardly entertainment. And it is very far from being instructional or enlightening. Such programs do, however, further degrade the level of knowledge about the Holocaust.

The situation is no better when one looks at middle or even high brow culture. Saul Friedlander's revealing study *Nazism: Reflection on Kitsch and Death* speaks about the impulse to "neutralize" Nazism. Friedlander's study arrives at the inescapable conclusion that in a variety of films and novels on both sides of the Atlantic, but especially in Europe, mass death has become kitsch. Alvin Rosenfeld's equally sobering study, *Imagining Hitler*, speaks about the domestication of Hitler in American popular novels. Among the details that Rosenfeld documents is popular culture's fascination with Nazi memorabilia; sales in the United States are in the multi-million dollar range. One may also turn to novels such as D. M. Thomas's *White Hotel* and discover that the Shoah has been "deconstructed," i.e. Yevtushenko's epic poem, *Babi Yar*, has been re-worked into a type of Freudian sex and death novel in which no one really dies, and the framing narrative is the bayonet rape of a [non]-corpse at Babi Yar, and George Steiner's *The Portage to San Cristobal of A. H.*

Steiner's novel is a case of studied ambiguity. The author elects to give Hitler the final say. Unsurprisingly, the tyrant mouths denier-type arguments; although he never denies the Holocaust.[17] Steiner has Hitler blame the Jews, relativize the Holocaust, and—irony of ironies—contend that he, not Herzl, should be credited with founding the State of Israel. The Jewish crime is in perpetrating the "blackmail of transcendence" on Western culture. Consequently, Jews have "infected our blood and brains with the bacillus of perfection." Therefore, A. H. contends, the "virus of utopia" had to be burned before it sickened Western civilization. Further, Stalin murdered thirty million, far more than perished in the Shoah. On the one hand, it can be argued that Steiner is attempting to demonstrate the murderous absurdity of these positions. But the truth is that bureaucracy and technology were just as significant as ideology in the destruction of European Jewry. Furthermore, and on the other hand, the Holocaust was not mono-causal and cannot be reduced to a single speech no matter how well crafted in the hands of a gifted novelist. Giving evil the final say is in itself a form of denial.

The Obtuseness of the Academy

A favorite technique of deniers is to place paid advertisements in college and university newspapers that, under the guise of freedom of inquiry, seek to raise doubt that the Holocaust happened. This effort, headed by Bradley R. Smith of the so-called Campaign for Open Debate on the Holocaust (CODOH), is an attempt both to rehabilitate National Socialism and to undermine the State of Israel. Smith intentionally targets college campuses because they are "fertile grounds" for his type of antisemitism. Seeking refuge behind the First Amendment, i.e., Freedom of Speech, Smith's ads have run in dozens of campus papers. These "advertisements" deconstruct the Holocaust by several means; citing as experts individuals who are known deniers [David Irving]; lying in attesting that confessions by German war criminals at war crimes trials were coerced; and falsely insinuating that there are two sides to the Holocaust, e.g. the presentation of "establishment historians" and the counter versions offered by "revisionist historians." All of this morally outrageous and historically wrong claptrap is couched in terms of the revisionists championing the cause of freedom to speak out in the face of coercive political correctness. In this reading revisionists portray themselves as victims; their ideas censored, they themselves "oppressed" because they reach conclusions different from establishment historians. Is it any wonder that, in responding to the decision of Northwestern University's student newspaper to invite Butz to publicly debate his "unorthodox view" of the Holocaust, the Harvard *Crimson* observed that (the *Daily Northwestern*) "had elevated... 'utter bullshit' to the level of a theory deserving of a forum."[18]

Sad to say, many university presidents and campus newspaper editors wrongly view the issue of revisionist ads in terms of the First Amendment. Lipstadt discusses this phenomenon with great precision and insight in her chapter "The Battle for the Campus." Fundamentally, revisionist ads have nothing to do with free speech. Editors routinely refuse to run certain types of advertisements. For instance, many ads for cigarettes are not run, some do not run brassiere advertisements, etc. The issue here concerns the role and function of the university. The president of a private university in the southeast told me that while he had lost a substantial pledge because the campus newspaper had run a revisionist ad, he was certain that the donor would eventually "come around," and that the university would receive the pledge. It struck me that the president's position betrayed a complete lack of awareness of both the pernicious nature of Holocaust deniers and the role of the university.

Responding to the president, I distinguished between revisionism as an honorable academic practice, and antisemitism. Historians, and others, constantly revise hypotheses based on new discoveries or alternate interpretations of extant data. This is the logic of intellectual curiosity and growth. Holocaust revisionists are, for their part, interested in neither intellectual growth nor furthering understanding of events. They are contemporary antisemites. Furthermore, the university is under no obligation to host liars and bigots. Free speech does not mean distortion of reality. Would the president endorse a campus newspaper advertisement stating the case for open debate on the moral usefulness of slavery? Arthur Hays Sulzberger had it right in contending that if your mind is too open, "your brains fall out."

The pernicious strain running through the contemporary academy is not restricted to Holocaust denial. The work of Mary Lefkowitz in her suggestive book *Not Out of Africa* provides an illuminating example of the excess and dangers of denial, A classicist, Lefkowitz critiques the position of Afrocentrist historians who contend that Aristotle stole his ideas from Egypt. This assertion, whatever one may think of its merits, raises central issues both for the academy and society-at-large. Specifically, Lefkowitz questions whether "alternate ways of looking at the past" justifies the Afrocentrists' demand that "ordinary methodology be abandoned in favor of a system of their own choosing." How one treats history speaks to the issue of university teaching. In Lefkowitz's trenchant words, "teaching what is untrue does not educate. Rather, it keeps people in a state of illusion."[19] What respectable institution of higher education would teach that the earth is flat or that slavery never existed? Further, if there are no commonly held assumptions about discourse, there is no community. Dialogue and the search for meaning deteriorate into vulgar exercises in triumphalism, obscene attempts at "comparative suffering," and disregard for the life of the mind. That certain people believe what is patently and demonstrably false, Lefkowitz attributes—in part—to the "present intellectual climate" in which academics "regard history as a form of fiction that can and should be written differently by each nation or ethnic group."[20]

Lefkowitz herself looks to the Holocaust as a confirmation of a bedrock truth. She correctly distinguishes between various, and frequently competing, interpretations of the truth, and the fact that some things are simply not true. "It is not true," she writes, "that there was no Holocaust." "There was a Holocaust," she continues, "although we may disagree about numbers of people killed."[21] It is precisely here that deniers seek to "validate" their bogus claims. Seizing on disputes among legitimate scholars, deniers contend that since reputable academics cannot agree on certain details, e.g., numbers of victims, the debate between functionalists and intentionalists, the precise role of anti-semitism, etc., this "proves" that the Holocaust is a hoax. There is all the difference in the world between survivors who, reflecting on the enormity of their experience, wonder if it really happened, and deniers who contend that there was no Shoah. Lefkowitz concludes by observing that people who are "prepared to ignore or to conceal a substantial body of historical evidence that proves [that Aristotle did not steal his ideas from Egypt] are travelling a dangerous path." Suppressing history inevitably means that "you can have no scientific or even social-scientific discourse, nor can you have a community, or a university."[22]

Responding

Responding to the phenomenon of Holocaust denial will go a long way in determining both the type of society America is and the type of university that we are willing to endorse. Franklin H. Littell asks the right question. "How do we structure the university," he writes, "in relation to society and internally that its graduates function as men and women of conscience and wisdom with a commitment to life—and not as mere cogs in genocidal machines?"[23] The deniers have launched their own continuation of the war against the Jews even as survivors live in our midst. What will happen as survivor ranks dwindle, and the testimony of witnesses, helpers, rescuers, and troops who overran the camps gradually becomes simply a part of the history that is "up for grabs?" Part of the answer lies in how university administrators view their task. Another major part of the issue is how to respond to the deniers themselves.

University administrators need to distinguish between public relations efforts and scholarly obligation. The latter involves a moral dimension. James T. Laney, former President of Emory University, astutely observes that "Educators are by definition professors of value. Through education," he continues, "we pass on to the next generation not merely information but the habits and manners of our civil society." Teaching has a moral dimension, the linchpin of which is respect for truth. Under this umbrella there is ample room for disagreement, debate, and competing interpretive positions. The value of free speech does not mean guaranteeing that "both sides" receive a hearing. The perniciousness of the denial phenomenon resides in the fact that, even if one does not follow the arguments, one walks away from a "debate" remembering that there were two sides. Writing in the context of the incivility of American campus life, Laney asks a question that applies equally to the issue of denier advertisements. He queries: "...should the university be a place of such severe neutrality about values that mere volubility or numbers can carry the day?" I would add to President Laney's question the following phrase, sheer mendacity and disregard for history.

After Auschwitz, all who espouse antisemitism, or acquiesce in its dissemination, are declaring themselves in favor of gas chambers. It is not the case that all ideas have equal value. Some have no value. Others possess negative value. Why treat them all the same? Nor, for that matter, is the denier phenomenon about ideas. Rather, it is about lies and deception. Far from being interested in assisting the learning process, Holocaust deniers cripple and pervert attempts to learn. Surely this is not what the university or its mission is about. Aiding and abetting suppression, distortion, and lying about historical events leads neither to good learning nor to responsible judgement. If reason were the guarantor of freedom from prejudice, why were so many academics involved in the "Final Solution" under Nazism? And why is there a disturbing increase in antisemitism and prejudice among the educated class today?

The academy can respond usefully to Holocaust denial in a variety of ways. For example, in terms of curriculum there is ample evidence that courses in the phenomenology of prejudice, the history of hatred, and the nature of anti-semitism are fully warranted. Further, faculty should discuss the deniers in the context of other historical examples of fascism and tyranny, all of which were based on lies and led ultimately to death and destruction for millions. In this context, it is important to teach about genocide's early warning signals. Scholars are increasingly involved in this enterprise.[24] Wherever feasible, students should be taken to the United States Holocaust Memorial Museum, or other reputable Holocaust museums, where they will be able to see documents and artifacts, view and listen to taped testimony of survivors, soldiers who overran the camps, and hear stories of the few who helped. Immersing oneself in the data of the Holocaust is the best way to combat denier mendacity. In addition, students should be sensitized to the nuances of media and public relations in concealing, rather than ventilating, the position of candidates and the meaning of issues. This would, in turn, lead to a heightened awareness of the insidious nature of camouflaged language in the political process. Hopefully, students will learn the necessity of critical thinking, informed judgements, and taking seriously their role as citizens.

What of the deniers themselves? The cardinal principle is, do not debate them. This grants them unwarranted legitimacy. But one cannot stop at this. Rather, it is crucial to know of what their lies consist and then to contradict these falsehoods with what actually is the case.[25] For example, it is true that Dachau was to a large extent rebuilt. It is also the case that many who died in Bergen-Belsen did so as a result of typhus rather than being gassed. It is also true that historians disagree about the number of Jews murdered by the Nazis and their many helpers. But this has nothing to do with Auschwitz-Birkenau, Maidanek, and other places of evil. Nor is it relevant to the Holocaust. Do not argue with revisionists. Rather, argue against what they say.

Conclusion

Education, like everything else after Auschwitz, needs to be re-evaluated. There is no greater challenge to the mission of the university than the denial phenomenon. If campuses are unable to define themselves in a way that distinguishes intellectual discourse, which at bottom is also moral discourse, from mendacity, then—as Lefkowitz observes—we have neither campus nor community. While denial affects a relatively small percentage of people, the struggle is always between the tenacity of antisemitism and hatred on the one hand and, on the other, the delicate nature of truth. Further, there are fiscal considerations involved. For example, in times of increasingly stringent library budgets, well-financed denier organizations send their professionally bound books to libraries without charge. How, and whether, these works should be catalogued is the topic of much discussion.

There is yet another element that may yet prove the deniers' ultimate ally. The passing of survivors coupled with the characteristically American distaste for history may combine to yield forgetfulness, which is the final denial. Thus there are elements of national character that combine, albeit in a muted way, with the intentional lying of the antisemites. Holocaust Denial must itself be denied. On the eve of the twenty-first century, it is increasingly clear that our relationship to Holocaust memory needs to be clarified. Memory of the Shoah may be redemptive. At the very least, it can help us be aware of when governments and institutions begin to go wrong. This, in turn, may be viewed as an early civilizational warning system. Denying or forgetting the Holocaust will, on the other hand, most certainly condemn civilization.

1. An earlier version of this paper was delivered as the Jacob Perlow Lecture at Skidmore College, July, 1996.

2. Hannah Arendt, *The Origins of Totalitarianism*, New Edition (New York: Harcourt, Brace, & World, Inc., 1966), p. 439.

3. I am indebted to the pioneering work of Deborah Lipstadt on Holocaust denial. Her groundbreaking study, *Denying the Holocaust: The Growing Assault on Truth and Memory* (New York: The Free Press, 1993), is indispensable for those wishing to understand the denial phenomenon. I follow closely her notion of the deniers embodying an attack on reason itself. Hereafter, Lipstadt's book will be cited as *Denying*.

4. Emil Fackenheim. Address delivered in Jerusalem, July 25, 1988.

5. Jeffrey Mehlman. Foreword to Pierre Vidal-Naquet *Assassins of Memory: Essays on the Denial of the Holocaust*. Translated and with a foreword by Jeffrey Mehlman (New York: Columbia University Press, 1992), p. xvi. Henceforth this work will be cited as *Assassins*.

6. See above, footnotes 3 and 5. In addition, see Kenneth A. Stern's helpful study *Holocaust Denial* (New York: The American Jewish Committee, 1993).

7. Nadine Fresco, "The Denial of the Dead: On the Faurisson Affair," *Dissent*, Fall, 1981, p. 467.

8. Op. Cit.

9. Ibid., p. 470.

10. Ibid., pp. 473-474.

11. Home Web page of Arthur R. Butz. Copyright A. R. Butz 1996, 1997, p. 1.

12. Vidal-Naquet, *Assassins*, pp. 18-19.

13. Mark C. Carnes, "Beyond Words: Reviewing Moving Pictures," in *Perspectives* 34:5, May/June 1996, p. 5.

14. Oliver Stone letter cited by Carnes, p. 6.

15. Alvin Rosenfeld, "The Americanization of the Holocaust" David W. Belin Lecture in American Jewish Affairs, Ann Arbor: The University of Michigan, 1995, fn. 42, p. 43.

16. Loc. cit.

17. It is instructive to note that Holocaust denial does not appear in Poland, the country where the largest and most deadly of the camps existed.

18. Cited by Lipstadt in *Denying*, p. 206.

19. Mary Lefkowitz, *Not Out of Africa: How Afrocentrism Became an Excuse to Teach Myth as History* (New York: Basic Books, 1996), p. 158.

20. Ibid., p. xiv.

21. Ibid., p. 161.

22. Ibid., p. 175.

23. Franklin H. Littell, "The Credibility Crisis of the Modern University," in *The Holocaust: Ideology, Bureaucracy, and Genocide*. Edited by Henry Friedlander and Sybil Milton, (Millwood, New York: Kraus International Publications, 1980), p. 271.

24. Representative works here include the following: Israel W. Charny, *How Can We Commit the Unthinkable? Genocide the Human Cancer* (New York: Hearst Books, 1982), especially chapter 13, "Toward a Genocide Early Warning System," written with Chanan Rapoport; Ephraim M. and Yochaved Howard, "From Theory to Application: Proposal for an Applied Science Approach to a Genocide Early Warning System," in Israel W. Charny, editor, *Toward the Understanding and Prevention of Genocide: Proceedings of the International Conference on the Holocaust and Genocide* (Boulder: Westview Press, 1984); and Franklin H. Littell, "Early Warning," in *Remembering for the Future: The Impact of the Holocaust on the Contemporary World* (Oxford: Pergamon Press, 1988).

25. I am grateful to my colleague Professor Aubry Newman of the United Kingdom for discussion on this matter.

BLIND BUT NOT IGNORANT
German Women During the Holocaust
Carol Rittner, R.S.M.

I first met Harry James Cargas, not in person but through his writing, when I was a graduate student at the University of Maryland, working on my MA in English and writing a thesis on Dan Berrigan, the Jesuit priest, poet, and peace activist. It was the early 1970s. The country was chaotic, divided over the war in Vietnam and the civil rights movement in America. Berrigan was the *enfant terrible* of the American Catholic Church, wanted by the F.B.I. for various acts of civil disobedience committed against the war in Vietnam. He had gone underground, popping up from time to time around the country at anti-war rallies, just long enough to be seen, but not long enough to be caught. My thesis included an extensive—everything I could find in English—annotated bibliography of works by and about Berrigan, so it was inevitable that I would meet Harry, whose St. Louis University doctoral dissertation, *Dan Berrigan and Contemporary Protest Poetry*, was an invaluable resource. It would be my first, but not my last encounter with him.

Harry Cargas thought, wrote, and spoke about Dan Berrigan, the war in Vietnam, Elie Wiesel, and the Holocaust long before I ever did. Always in the forefront, he has been asking questions, grappling with issues, and challenging conventional thinking long before most of us even gave such topics much thought. A greathearted man of character, Harry never has been afraid to face difficult and confounding questions. He is not afraid of the truth, even when "the truth," as Gitta Sereny writes, "is a terrible thing to live with." In Harry James Cargas, there are no "gray zones," no blank spaces between knowing and *not* knowing, between knowing and *not wanting* to know. There is only curiosity, integrity, and honesty.

When I originally read Gitta Sereny's book, *Albert Speer: His Battle with Truth* (New York: Alfred A. Knopf, 1995), I'll admit that Harry Cargas was not really on my mind, but in thinking about this essay, I thought again about the questions that hounded me as I read Sereny's book: Who *knew*, and who *didn't want to know*? How was it possible for anyone in Hitler's inner circle to claim ignorance about the atrocities perpetrated by the Nazis and their collaborators

47

against the Jews, and others, as Nazi Germany set about trying to racially and ethnically "cleanse" Germany, and later, German-occupied Europe, of peoples they considered *untermenschen* ("subhuman")? Reading Alison Owings' book, *Frauen: German Women Recall the Third Reich* (New Brunswick, NJ: Rutgers University Press, 1993) surfaced those questions in me once again.

In both books, the reader encounters a variety of women, although, unlike Owings, Sereny does not focus specifically on women in Nazi Germany. Still, in Sereny's book, one does "meet" Albert Speer's wife Margret, as well as a few other women; Anni Brandt and Maria von Below, for example, both of whom, like Margret Speer herself, were married to men in Hitler's inner circle. In Owings' book, one meets a broad spectrum of German women, some of whom also were married to Nazis. Though not as elite as those in the Hitler circle, they were elite enough members of the SA (*Sturmabteilung*) and the SS (*Schutzstaffel*), Hitler's instruments of terror. How carefully these women avoided asking their husbands—or each other for that matter—questions of significance. That they chatted about many things—family, friends, films, art, etc.—that they gossiped about each other and about others seems clear enough, based on what they told Owings and Sereny, but that they ever discussed with their spouses or with each other what they knew, or guessed, or sensed about what was happening around them, they never admit. Indeed, these women, both the extraordinary-privileged whose husbands were part of Hitler's inner circle, and the ordinary-privileged whose husbands were "merely" members of the *SA* and *SS* during World War II and the Holocaust, transformed the art of small talk into the art of avoidance. They avoided asking questions of consequence, questions that would have disturbed their spouses, themselves, or their private world of public indifference.

Unlike the women married to men in Hitler's inner circle, *Frau* Ellen Frey, interviewed by Alison Owings for *Frauen*, was married to an "ordinary" Nazi. Her husband was a member of the *Sturmabteilung* (SA), the Nazi "brown shirts." Did she know what her husband did during the war, Owings once asked her. No, She really did not know, she said. "She really did not know what he did in Germany, or in France, or in Russia, except to be a regular soldier" (p. 177). When he was home on leave, they spoke little of politics, Ellen Frey said, although she herself was not politically naive, having read Hitler's *Mein Kampf* and Hans Grimm's *Volk ohne Raum* ("People without Space"). Why had they not discussed politics, Owings asked. Because, Ellen Frey replied, "You know, in the war, when things with the Jews probably also were going on, we had so many problems ourselves. To keep our heads above the water, that one had enough to eat, or got everything the children needed. One really had so many problems and. . . ." (p. 179) One day when her tape recorder was turned off, Owings asked *Frau* Frey if she wanted to know what her husband did during the war. Apparently she did not, because, as Owings writes, Ellen Frey never "did take me up on an offer to find out" (p. 177). But others did want to know.

Frau Frey told Owings that her son used to question her about the war years, about what his father did and did not do. She always told him that his father was an ordinary soldier like so many other German men. When he asked her about what had happened to the Jews of Germany during the Third Reich, she told him that she did not know about such things, because she herself never saw anything terrible happening to people around her. But her son didn't believe her. "My son always says, 'I know exactly how it was. You didn't want to see it.' That's not *true*. I really didn't see it. He says, 'In your subconscious you didn't want to.' But I say *no*, 'I really didn't see it'" (p. 179).

After her first husband died, Ellen Frey remarried, this time to a man who had been a member of the SS during Hitler's Third Reich, but they apparently never discussed politics or talked about what he did during the war either, because she steadfastly maintained that she did not see or know about the horrors of the Holocaust or the fate of the Jewish people during the Nazi years in Germany. How was it possible for *Frau* Frey *not* to see what was happening to so many people in Germany—Jews, Gypsies, and many others—unless it was that she chose not to look? What was she thinking when people—Jews particularly, but others as well—began disappearing from the streets, villages, towns, and cities of Germany, when she no longer met them in schools or hospitals, in universities or civil service offices? How was it possible for her *not* to know unless it was that she *did not* want to know? If *Frau* Ellen Frey, married to two "ordinary" Nazis, was ignorant about the fate of the Jews during World War II and the Holocaust, what about other women, like those who were married to the men in Hitler's elite inner circle, the women, who with their husbands often socialized with Hitler at the Berghof during the war? What did they know?

Gitta Sereny sought out some of the women who had been part of Hitler's entourage, women who had been part of his staff (secretaries, for example) and those who were married to members of his staff. Many had been largely ignored after the war because researchers thought the information they could provide seemed trivial, but Sereny, following in the footsteps of Claudia Koonz, who wrote *Mothers in the Fatherland: Women, the Family, and Nazi Politics* (New York: St. Martin's Press, 1987), thought otherwise.

Sereny spent many, many hours interviewing Albert Speer. She met various members of his family, including his wife Margret. (Her given name was Margarete, but Speer called her Gretel and referred to her as Margret.) Albert Speer was Hitler's favorite architect, a man well placed in the Nazi bureaucracy. During the war, he was Hitler's Reichminister for Armaments and Munitions (as of February 1942), as well as his Minister for Armaments and War Production (as of September 1943). He helped to keep the Nazi war machine running—with conscripted foreign laborers from the occupied territories and with Jewish and non-Jewish slave labor from the Nazi concentration camps. He was in a position to know many things during World

War II and the Holocaust, although during the Nuremberg War Crimes Trials, he steadfastly maintained that he did *not know* about the terrible things happening during WW II and the Holocaust to the Jews and others despised by the Nazis. He accepted his share of "collective responsibility" for the crimes of the Nazi regime, but he vehemently denied any allegations of complicity in specific crimes. He escaped the hangman, serving, instead, twenty years in Spandau Prison for his part in Nazi war crimes.

Sereny wrote *Albert Speer: His Battle With Truth* because she wanted "to understand" Speer, to put into context all the crimes against humanity which Hitler initiated, which continue to threaten us today, and of which Speer, who was in many ways a man of excellence, sadly enough made himself a part (pp. 14, 15).

One day when he was talking to Sereny, Albert Speer excused himself so that he could take care of some urgent correspondence requiring his attention. Gitta Sereny and Margret Speer were left on their own. Sereny knew from what Speer had told her that his wife feared Sereny one day would ask her about the Jews. Until that moment, they had avoided such conversation, but when Albert Speer left the room, Gitta Sereny began to question Margret about the Hitler years. What was it like, she wanted to know, for the women who lived under Hitler's shadow? What did *you* know? Margret Speer responded, "Well, you know, it *was* heady living in that circle. [Hitler] was always very gallant to women, very Austrian." Her sentences, recalled Sereny, were interrupted by long pauses, reflections and retreats, to allow her, it seemed, to catch her breath. "One never . . . we all just chatted and we watched films." Sereny asked Margret if she ever questioned Hitler, or had a serious or personal conversation with him during any of those many evenings around the fire at the Berghof. Margret Speer became desperately uncomfortable. "Not conversations—it wasn't like that," she said looking away from me. "He talked. We listened" (p. 193).

During that same conversation, Sereny asked Margret about her best friend, Anni Brandt, the wife of Dr. Karl Brandt, Hitler's personal physician, who early on was involved in the Nazi Euthanasia Program. Later, Brandt would direct some of the appalling medical research carried out on concentration camp inmates. She also asked about Maria von Below, the wife of Hitler's long-time adjutant, Nicolaus von Below. These wives of the Nazi elite constituted a unique circle of their own, unconnected with the women on Hitler's personal staff. What did they talk about when they were together, on their own? Did they ever discuss politics, the war, some of the troubling things that began happening as of 1934? "Not really," Margret Speer said (p. 194).

Sereny pressed her. Was she saying that the conversation among the elite women of Hitler's Third Reich was entirely restricted to *kinder, kirche, kuche* (children, church and kitchen)? It was a direct, stinging question, and when Margret finally responded, there was annoyance and frustration in her voice. "Well, no. Of course one discussed daily events but not. . . ." Full stop. I waited. "You know," she finally continued, "one just talked about people, gossip really, and about plays, films, concerts and a lot of talk about artists." She paused. "One talked about one's children" (p. 195).

Gitta Sereny was not a hostile interviewer, but she was a determined focused one. She probed and pushed, always moving firmly, step by step until she uncovered what she was after:

> "When things happened everyone knew about," [Sereny] said, "such as people being sent to concentration camps, was that never mentioned between them?"
>
> "I didn't know anyone who was sent to a KZ" [concentration camp] she said. "We . . . we really did live very much on the outside. You can't imagine that, I think."
>
> I said that, yes, I could imagine this golden circle, but was she saying they didn't know there were concentration camps?
>
> "Of course we knew," she said almost angrily, "but if one thought about them at all, it was as prison camps, for criminals. I mean," she said quite tartly, "you have no objections, have you, to criminals being sent to prison?"
>
> She said she didn't know people were sent there for political reasons, people opposed to the Nazi ideas, such as priests, for instance. . . .
>
> Her husband had certainly known it, I said.
>
> "I suppose so," she said, now beginning to sound weary. "But that wouldn't have been a subject for discussion between us."
>
> There were things, I said, which much if not most of the German population knew about, such as killing the handicapped in 1940 and 1941. Did she and her friends really never discuss Hitler's Euthanasia Program and its moral and religious implications? And Bishop Gallon's famous sermon against it at Munster Cathedral on August 3, 1941, which became so widely known? Did all this bypass them altogether?
>
> She didn't answer, looked past me out of the window at the snow-covered fields, looked at her tightly folded hands in her lap. I had gone too far.
>
> "Would you like some coffee?" she finally asked, her voice tremulous (p. 195).

What can one say about such seeming ignorance? Was Margret Speer ignorant because she did not want to undertake to discover what reality lay behind rumors that were circulating and that she admittedly had heard? Was she ignorant because she was filled with an awful anxiety before a truth she feared she could not face? Or, was she ignorant because she *knew* a monstrous event was taking place and she did not oppose it? Whatever the answer to such questions, one can only conjecture, for these were questions Margret Speer could not face, or at least, could not discuss with Gitta Sereny, although as her daughter Hilde once told Sereny, "There is so much in her, so many guilt feelings of her own which need to come out to give her peace" (p. 691). But it was not to be. Margret Speer died of cancer in the 1980s, silent about what she knew and did not know.

Anni Brandt was Margret Speer's closest friend. Her husband, Karl was a close personal friend of Albert Speer. In 1939, Hitler appointed Karl Brandt Joint Chief of the Euthanasia Program. Throughout the war, except on those occasions when Brandt accompanied Hitler to his field headquarters, Frau Brandt shared her husband's life. What did *she* know? Gitta Sereny posed that question to Albert Speer. Did he consider it possible that Anni Brandt would have known nothing about her husband's activities? As difficult as it may be to believe, Speer insisted that such a topic "would not have been a subject for discussion between them" (p. 199).

Sereny spoke personally to Maria von Below, wife of Hitler's longtime adjutant, Nicolaus [Klaus] von Below. Only nineteen when she married Klaus von Below, her world, she said, encompassed "wonderful Klaus," not the political machinations of the Third Reich. "I had no interest in politics whatsoever," she asserted. Like the other women married to the men in Hitler's inner circle, she was part of the social scene at the Berghof, often was in the presence of Hitler, and frequently in the presence of other high ranking Nazis. She met regularly with Margret Speer and Anni Brandt, but, according to her own testimony, she was unthinking, uncritical, non-judgmental, or at least so she says:

> "My children keep asking me how I—how we—could bear it. But my God, it was a different world then. For me, married for two months then to the most wonderful man I could imagine, the world was Klaus; in a way, Hitler was immaterial to me. I suppose you would have thought me rather lightweight, flippant. . . . Of course, the more involved [Klaus] became with Hitler, the more difficult it all became. As what Hitler did, thought and also his moods became increasingly important to Klaus, he of course became increasingly important to me too." . . . she was flabbergasted when I interpreted this as her having begun to think critically of Hitler. "Oh, no," she said quickly, "I was in no position to judge him . . . "(p. 114).

What about other German women Sereny spoke to, women married to men in important positions, but not part of Hitler's inner circle at the Berghof? One such woman was the wife of Theo Hupfauer, Commandant of the Ordensburg Sonhofen, an elite college of political education, where "hereditary health" and "racial purity" were prominent parts of the educational program. What did Frau Hupfauer know? Indeed, what did either one of them know about the crimes and misdemeanors of the Nazi Third Reich? If one believes Frau Hupfauer, her realm was the house and their children, his was the school. When Sereny asked them what they had known about the euthanasia program, Herr Hupfauer replied,

> "I was only the Commandant . . . I didn't know about euthanasia. . . . There was a notice on the wall of every office during those years," he said . . . .It said, "Every man need only know what is going on in his own domain." Sonthofen *was* his—and his wife's—domain as of April 1941. They had proudly shown me a stack of beautifully printed *SonthofenHefte* (magazines).

The first issue carried three patriotic proclamations: one by Hitler, the second by Hupfauer as Commandant, and the third by Frau Hupfauer. She wrote it herself, she said proudly. And did she know about euthanasia? "No, never," she said, "You know, I was busy with the house and children." She and her husband looked at each other.

"We had an arrangement," said Hupfauer, "She looked after the family; I looked after politics and the war. One of us in politics was enough" (pp. 201-202).

In a bureaucratized world like Hitler's Third Reich, it was possible for Nazi men to separate themselves from their public deeds because, at the end of the day, they could go home, where their women awaited them, ready to soothe them and help them to forget their work for *Fuhrer* and Fatherland, or at least not remind them of it. German women like Ellen Frey, Margret Speer, Anni Brandt, Maria von Below, Frau Hupfauer, and many others, far from wanting to know the details of their men's public lives, cultivated instead their own private worlds of pleasure. They gossiped, enjoyed art and films, took care of their homes and children, entertained and socialized, looked after their husbands, and carefully avoided asking difficult or confounding questions. In this way, they cultivated their own blindness and helped their men to avoid facing responsibility for participation in the Holocaust. After the war—even many years after the war—they pleaded ignorance, said they never saw anything terrible happening to the Jews, Gypsies, or others in Nazi Germany, they never knew about the terrible things done in the name of Hitler and the Nazis. Like their Nazi husbands, these women failed an enormous test of morality, courage, and intelligence. To pass that moral test would have required at the very least for them to have had less trust in Hitler, the Nazis, and their spouses, and more bravery, curiosity, insight, and rebelliousness.

As Claudia Koonz writes in *Mothers in the Fatherland*, women married to Nazi men "contributed mightily to the atrocious success of the Third Reich." They did so by keeping the Nazi flame alive and/or the home fires burning. In that way, "German women enabled German men to set the other conflagrations, those that burned ghettos, barns, countries and corpses." That support was engendered by a split between private and public life that Nazism encouraged. The Nazi system urged women to create home environments that kept the private, feminine world of the family cocooned from the public, masculine sphere of political duty. The later often required, as Koonz points out, "brutality, coercion, corruption, and power"—the unpleasant work that somebody had to do if the Third Reich's "glory" was to be maintained. Women like Ellen Frey, Margret Speer, Anni Brandt, Maria von Below, and *Frau* Hupfauer, simply by staying in their place, focusing on their spheres of influence—*kinder, kirche, kuche*—and refusing to open their eyes to see what was happening to Jews in Germany and Nazi occupied Europe during World War II and the Holocaust cultivated their own blindness, helped keep their men undisturbed, and after the war, pleaded ignorance.

MAKING SENSE OF EVIL
Reflections on Hate, Intolerance and Responsibility
Jacob Neusner

Who is responsible, and for what? That question, whether addressed to humanity or asked to God, sparks huge discussions when the Holocaust comes to the forefront: who did these things, and who bears responsibility for them? Hitler alone, as the surviving Nazis wanted us to think, or the perpetrators, or those who helped, or those who did not hinder, or those who before World War II prevented the victims from finding refuge, or those who for a century propagated doctrines of racism, hatred, and intolerance? Assigning responsibility stands for no abstraction. If we ask people, who killed Anne Frank? or more generally, who is responsible for the systematic murder of nearly six million children, men and women in German-occupied Europe in World War II? the answers range from everybody in Germany to nobody in particular—it was just "the system." The "everybody"-answer usually means, all Germans of that time, with their allies. In the case of Anne Frank, was it the Dutch police who did the job, the Germans who gave the orders, the Dutch people who, in the mass, did little to intervene but produced what was proportionately the largest contingent of Nazis of any of the occupied countries? Where does the list end, and whose name can be left off? That is the chapter in the large, this-worldly question confronting thoughtful people: who is responsible for evil?

The Goldhagen Debate

Just now a young political scientist named Daniel Goldhagen created a stir with an emotional account of how a single battalion of ordinary Germans murdered thousands of people. On the basis of that case he proposed that exterminationist-antisemitism was so deeply rooted in German culture that Germany is responsible, as a cultural and political collectivity. Easy answers win vast audiences, especially when a just-beneath-the-surface hatred of Germany flows freely in the west. So Goldhagen got a huge hearing—especially in Germany. The "nobody-in-particular"-answer matches. But instead of labeling a whole nation as mass-murderers, the other extreme speaks of the human condition, modern culture, or some other abstraction. Richard L.

Rubenstein's *Cunning of History* and *After Auschwitz* represent in a far more sophisticated and literate way the counterpart and opposite to the Goldhagen position. For he argued that the system of Western civilization reached its culmination not in a concert hall where a symphony orchestra exquisitely reprised a Brahms' symphony, but in gas chambers in a symphony of stifled screams.

Clearly, where answers to an urgent question take every position and its opposite, we deal with a failure of intellect. People answer the question before they have analyzed it, they respond with their heart and not their mind, and they permit ultimate questions to suffer trivialization through the medium of shallow discussion and superficial thinking. But the western tradition of thought, beginning with ancient Greece and continuing without interruption through Rome and via Christianity, Islam, and Judaism, into our own times—a continuous tradition of reflection and criticism—has prepared us to think about tough questions, whether of science or of morality. We do have philosophical media through which to conduct our thought, and when we identify the right, the relevant one, we may find our way through the complexities of even the most intractable problem. That is the meaning of receiving, enhancing, and handing on a great tradition of thought: we do not have to invent the wheel every morning. The past has given us a heritage of not only experience and wisdom, but also, and especially, rules of clear and cogent thinking. It is because, in the face of the Holocaust, emotionalism and sentimentality have replaced rigorous thought that now, a half century later, history flourishes but philosophy languishes. That is to say, the story of what happened is told eloquently and accurately and responsibly. But thinking about what happened remains at its elementary stages, which is why a mountebank like Goldhagen gets a hearing by packaging familiar facts in incendiary ribbons.

Thinking Philosophically about the Holocaust

Do we have a case that points us toward a rule—an example of how thinking about the Holocaust ought to go forward, not in novels and in historical narratives but in the conclusion-drawing, generalizing framework of intellectual life in the West? I will gave a case and then generalize.

Let me contrast the treatment of the question of responsibility and blame, which I think exemplifies a failure of intellect, with the recent discussion of the question of the classification of the Holocaust. There, a first rate, trained philosophical mind, Stephen T. Katz (Boston University) in his multi-volume *Uniqueness of the Holocaust*, pursues the question, is the Holocaust comparable to other events or in some ways must it be deemed unique? Katz does not answer the question; he analyzes it and thinks deeply about the requirements of an answer. He then proposes his own program; "an...investigation of the relevant history of mass murder and genocide in all its diversity and expansiveness." To do this he has created "a series of analytical case studies of the major events that are relevant to...the complex process of answering the uniqueness question." But it is the power of vigorous and penetrating thought that really gains the reader's respect. Katz identifies the important questions and deals with them, locates the potential weak points in his argument and addresses them; does not merely announce propositions but amasses arguments and evidence. Here is what scholarship should offer.

The critical issue is addressed at the outset: what can we possibly mean by "uniqueness," and how absent a complete repertoire of genocide in all of recorded history should we know that a given national calamity is without parallel? Katz phrases his definition of uniqueness in terms on intentionality; here alone, genocide applies "the actualization of the intent...to murder in its totality any national, ethnic, racial, religious...group...as these groups are defined by the perpetrator, by whatever means." This is what separates genocide from other forms of mass murder (p. 134). Katz's main point is, "Employing this definition, we can begin to recognize that Assyrian, Babylonian, Persian, Hellenistic, Roman, and Crusade policy was cruel, but not every cruelty is genocide." Being a trained philosopher, Katz proceeds to a negative inquiry: "cultural genocide: what the Holocaust is not;" then "what anti-Semitism is not." Because Katz proves that the Holocaust is a question worthy of rigorous philosophical thought, let me quote his language as a model for what the issue of responsibility requires:

> Three interlocking questions now require investigation: does the inhumane history of pre-Nazi antisemitism... include occasions of physical genocide? Or, conversely...is the Hitlerian intention to exterminate the entire Jewish people a crime without precedent? Does the delimiting category of physical genocide serve to individuate the Shoah as an historical novum within—and without—the boundaries of Jewish history. The determinative, interdependent answers to each of these three questions is clear: there were no prior instances of physical genocide perpetrated against the Jewish people...; Hitler's...biocentric design was unprecedented...the category of physical genocide will serve to individuate the Shoah as an incommensurate moment within the parameters of Jewish history.

So Katz defines his work, systematically, rigorously, critically. Here is the kind of philosophically-rigorous analysis that characterizes the work throughout.

I point to Katz to prove that discussion of the Holocaust and its meaning for humanity does not have to degenerate into mindless emotionalism and finger pointing. There are useful lessons to be discerned, important conclusions to be drawn. There is civilization to be served. But if we approach the dreadful, painful subject as though thinking commenced this morning, we shall have to recapitulate the entire intellectual history of Western civilization, and along the way, we are going to give up. Then we shall be left where we now stand, which is, in a state of utter confusion, producing contradictory answers without the capacity rationally to show how one is right, the other wrong. So we are left with everybody is guilty and no one is responsible, with every possible possible in-between.

Before proceeding to my proposed approach to this matter of responsibility, I want to allow for a contrast between the wrong way and the right way to think. Only when we see the choices do we appreciate the opportunities. So let me introduce the position that is at this moment quite sensational, the one of Daniel Goldhagen. Only with his reading of matters in hand will the genius of philosophy to think rationally and clearly be set forth in proper contrast.

What we find in Goldhagen is an exercise in cultural determinism: Germany was going to perpetrate the Holocaust, because it was in the nature of German culture that the Jews should be exterminated. Goldhagen's thesis is: "In the middle ages and the early modern period, without question until the Enlightenment, German society was thoroughly anti-Semitic," and, consequently, the Holocaust testifies not to the work of a single generation but to the worth of an entire country. Goldhagen never asks whether or not the same statement applies, too, to Russia, Poland, Ukraine, Rumania, Hungary, Austria, and numerous other territories in Europe. But everyone knows that it does. That is why, formulated in terms of a particular country as sinful beyond all others, such a statement about a particular "race" on the face of it is racist: the condemnation of an entire culture, people, and nation must be treated no differently. Let us not mince words: this is a book nourished by, and meant to provoke, hatred of Germany. Were its topic the Jewish people, its method—give a few cases, in a special situation, to characterize the whole in all times and places—would qualify for out-of-hand rejection as naked antisemitism of a gross and repulsive, intellectually contemptible order. In my view, anti-Germanism differs in no important way.

What Goldhagen asks us to believe is that Germany was uniquely antisemitic. Then, to prove his point, he simply ignores that antisemitism was an international political phenomenon, on the one side, and insists that what happened in the National Socialist period can be explained only in continuity with pre-Hitler Germany. That is a considerable claim, and one that, in my view, Goldhagen not only does not, but cannot, substantiate. For the work of comparison and contrast—German antisemitism in the National Socialist period compared with that prevalent in prior periods in German history, and, more important, German antisemitism contrasted with the antisemitism of other countries—simply is not done. But without comparison and contrast, all of Goldhagen's fulminations against German culture—a distinctively German mode of Jew-hatred—lose all purchase on reality.

Now from our perspective, what is at issue is not the character of Germany or even the Holocaust, but the character of the thought, the rationality, the argument. Shall we blame Germany because of its culture? or exculpate Germany because its culture left no choices? Determinism takes the view that "whatever happens has all along been necessary, that is, fixed or inevitable."

But then, how can we blame the Germans who did the deed, or those who helped, or those who did not hinder it, if they had no choice, if what they did was made necessary by who they were, by the culture that defined them? The cultural determinism implicit in Goldhagen's position renders the issue of blame moot and inert: no one is culpable, if it is a matter of cultural necessity, if no one made choices or could have.

Necessity, Cause and Blame

Over twenty-three hundred years ago, the founder of philosophy in the West, Aristotle, asked in general and abstract form the question that confronts us, and he made the connections that show us a way to think about that question. When we do our homework and learn what he taught, we find a structure of thought, a program of analysis, that will allow us to do in a right and rational way the intellectual business of the moment. How would Aristotle have answered the question, who killed Anne Frank? For my exposition of the answer, I turn to a great scholar, Richard Sorabji, who expounded Aristotle's theory of responsibility in a classic work, *Necessity, Cause, and Blame: Perspectives on Aristotle's Theory* (Ithaca, 1980: Cornell University Press). I claim that when we have followed Aristotle's way of framing issues as Sorabji expounds it, we shall have some of the intellectual equipment to pursue our discussion in a rational way. We shall no longer have to resort to sentimentality and emotionalism, airing prejudices against Germany, on the one side, or ventilating a vacant cynicism about Western civilization, on the other.

To state the issue frontally: we are responsible for what we do and what we cause, but we are not responsible (or not responsible in the same degree) for what we cannot control. We are responsible for what we do, but how do we assess responsibility? We have forthwith to introduce the issue of causation: how does our action or lack of action relate to the consequence of what we do or not do? That brings us to how we assess responsibility. The issue concerns necessity, cause, and blame. Everyone understands we are responsible for what we do, but how do we know what we do: what is the nature of causation? These three then hold together in an uneasy, unstable balance. The relevance to the Holocaust is now clear: Goldhagen argues that the Holocaust came about within a process that was culturally determined for centuries before the process reached its culmination in the Holocaust.

Necessity, cause and blame, the categories provided by the great Aristotle scholar, Richard Sorabji, form the grid that serves philosophy in its sorting out of questions of responsibility, a subdivision of the theory of causation. A brief account of the matter of responsibility as set forth by Aristotle suffices to make the point that the Mishnah's category-formation governing necessity, cause and blame conforms to the lines of structure, with special attention to the governing distinctions, set forth by Aristotle. The issue of responsibility has to be set forth in two parts, first, in the context of Aristotle's general theory of causation—if we don't know that an act has caused a result, we cannot hold responsible the person who has done the act for the consequences he has brought about—and only then, second, in the setting of the specific, juridical position set forth by Aristotle.

A bit of patience is now needed to review the basic theory; only afterward do we return to the issue that faces us. First, as to causation in general: Aristotle discusses causation in the context of physics, not relationships or events in the social order. He finds, in accounting for changes in nature, four causes: [1] form, [2] matter, [3] moving cause, and [4] final cause. These are explained by G. E. R. Lloyd as follows:

> Take first an example of artificial production, the making of a table. To give an account of this four factors must be mentioned. First matter, for the table is made out of something, usually wood. Secondly form, for the table is not just any lump of wood, but wood with a certain shape. Thirdly, moving cause, for the table must be made by someone, the carpenter. Fourthly, the final cause, for when the carpenter made the table, he made it for a purpose.[1]

These same factors are taken into account in describing change from potentiality to actuality:

> The seed of a tree is potentially the mature tree; it is potentially what the mature tree is actually. This doctrine draws attention to the continuity of natural change. The goals towards which natural changes are directed are the ends of continuous processes. But while the ideas of potentiality and actuality are obviously relevant in this way to natural growth, Aristotle generalizes the doctrine and applies it to other types of change as well. A hunk of wood in a carpenter's shop is potentially a table or a chair or a desk...

Now to what is to us the important classification of cause, the efficient cause, the point at which culpability will enter in the transactions of the social order come under consideration. The efficient cause is the "whence the change begins," and the final cause is the "for-the-sake-of-which", or the goal.[2] In natural processes, Edel says,

> the final cause is the mature development of the form itself in the particular materials: the acorn grows into an oak tree whose end is simply to express in its career what it is to be an oak tree...

The efficient cause is "always some activity of the same type that the developed form exhibits." At the same time, in the consideration of causation, we take up the matter of chance, when something happens "by accident." Randall explains, "Chance is the name given to all events caused by factors that are not relevant to the ends of natural processes, by all the non-teleological factors, the brute events interfering with the natural working out of a process, or achieving a quite different end incidentally..."[3] Chance will take its place in the grid to be placed over an event so as to affix responsibility. Any account of responsibility will have chance on the one side, total responsibility, based on volition expressed in wholly successful intention, on the other; but then, responsibility also will be modulated, with gradations from the one pole to the other.

Of the four causes, the one of greatest interest to us is efficient cause. From this point forward Sorabji provides the account upon which we shall rely; everything that follows concerning category-formation depends upon his exposition. As to the definition of efficient cause, Sorabji explains: "The efficient cause is defined by reference to change; it is that whence comes the origin of change."[4]

Sorabji categorizes the treatment of efficient cause as the real point of Aristotle's contribution to legal theory.[5] Concerning Aristotle's contribution as a whole he states:

> It lies in his whole enterprise of trying to classify the different kinds of excuse and of culpability. This important step drew attention to whole classes of cases, not only to the general categories of voluntary and involuntary, but also to overwhelming external force, fear of a greater evil, non-culpable ignorance of what one is doing, culpable ignorance, negligence, acts due to natural passion or to unnatural passion, acts due to deliberate choice...[6]

Sorabji further comments:

> [Aristotle] introduces the criterion of what is not contrary to reasonable expectation, and so he turns the category of mistakes into a category of negligence... Aristotle further divides injustices into those that are merely voluntary, and ones that are in addition inflicted because of a deliberate choice.[7]

Aristotle's treatment of negligence is set forth by Sorabji in these terms, which at last lead us from the territory of metaphysical theory to incorporated society: issues of the social order, such as those with which the Mishnah is concerned:

> Aristotle starts by distinguishing two kinds of injury inflicted in ignorance (and therefore involuntary). The first is a mere mishap; the second is called a mistake... a culpable mistake. It is distinguished by reference to two ideas. First, the injurious outcome is not contrary to reasonable expectation, as it would have been in a mere mishap. Second, the origin of the cause... lies within the agent, not outside, as it would in a mere mishap. Aristotle's remaining categories of injury are two kinds of injustice. They are distinguished from the first two categories by the fact that the agent acts knowingly.[8]

What makes important Aristotle's conception of responsibility as Sorabji spells it out is his classification of different kinds of "excuse and culpability," which corresponds to the matter of responsibility.

What this set of directions yields are these gradations between total culpability or blame, by reason of one's forming the efficient cause without mitigating considerations, and total absolution from culpability and blame, by reason of one's bearing no responsibility whatsoever for what has happened:

[1] Responsibility for all damages done, because the event that has caused loss and damage is voluntary and foreseeable, not the result of overwhelming external force; preventable; brought about by willful action; the result of culpable knowledge; deliberate choice, not mere negligence;

[2] Responsibility for the greater part of the damages that are done, because the damage is foreseeable; not the result of overwhelming external force; preventable; thus in the event the ignorance is classified as culpable, but not voluntary;

[3] Responsibility for the lesser part of the damages that are done, because the damage is foreseeable; but the result of overwhelming external force and not preventable, thus; involuntary, but the result of culpable ignorance and negligence;

[4] No responsibility at all, the event being involuntary, the result of overwhelming external force, not foreseeable, hence, inculpable ignorance; e.g., pure chance.

We therefore identify three operative criteria—points of differentiation in the analysis of events and the actions that produce them, which form a cubic grid, with, in theory, nine gradations of blame and responsibility and consequent culpability:

[1] An event produced by an action that is voluntary vs. involuntary;

[2] An event that is foreseeable vs. not foreseeable, or an action the consequences of which are foreseeable vs. not;

[3] An event that is preventable vs. not preventable; or an action that is necessary and therefore blameless, or one that is not.

Thus we may construct a grid of three layers or dimensions, one grid formed of considerations of what is voluntary vs. involuntary, the second, of what is foreseeable vs. not foreseeable, the third, of what is preventable vs. not preventable, lines: a cube, with lines at each of the three intersecting levels drawn by the vertical of voluntary and the horizontal of involuntary, so too at the other layers, the whole then corresponding to the three categories just now given. One such mixed grid then will permit us to adjudicate complex cases of culpability and therefore compensation along lines projected at each of the layers. That permits us to identify an efficient cause that is voluntary, foreseeable, and preventable; voluntary, foreseeable, and not preventable; involuntary, foreseeable, and preventable; involuntary, not foreseeable, and not preventable, and so on for the rest. The nine possible combinations then allow us to sort out all situations that can arise; that is the compelling claim of philosophy that is "generalizable" or "universalizable."

Who Killed Anne Frank?

We are responsible for the choices we make, but we bear diminished responsibility for choices that we do not control. Did we mean it, did we foresee what would be the consequence of our action, did we do it? Then we are responsible and bear the blame. Necessity played no role. There was no possibility other than the one that our actions realized. We have identified four classifications of responsibility, therefore of blame:

[1] Responsibility for all damages done, because the event that has caused loss and damage is voluntary and foreseeable: the persons who actually participated in the entire process of the murder of the Jews; of these we say: forgive them not, O Lord, for they knew exactly what they were doing;

[2] Responsibility for the greater part of the damages that are done, because the damage is foreseeable: those who collaborated, the French police, for example, who knew, or should have known, the destination of those they rounded up; of these we say, Forgive them, O Lord, if they acknowledge their complicity;

[3] Responsibility for the lesser part of the damages that are done, because the damage is foreseeable, but the result of overwhelming external force and not preventable, thus: involuntary, but the result of culpable ignorance and negligence: the German people who supported the war, and who from 1942 onward knew fairly well what was going on with the Jews; and the various countries of Europe that did nothing to prevent the catastrophe; of these we say, Leave them with their shame, O Lord;

[4] No responsibility at all, the event being involuntary, the result of overwhelming external force, not foreseeable, hence, inculpable ignorance; e.g., pure chance: people too young to have known or too old to have acted.

This brings me back to the issue of responsibility: who is not responsible? When I gave a seminar at Gottingen University in 1995, the students asked me whether I thought they were responsible for the Holocaust? My answer was in two parts. First, no reasonable person can maintain that contemporary Germany bears any responsibility for events of half a century ago. Germany has done everything anyone can expect to repudiate those monstrous actions and so far as possible make reparations. But, second, so far as a nation receives as its heritage a history out of the past, Germany is going to bear shame for the Holocaust, as much as our own country must bear a heritage of shame for slavery, and Germany will continue to follow a national policy of nurturing tolerance of difference just as we are going to do what has to be done to overcome the legacy of slavery.

But from the perspective of religion, guilt is not indelible, and sin can be overcome. Christianity will speak for itself. For Judaism it suffices to cite the passage of the Talmud that says,

> Grandsons of Haman studied Torah in Bene Beraq. Grandsons of Sisera taught children in Jerusalem. Grandsons of Sennacherib taught Torah in public. And who were they? Shemaiah and Abtalion [teachers of Hillel and Shammai]. (*Bavli Gittin* 57B)

To understand the power of this statement, we have only to say, "Hitler's grandson teaches Torah in a yeshiva of Bene Beraq." Or: "Eichmann's grandson sits in a Jerusalem Yeshiva, reciting prayers and psalms and learning Talmud." We may then go onward with Sennacherib, who can stand for Himmler, and Shemaiah and Abtalion, the greatest authorities of their generation, who can stand for the heads of the great yeshivas and theological courts of the state of Israel, Himmler's grandsons are arbiters of the Torah, that is to say, Judaism, in the State of Israel. These are not matters of theory. I have met, and know well, a fourth cousin of Adolph Hitler himself, a man who teaches the history of Judaism at Tel Aviv University.

True, Scripture says "...visiting the guilt of the parents upon the children, upon the third and upon the fourth generations of those who reject me" (Ex. 20:5). But the Torah—the oral Torah reading the written Torah—qualifies that judgement: if the third and fourth generations continue the tradition of the fathers in rejecting the Lord, they too suffer punishment—for their own sins. This remarkable statement from the Talmud shows that sin is not indelible either upon one's family or upon oneself. Haman then stands for Hitler now. Sisera stands for Petlura, who murdered tens of thousands of Jews in Ukraine after World War I. Sennacherib represents Nasser, who in 1967 undertook to wipe out the State of Israel. The sinner should be, and is, punished; but sin is not indelible. If the sinner repents the sin, atones, and attains reconciliation with God, the sin is wiped off the record, the sinner forgiven, the sinner's successors blameless. The mark of repentance comes to the surface when the one-time sinner gains the chance to repeat the sinful deed but does not do so; then the repentance is complete. To translate into our own times hardly is necessary; indeed, it defies imagination.

Hate the Hun?

This brings us back to our starting point, Daniel Goldhagen's indictment not of those who acted and those who helped and those who did not hinder, but of the entire culture of a nation: the nation itself. In 1945 Goldhagen would have found much evidence to sustain his judgment. Right after the war the German message came through loud and clear: "We knew nothing, we saw nothing, we heard nothing, it was all done in secret." Nobody today entertains that proposition, which was self-serving and deceitful. No one claims that Germany before Hitler knew no antisemitism but that Hitler invented it. Everybody has long recognized that, along with the rest of Europe, important elements in German society—the clergy, the army, the universities for example—maintained bitterly antisemitic attitudes and adopted antisemitism as a philosophy and a program. But the same attitudes flourished elsewhere, and Goldhagen does not even pretend to undertake the work of comparison and contrast that would have rendered his thesis plausible. I have heard survivors of concentration camps debate with greater rationality and reason whether Auschwitz was "worse" than Treblinka, or Buchenwald than Dachau.

What Goldhagen asks us to believe is that Germany was uniquely anti-semitic. That would render Germany Aristotle's "efficient cause." But to prove his point, he simply ignores that antisemitism was an international political phenomenon, on the one side, and insists that what happened in the National Socialist period can be explained only in continuity with pre-Hitler Germany. That is a considerable claim, and one that, in my view, Goldhagen not only does not, but cannot, substantiate. For the work of comparison and contrast—German antisemitism in the National Socialist period compared with that prevalent in prior periods in German history, and, more important, German antisemitism contrasted with the antisemitism of other countries—simply is not done. But without comparison and contrast, all of Goldhagen's fulminations against German culture—a distinctively-German mode of Jew-hatred—lose all purchase on reality.

But when we come to logic, Goldhagen's case proves still worse. For he maintains that, since the Germans in the National Socialist period perpetrated such monstrous deeds, as Goldhagen says, "its [the Holocaust's] commission was possible...because Germans had already been changed." *Post hoc, ergo propter hoc!* Because one event follows another, the earlier has caused the latter. Goldhagen thus recapitulates the simple logical fallacy described in the words, *post hoc, ergo propter hoc*, should have alerted his teachers. Everyone knows that causation is more complex and that explanation demands more nuanced and searching analysis. If as Goldhagen insists, Germany was permanently poisoned by an indelible heritage of antisemitism, then how do we account for the Germany that from 1945 has taken its place as a major power in world culture? Everyone knows that of all the countries that were party to the Holocaust, those most guilty, the Germans, also have most thoroughly addressed the Holocaust, repaired such damage as could be remedied, and undertaken to build for themselves a political culture as free of racism and antisemitism as exists in the world today. No country has done more to learn the lessons of the Holocaust, and none makes a more systematic effort to educate new generations in those lessons.

France has yet to address the complicity of its own government in the Holocaust; its police, not German ones, rounded up the Jews. The Netherlands produced out of its population a higher proportion of Nazi Party members than any country in Europe. Everyone knows that the USSR denied the Jews even the manifest right to claim they had been singled out for special handling. Austria happily calls itself Hitler's first victim, as though no one saw the movies of the wild reception Vienna gave him in the *Anschluss*. In all of Europe, as Judith Miller showed in her *One by One by One*, only Germany has frankly examined its past, expiated its guilt through acts of genuine atonement, and acknowledged its enduring shame, much as we Americans acknowledge the enduring shame of slavery. That is why the new Germany also has built upon granite foundations uncovered in the hidden heritage of the old, a heritage that survived the National Socialist period. After all, Adenauer was a German, but Hitler, an Austrian (once more to argue from a single case!). True, the damage done by the National Socialist period to the enduring institutions of the country required long decades for reconstruction; in my experience at Tübingen, Frankfurt, and Göttingen I learned that the universities have not fully recovered. But Germany in a half century overall has accomplished that reconstruction. It has acknowledged its history of shame, but it has removed from its shoulders the burden of guilt for deeds that the current generation did not do and would not repeat and has repudiated in every possible way.

Now how are we to explain that fact—which even Goldhagen acknowledges, if grudgingly, in a sentence or so? For if Germany were as Goldhagen wishes us to think it was, irremediably, irrevocably tainted at the very roots of its culture and politics, then whence the sources for regeneration and renewal that, manifestly, have found ample nourishment in the country and its culture from 1945? I do not think we can explain Germany from 1945 onward without uncovering in pre-National Socialist Germany—whether in 1848, whether in Weimar—alongside the abundant sources of murderous antisemitism, also sustaining resources for a humane and liberal German political culture. The consensus of learning has concluded that National Socialism competed with other political traditions, vanquished them, and ruined Germany. That seems to me a much more plausible picture than Goldhagen's, which, if adopted, leaves us unable to make sense of today's Germany.

To treat Germany as the sole venue for "eliminationist antisemitism" requires us to ignore the rest of Europe, on the one side, and to dismiss as an important basis for explaining what happened the actualities of the National Socialists and their history from World War I onward: a special case, to be explained within the framework of its time and place, not a general symptom of the moral evil of an entire society and its history into recent times. In this context, we must wonder, what of the systematic destruction of Judaism by the Communists in exactly the same time? For while they preserved the Orthodox Church to serve their purposes, they rooted out the practice of Judaism in the USSR as thoroughly as Germany would hunt down and kill Jews. How does anti-Judaism fit into the picture? In my view, it complicates matters, and so is best omitted to make the case Goldhagen wishes to make.

Rehearsing dreadful, but familiar cases of brutality beyond all rational purpose, Goldhagen sets forth as his thesis that "eliminationist antisemitic German political culture...was the prime mover of both the Nazi leadership and ordinary Germans in the persecution and extermination of the Jews and therefore was the Holocaust's principal cause." Framed in that way, the thesis emerges as both unexceptionable and also unexceptional; no one can find it surprising. For two generations, now, the argument, "we heard nothing, we knew nothing, we saw nothing," which I heard in Frankfurt in 1953 as a young Oxford student come to see with my own eyes the people who had done such things. Today's Germans know better.

What goes wrong, then, is that, along the way, the thesis of a generation of Germans' broad and enthusiastic complicity in mass murder extends its reach and turns into an indictment of an entire country and its history and culture, past and future, as though National Socialism were the inevitable outcome instead of a special situation. It is to that incubus, taking over what is otherwise a perfectly ordinary historical narrative, that I strenuously object. My objection is because the dissertation proves much less than it alleges. It demonstrates that Nazism penetrated into the deepest layers of Jewish life, that many Germans, at some points surely a majority, supported the National Socialists, and that Germany at that time united in support of its leader's program. But the dissertation then does not prove what it sets out to demonstrate, which is the inevitability of the Holocaust in Germany and no where else, the peculiar traits of German life and culture rendering Germany the unique and sole venue for such an event. As I said, a dissertation meant to prove that point would have included long and thorough studies aimed at the international comparison of antisemitism, in theory and in practice, in culture and in politics, in all of the countries that adopted that philosophy as a principal medium for social organization and expression, not just Germany.

When, on Easter, the Passion Narratives resound in the Churches, with "the Jews" identified as the evil actors in the condemnation and murder of Jesus, Christians over the centuries have found difficult the distinction that sets apart for condemnation those people in that generation, then and there, but that treats as unblemished by the ancient deed all later generations of Israel, the Jewish people. That is how, nurtured every day for 2,000 years, antisemitism transformed into a massive, mythic construct the calamitous deeds of a handful of people in a specific place at a determinate time. Anti-Germanism differs in no important way, when the Holocaust is used as a weapon to discredit Germany through all time, instead of the Germany at that time and in that place.

Who killed Anne Frank? A government and a great many people at a given time and place—not a system reaching back into remote time, not a circumstance that cannot have been avoided, not everybody, not nobody. If we wish to apportion responsibility, and we should, we have then to identify the efficient cause(s), not blame everybody, not blame nobody, not blame abstractions such as "the system," and not blame "Western civilization" or "Christianity." Hatred and intolerance represent choices people make, not necessities that circumstance dictates. So too do racism and antisemitism and bigotry: we are responsible for what we do, and for what we do not do—but not for what we cannot have caused or prevented. There are limits.

1. G.E.R. Lloyd, *Aristotle: The Growth and Structure of his Thought* (Cambridge, 1968: Cambridge University Press), pp. 58-9.
2. Abraham Edel, *Aristotle and His Philosophy*, (Chapel Hill, 1982: University of North Carolina Press), pp. 61-62.
3. Op. Cit., p. 183.
4. Richard Sorabji, *Necessity, Cause and Blame. Perspectives on Aristotle's Theory* (London, 1980: Duckworth), p, 42.
5. Sorabji, pp. 291ff.
6. Sorabji, p. 291.
7. Sorabji, p. 293.
8. Op. Cit., pp. 278ff.

RE-READING THE STORY
OF SODOM AND GOMORRAH
In the Aftermath of the Holocaust
Rachel Feldhay Brenner

The notion that the destruction of Sodom and Gomorrah is "a story" is essential to this post-Holocaust re-reading of the biblical episode. As a literary text, the biblical story opens up to interpretive commentary. The fictional component grants the liberty of search and research for the story's relevance today. As Walter Brueggeman argues, "[t]he biblical story can be told in more than one way. It has more than one meaning, depending on the way it is told and the way it is heard."[1] The way in which the story is told and heard is predicated upon the historical situation in which it is invoked. The biblical story remains viable as a relevant voice commenting on evolving circumstances.

The narrative of the biblical story, especially its dramatic properties, sets the reader's memory and imagination free, engendering an interaction between the text and the historical situation. The midrashic interpretation sheds a new light on the particular reality into which the story is summoned. At the same time, it reveals the hitherto unexplored facets of the story itself.

On the one hand, our engagement with the biblical story in the aftermath of the Holocaust reflects the desire to continue the midrashic tradition despite the consciousness of the catastrophe. On the other hand, however, the Holocaust consciousness raises doubt as to the validity of the midrashic interpretation of the biblical story. We therefore vacillate between desire and doubt. While still hoping for guidance from the story, we are no longer certain of its pertinence in today's world.

This is especially true of the story of Sodom and Gomorrah. Its representation of total destruction indicates a seemingly obvious parallelism with the Holocaust catastrophe. I would argue that, in its wisdom, the story steers us away from the analogy. While refusing to be associated with the apocalypse, it structures a framework of reference which encompasses both Testaments and makes an alternative interpretation of the story possible. I suggest that a different midrashic interpretation of Abraham's role in the story redefines the concept of justice. This perception situates the relevance of the story today in the linkage between the two Testaments.

At first sight, the destruction of Sodom and Gomorrah appears to establish obvious correspondences with the tragedy of the Holocaust. The motif of violent, total annihilation of human proportions establishes a plausible common denominator. The hopelessness of the doomed European Jewry echoes the futility of Abraham's pleading for the cities whose fate had already been decreed.

The closure of the Sodom and Gomorrah episode points to another common aspect. Through Abraham confronting the enormity of the destruction, we witness "the smoke of the land [going] up as the smoke of a furnace" {19:28}. The images of fire and furnace associate with the death camps' crematoria chimneys.

Furthermore, in both catastrophes we find a similar interpretation of God—it is a God who distances Himself from suffering humanity. Abraham's intercession on behalf of the doomed cities ends in God's abrupt departure, followed by the total destruction of the Plain. The unrelieved horror of Jewish victimization in the Holocaust points to the silent or the absent God. Merciful Providence is not to be found in either scene of suffering.

One could disprove the relevance of these analogies, arguing that the people of Sodom and Gomorrah were "other nations," not Israel. Such an argument, however, is not supported by the subsequent development of the Sodom and Gomorrah tradition. In both Testaments the destruction of the sinful cities of the Plain is unequivocally recalled in reference to the punishment of Israel for its transgressions.

For instance, in Deuteronomy, Israel's punishment for forsaking the covenant is compared to the fate of Sodom and Gomorrah. Worship of other gods, wickedness, and corruption will evoke God's wrath; the people will be cast into exile and the countryside will turn into wasteland. (29:21-27)

Isaiah refers to Sodom and Gomorrah in his opening description of the sinful people of Israel and the devastation of the land:

> Your country is desolate;
> Your cities are burned with fire...
> Except the Lord of hosts
> Had left unto us a very small remnant,
> We should have been as Sodom,
> We should have been like unto Gomorrah. (1:7-9)

In the following verse, the prophet makes sure that the day of doom is approaching when he addresses Israel as "Ye rulers of Sodom," "Ye people of Gomorrah." The identification of Israel's conduct with the ultimate wickedness of Sodom and Gomorrah leaves little doubt as to the tenuousness of Israel's existence.

In the New Testament, the reference to Sodom and Gomorrah depicts an even more radical vision of the destruction of Israel. The description of the punishment of the Jews who will not welcome the disciples carrying the word of Jesus is identical in Matthew and Luke. "I assure you that on the Judgment Day God will show more mercy to the people of Sodom and Gomorrah than to the people of that town [which did not welcome the disciples]" (Matt 10:15).

As Matthew sees it, the final destruction will be preceded by a breakup of terrible violence, whereby the Jews and the new Christians will turn against each other and "a man's worst enemies will be the members of his own family" (10:36). Like God in the story of Sodom and Gomorrah, Jesus emerges as a punitive force when he declares through Matthew: "I did not come to bring peace, but a sword," (10:34), and promises to take revenge on those who will not take up his cross (10:39).

Theologians try to attenuate the prophecy of doom. In his thorough investigation of the Sodom and Gomorrah theme in early Jewish and Christian writings, J. A. Loader argues that "the Sodom and Gomorrah tradition functions in an eschatological context" and, therefore, "in this literature" the focus is on "examples of fire as eschatological punishment."[2]

Loader's argument draws a clear distinction between the "eschatological context" and the context of human history. The punishment of the Jews who refused the word of Jesus will take place on the Day of Judgment and therefore should be understood as a figure of speech, rather than an historical possibility. Such a realization posits the correlations between Sodom-Gomorrah and Israel in both Testaments as a rhetorical strategy typical of the oratory of exhortation.

The event of the Holocaust, however, eliminates the distinction between eschatology and history. Tragically, the Holocaust demonstrated the plausibility of eschatological prophecies in the realm of world history. The annihilation of the Jews presented humanity with the hitherto unthinkable moment whereby history and eschatology converged. This convergence denoted the end of human history.

As Frank Kermode claims, "the consciously false apocalypse of the Third Reich"[3] signified the actualization of the paradigm outlined by the biblical story which starts with creation and ends in the apocalypse. The common knowledge that the apocalypse is constantly deferred, that it is "immanent rather than imminent,"[4] was transformed in the reality of the Final Solution. In an historical nightmare that neither the prophets nor the apostles could have envisioned, the improbable prophecy of Israel suffering the fate of Sodom and Gomorrah became real.

The actualization of the prophecy of the apocalypse in the historical time pronounces the deadness of the biblical story. In the reality of the day of Judgment the text and its midrashic interpretations are no longer relevant because the fulfillment of the prophecy supercedes history. The a-historicity of the apocalypse obliterates the past, precludes the future and, effectively, declares the end of the story. When history comes to its end, the story loses its midrashic *raison d'être* to elucidate the ever-changing reality. The apocalyptic *denouement* leaves nothing to either memory or imagination.

It follows, therefore, that to read the biblical tradition of Sodom and Gomorrah as a prolepsis of the Jewish destruction leads to a dead-end. The review of the story as a preview of the Holocaust ends the midrashic tradition and thus fossilizes the biblical text.

The biblical canon, however, insists upon survival. The intratextual reshaping of the Sodom and Gomorrah convention reaffirms its viability. An alternative referential trend undermines the exclusivity of the interpretation of the story of Sodom and Gomorrah as a harbinger of eschatological devastation. The use of Sodom and Gomorrah in both Testaments in the context of consolation, rather than destruction, suggests a perspective which countervails the apocalyptic ending.

A different vision of the future in the biblical text delineates an alternative course of human destiny. This course of hope and consolation subverts the trend which heads toward irrevocable destruction. The Sodom and Gomorrah imagery revokes the terror of implacable punishment when it transforms into an illustration of boundless divine love and mercy. The rhetorical genius of the story turns condemnation and rejection into acceptance and forgiveness. In contrast with the finality of the devastation, nothing is irredeemable in the vision of consolation.

Whereas Deuteronomy threatens Israel with destruction for violating the covenant, in Ezekiel's vision Israel's forsaking the covenant will be forgiven. Even though sinful Israel has become the sister of Sodom, she will regain the favor of the Lord, and even Sodom will be restored through divine grace: "And thy sister, Sodom and her daughters shall return to her former estate... and thou and thy daughters shall return to your former estate... I will remember My covenant with thee in the days of thy youth, and I will establish unto thee an everlasting covenant" (16:55; 60).

A complete dissociation of Israel's fate from the fate of Sodom and "her daughters" marks Hosea's vision of consolation. By recalling the cities Admah and Zeboim, which were destroyed together with Sodom and Gomorrah, the prophet conveys the vision of infinitely merciful God:

> How shall I give thee up, Ephraim?
> How shall I surrender thee, Israel?
> How shall I make thee as Admah?
> How shall I set thee as Zeboim?...
> My heart is turned within Me,
> My compassion are kindled together....
> I will not return to destroy Ephraim (11:8-9)

Matthew juxtaposes the prophecies of divided, warring families with Jesus' preaching of brotherly love, a love which precedes the worship of God: [G]o at once and make peace with your brother, and then come back and offer your gift to God" (5:24). In contrast with the prophecy that Jesus has come to set sons against their fathers and daughters against their mothers (10:35), Matthew demonstrates that the commandment to respect parents is crucial in Jesus' exhortations: "And why do you disobey God's command...Respect your father and your mother...In this way you disregard God's command, in order to follow your own teaching. You hypocrites!" (15:3-7)

Most pertinent to our re-reading of the Sodom and Gomorrah tradition is Paul's Letter to the Romans. The apostle is explicit about Israel's intact position of the chosen nation despite her rejection of Jesus. Here, in diametrical opposition to Matthew's and Luke's vision of Israel's total destruction, the apostle reaffirms the survival of Israel. He re-interprets Isaiah's view of the remnant of Judah as a promise of Israel's salvation. According to Paul, the remnant of Judah is a providential sign of Israel's rescue from the fate of Sodom and Gomorrah (9:29).

The apostle reasserts Israel's chosenness: "God has not rejected his people, whom he chose from the beginning" (11:2). Even though they did not accept the word of Jesus, the Jews maintain their special position vis-à-vis God: "Because they reject the Good News, the Jews are God's enemies for the sake of you Gentiles. But because of God's choice, they are his friends because of their ancestors. For God does not change his mind about whom he chooses and blesses" (11:28-29).

The transformation of the message of destruction into a message of consolation and redemption refutes the analogy between the biblical story of Sodom and the annihilation of the Jews in the Holocaust. Tragically, history embarked on a different pattern, enacting the prophecy of eschatological doom.

The finality of the Holocaust destruction, therefore, does not signal the end of the evolving biblical-midrashic tradition. On the contrary, in its spectrum of prophecies, whereby the hope of rebirth and renewal offsets the menace of ending, the biblical text manifests versatility which subverts the intransigence of the absolute. The confluence of the seemingly irreconcilable extremes of destruction and redemption in a single tradition, the tradition of Sodom and Gomorrah, offers the alternative of an adaptable and therefore relative perspective. Such a perspective disconfirms the uncompromising division between good and evil, between reward and punishment.

In fact, even the canonic version of Sodom and Gomorrah itself, presents us with a bold attempt to alter that which, by definition, is unalterable. Abraham tries to change the divine decree despite the full knowledge of God's resolve when he intercedes of behalf of the cities. In addition, he suggests a different solution to the problem. Since this solution antagonizes the divine decree, Abraham's suggestion implies a criticism of God's plan and perception of justice. In fact, Abraham's concept of a just judgment projects a hardly concealed doubt about the ethics of God's judgment.

The confrontation of the two systems of justice, that of God and that of Abraham, is of utmost significance. Despite Abraham's failure to save the cities, his query of God's judgment signals the possibility to assert difference even vis-à-vis the divine. Such a possibility counteracts the tenets of immutability and finality.

Such possibility raises an essential question in terms of our discussion. To what extent does Abraham's antagonistic response to God's judgment remain meaningful for us today? Or, to recall Paul's affirmation of God's friendship with Israel for the sake of the ancestors, in what way does Abraham's position vis-à-vis the condemned cities, validate the friendship in post-Holocaust reality?

In order to approach these issues, we need to investigate the philosophical underpinnings of Abraham's argument. Abraham starts with the conventional notion regarding justice: "Wilt Thou indeed sweep the righteous with the wicked?" (18:23), a rhetorical question which presupposes a clear-cut distinction between the virtuous and the wicked in terms of punishment and reward. In the next phrase, however, the accepted view of justice is overturned: "Peradventure there are fifty righteous within the city; wilt Thou indeed sweep away and not forgive the place *for* the fifty righteous that are therein?" (18:24)

This is not mere rhetoric. Abraham questions the universally accepted principle of justice which holds the individual responsible for his or her deeds. He substitutes the notion of justice meted out to individuals with a concept of collective justice, whereby the wicked would be saved *for the sake* of the righteous. The assiduity with which Abraham pursues his argument leaves no doubt as to the seriousness of his disagreement with God's position regarding the cities.

We are puzzled by Abraham's determination. But even more bewildering is the argument that he presents. We note that Abraham is not asking for forgiveness for the wicked. Nor is he imploring God for a merciful treatment of the sinners. He does not deny that the inhabitants of the cities are wicked. Nor does he promise their rehabilitation.

It seems important to note that Abraham's request does not foreshadow the legend of the *Lamed Vav*, 36 Righteous Men who will save the world. While the *Lamed Vav* work for the salvation of a naturally imperfect and unworthy humanity, the inhabitants of Sodom and Gomorrah commit acts of evil that are fully premeditated.

What Abraham proposes, in fact, is a redefinition of the concept of justice which traditionally assigns reward to the righteous and punishment to the wicked. He suggests that righteousness should be capable of saving not only those who practice it, but those who, in their wickedness, wish to destroy it.

This view of justice leads to what seems an absurd conclusion that the salvation of the wicked will demonstrate the victory of good over evil.

But the story does not allow an easy dismissal. Both its form and content insist on a serious consideration of the argument. In terms of form, the dramatic dialogue between man and God and the repetition of the question underline the significance of Abraham's intercession. In terms of content, the courage of questioning God's judgment communicates the immense importance that Abraham ascribes to his claim. God's willingness to listen and the concessions that He grants Abraham before His departure confirm the seriousness of Abraham's reasoning.

The concreteness of the case is significant. We are not witnessing a theoretical debate of matters concerning jurisprudence. The new vision of justice is presented as a debate over an actual piece of jurisdiction. The case before us enables us to examine Abraham's argument in light of the particular transgression of the inhabitants of the cities.

What is, then, the crime in question? The way in which the story frames the debate leaves no doubt that the transgression of the people of Sodom lies in their cruel rejection of the strangers in their midst. Chapter 19, which follows the debate between God and Abraham, presents us with a concrete example of Sodom's vicious treatment of the two guests/angels that Lot hosts in his home. The description of Abraham extending hospitality to the guests/angels in the scene preceding the debate accentuates the enormity of the Sodomites' wrong.

The story is very specific as to the reasons for Sodom's abuse of the virtue of hospitality. The angels disguised as humans are not strangers in need of charity. They ask for nothing and accept Lot's hospitality only after he pleads with them to rest in his house. The sin of the Sodomites, therefore, can hardly be explicated in terms of an aversion to share food, or other goods with the needy.

What, then, motivates the Sodomites' uncontained, violent hostility towards the strangers? Let us consider their response to Lot's pleading to leave his guests in peace: "bring them out to us, that we may know them" (19:5). The verb "know" in its literal meaning—make acquaintance with the strangers— assumes an ironic dimension in view of the scene of violence and hatred that follows. An understanding of "know" in its sexual connotation is reinforced by Lot's use of the same verb when he offers his daughters "that have not known man" (19:8) to the Sodomites. In this case, to "know" designates rape. Indeed, Augustine accepts the sexual connotation and reads "know" in terms of homosexual practice.[5]

Thus, either meaning of "know" indicates infliction of suffering and destruction of the strangers. The Sodomites' rage at the presence of the strangers in their city, their ruthless insistence on having Lot's guests delivered to them in the middle of the night, their fury directed at Lot for his unwillingness to do so—all these reveal deep hatred and fear of that which the

Sodomites do not know. What motivates the Sodomites' murderous attempts is their xenophobic fear of anything foreign and strange.

It is interesting to note here that Matthew's prophecy of the destruction of the Jews who do not welcome the apostles seems to arise from the fear of such xenophobic treatment of the disciples. Like the angels in the Sodom story, the apostles will not beg for charity, nor will they ask for any special favors: "[D]o not carry a beggar's bag for the trip or an extra shirt or shoes or a walking stick. A worker should be given what he needs" (10:10). All they require is to be welcomed and listened to.

It is significant that the emphasis in the chapter, especially in the first 10 verses, is not upon accepting the word, but upon hospitality extended to the stranger: "If the people in that house welcome you, let your greeting of peace remain; but if they do not welcome you, then take back your greeting" (10:13).

The extremity of the punishment for the vicious treatment of the "other" is indicative of the importance that the biblical story attaches to generous, respectful, and sympathetic attitude toward the stranger. Undoubtedly, transgression of this fundamental rule of human behavior requires a punitive response. Still, the implacable retribution inflicted upon the Sodomites raises the question of the ethics of justice. In a way, the destruction of the Sodomites mirrors their own uncontrollable desire to destroy the strangers. The common denominator of unmitigated violence directed against human beings underlies both sin and retribution.

In psychological terms, the reflection of the committed violence in violent punishment projects the virulent treatment of the stranger as a process of self-destruction. The abhorrence of the stranger arises from a deep fear of the recognition of one's own humanity in the unknown "other."

The recognition of a stranger would require a drastic change of the individual's attitude toward his or her fellow-beings. It would amount to an acknowledgment of one's indelible affinity with the other and therefore of one's responsibility for the other's well-being. In Levinas' terms, the consciousness of responsibility makes the individual the "hostage" of the other,[6] because one's humanity is predicated upon the obligation toward the other.

Hence, metaphorically, the blindness with which the angels smite the Sodomites becomes the representation of the denial of their humanity. The Sodomites are blinded when they are about to face their victims. Their failure to see communicates their inability to face the other. A glance into the stranger's eyes will reflect their own humanity connecting them with other human beings.

"The other," Levinas argues, "is known through sympathy, as another (my)self, as the alter ego."[7] The Sodomites' hostility toward the other signifies rejection of their own humanity. The desire to eliminate the other annihilates, in fact, their own inner self. In this sense, destruction brings forth self-destruction.

Sodom's sin of xenophobia elucidates Abraham's concept of righteousness. Righteousness lies in the ability to face strangers, to see them as the reflection of our self, and to protect them against those who can only hate. In other words, righteousness amounts to an acknowledgment that our affinity with other human beings signifies an obligation that supersedes all differences.

This definition of righteousness helps clarify Abraham's seemingly absurd notion of justice. As I mentioned above, Abraham's argumentation against destruction for the sake of the righteous implies that the power of righteousness will be measured by the salvation of the wicked. The destruction of the wicked will therefore demonstrate the weakness of the righteous.

Hatred of the other amounts to self-hatred; destruction of the other signifies self-destruction. By protecting the other from the wicked, the righteous protect the wicked from themselves. So long as the righteous can ensure the safety of the other, the wicked preserve their humanity that they are unable to acknowledge.

Righteousness, therefore, denotes not only the responsibility for the stranger, but the responsibility for the hater of the stranger. The destruction of the wicked thus demonstrates the inability of the righteous to save the wicked from themselves. Paradoxically, the obliteration of the wicked pronounces the victory of evil.

The story presents two examples of such paradoxical attempts of the righteous to overcome evil by saving the wicked. Both Lot's physical struggle and, on a much larger scale, the conceptual struggle of Abraham with God illustrate the implications of a responsible, righteous stance. The narratives of Lot and Abraham demonstrate the enormity of the sacrifice that the righteous act entails.

In his desperate confrontation with the Sodomites, Lot risks his possessions, his family, and his life. Considered in the social context of the time, the offer of his daughters to the Sodomites signifies an immense sacrifice. The daughters carry the promise of generational continuity. The rape, which in terms of women's social position precludes marriage and signifies life in disgrace, will terminate the family line.

Let us note that, to a remarkable extent, the consequences of Lot's offer to the Sodomites, of which he is quite aware, do not differ significantly from the consequences of Abraham's forthcoming sacrifice of Isaac. In terms of his position as a *pater familias*, Lot's assumption of responsibility for the strangers and, inadvertently, for the Sodomites themselves, amounts to the sacrificial loss of his posterity and therefore to self-sacrifice.

In terms of his unique destiny as a patriarch, Abraham's intercession for the cities projects a loss on a global scale. His persistent query intends not only to change God's decree, but to transform the definition of justice. Abraham's provocative position imperils the promise of chosenness that, to recall Paul, will make his descendants eternal "friends of God" for the sake of the patriarchs.

It is of extreme importance that Abraham's disagreement with God's sentence of death and destruction is reported immediately after his legitimacy as a patriarch had been reconfirmed. He had been promised a son. The birth of Isaac would actualize the blessing. To antagonize God might provoke God's wrath and result in the obliteration of Abraham's chosenness as the father of nations. Unlike Lot, who consciously risked all for the strangers, Abraham consciously risks all for the sinners.

What Abraham is unconscious of, however, is the test to which he is being submitted, whereby a prudent decision not to risk God's anger would have failed him. While quoting the divine stream of consciousness, the story implies that due to his chosenness, Abraham was indeed expected to present his argument on behalf of the condemned cities. We hear God explaining why He will inform Abraham about the plans for destruction: "Shall I hide from Abraham that which I am doing; seeing that Abraham shall surely become a great and a mighty nation, and all the nations of the world will be blessed in him?" (18:17-18).

God's decision to share the plan to destroy the cities clearly intends to elicit Abraham's response as the father of nations. Rather than privileges and rights, Abraham's elevated position brings forth a crucial test of his ethics of responsibility. In effect, God's acceptance of Abraham's discourse signals approval of Abraham's courageous stance. The fact that God ends the discussion attests to Abraham's determination to continue to plead for the cities as long as possible. God leaves, once He is satisfied that Abraham has proven himself worthy of his patriarchy.

The Sodom and Gomorrah story crystallizes the ethical role of the future father of nations. This ethics is articulated succinctly in Jesus' exhortation of love for enemies: "Why should God reward you if you love only the people who love you. Even the collectors do that! And if you speak only to your friends, have you done anything out of the ordinary? Even the pagans do that" (Matt 5:46-47). Abraham both anticipates and provides a model for Jesus' teaching by extending his care and attention not only to Lot but also to those who resist God.

The story makes clear that Abraham's behavior toward Lot, whom he calls his brother, is exemplary. He lets Lot have the better piece of land (Gen 13:8-12), and he saves him from captivity (14:14). The test of true love, however, consists in risking the entire future, his own and that of the generations after him, to assert righteousness through salvation of enemies. That is why Abraham's failure to prevent the destruction marks the tragic irony of his enormous effort. The smoldering landscape of the Plain on the morning after the destruction confronts Abraham with the futility of his endeavor.

The event of the destruction reiterates the problem of the relevance of the text to us today. In what way is Abraham's argument meaningful in view of the eventual destruction of the cities? While Abraham's intercession failed to save the cities of the Plain, it certainly established him as father of nations. The biblical tradition, as we have seen already, insists on his view that righteousness be reasserted through extension of love to those who transgress, as well as those who love us.

Let us turn once again to Paul, the Christian patriarch. Paul insists that Israel, despite her refusal to accept the word of Jesus, maintains her friendship with God thanks to the ancestors and that God will never renege on the blessing that He conferred upon Abraham. The teaching in Abraham's intercession for the cities seems to re-echo in Paul's argument. Furthermore, through his insistence on the blessedness of Israel, the apostle actually emulates Abraham's unconditional love and responsibility for humankind, whatever their creed might be. Significantly, rather than setting himself apart from Jewish tradition, Paul affirms his connection to Israel. As the father of the Christian nations, he wishes to shape his patriarchy after the model of the father of all nations.

It is extremely important to note that the Second Vatican Council, in *Nostra Aetate*, places emphasis on the link of Christians and the descendents of Abraham. This dramatic change is grounded in Paul's view that we have noted above:

> In 1964 Second Vatican Council in Dogmatic Constitution on the Church (*Lumen Gentium*) declared that "on account of their fathers this [Jewish] people remains most dear to God, for God does not repent of the gifts [God] makes nor of the calls [God] issues (cf. Rom 11:28-29)." In a single phrase the Roman Church reversed at least sixteen centuries of popular Christian teaching, typified by Chrysostom's "God hates them and always hated them."[8]

Through its midrashic interpretations, the biblical story keeps alive. Its continuing viability lies in its resistance to connect with the tragedy of the Holocaust. But while it refuses association with the apocalyptic destruction of the Final Solution, the story does communicate a meaningful message to the post-Holocaust world. In view of our consciousness of the possibility of destruction, it commands us to explore the profound and difficult lesson in reaffirmation of righteousness through the ethic of responsibility.

1. Walter Brueggeman, *Genesis: A Biblical Commentary for Teaching and Preaching* (Atlanta: John Knox Press, 1982), p. 4.

2. J. A. Loader, *A Tale of Two Cities: Sodom and Gomorrah in the Old Testament, Early Jewish and Early Christian Traditions* (Kampen, Netherlands: J. H. Kok, 1990), p. 119.

3. Frank Kermode, *The Sense of Ending* (New York: Oxford University Press, 1967), p. 39.

4. Kermode, p. 30.

5. Loader, p. 136.

6. Seán Hand, ed. *The Levinas Reader* (Cambridge: Basil Blackwell, 1989), p. 113.

7. Levinas, p. 47.

8. Philip A. Cunningham, *Education for Shalom: Religion Textbooks and the Enhancement of the Catholic and Jewish Relationship* (Philadelphia: The American Interfaith Institute, 1986), p. 35.

KNOW SODOM, KNOW SHOAH
Zev Garber

Harry James Cargas nas brought many years of learning, teaching, writing and hands-on experience to his scholarship on the Shoah and produced one of the best assessments by a Catholic scholar on the Church's responsibility, sans apology and theological cliché, in a post-Auschwitz age to the Jewish People. Multiple levels of reality, intermixing of illusion and fact, and emotions jumping in and out of the years of the Shoah are all parts of Cargas' agenda. He is cosmopolitan, his artistic approaches vary from historiography to oral history testimonies to interviews and investigative reporting—and his overriding theme is the exploration of the Shoah and genocide. Our honoree's gift is in granting extraordinary events ordinary causes, cloaking them with the potent poetic license of *j'accuse*! To read Harry James Cargas is an invitation to discover his character within his prose style. He is sensibly even-handed about this, choosing not to place style over character, but to use the former as the key to the latter. His generous soul, indeed his life, is a testimony to bridge building between Christians and Jews on issues that divide us. In appreciation of the efforts made by this self-styled "post-Auschwitz Christian," I contribute this essay on Genesis 18-19 juxtaposed with Matthew 10 as a hermeneutical exercise in re-reading Scriptures from the ashes and by the fire of Shoah.

We begin by assessing the Biblical Setting of Genesis 18-19 as received in the tradition of Synagogue and Church and proceed from Sodom to Shoah, where exegesis and hermeneutics combine to offer existential observation juxtaposed to the text, which may or may not be consistent with classical rabbinic interpretation. The image of Sodom in Matthew 10 is linked with Jesus' condemnation of soul-patriots, even as responsible members of Church and Synagogue choose to forget on their way to rapprochement. Consider the word *Christ*, used so frequently in discussions and depictions of Jesus; when the battle over its meaning has been as intense as any Christian war on words and doctrines in Church history, what may an outsider add? But the decision of the apostolic writers to etch the memory of the Christ-event in Jewish history propels us to go beyond Christian theology and religion and ask, What kind of Jew is Jesus? Jesus reconsidered proposes if there is a midrashic will, there is a redeemable way.

Rethinking Genesis 18, 19

I. *Biblical Setting*

1. The Cause for the Destruction of Sodom and Gomorrah and Other Cities of the Plain (Admah, Zeboiim, Lasha and later, Zoar) in terms of Factuality and Actuality.

    A. Factuality: Geographic upheaval south of the Dead Sea brought about by a natural catastrophe (possibly, earthquake accompanied by an eruption of underground petroleum gases), sometime after the Patriarchal Period.

    B. Actuality: Destruction brought about by a citizenry that lived in wickedness and sinfulness. The nature of the abominations and depravities: Sexual depravity (Gen 19:4-9); social oppression (Is 1:10; 3:9); adultery, lying, encouraging the criminal (Jer 23:14); disregard of the needy (Ezek 16:49).

2. The Role of Abraham

    A. The Covenant of Circumcision, an everlasting partnership between God and the seed of Abraham throughout the generations (Gen 17:7 ff.).

    B. From whose seed sprout the blessing and the curse: "I will make you a great nation, and I will bless you, and make your name great; and be you a blessing. And I will bless them that bless you, and him that curse you will I curse; and in you shall all the nations be blessed" (Gen 12:2-3). See also Gen 18:17; 22:18: 27:29.

    C. "The Father of a multitude of Nations" (Gen 17:4).

    D. Prophet (Gen 20:7), though not in the service of advising his people of a divine decree as the People of Israel is not yet in history.

3. *HaShem*'s Soliloquy

    A. The way of the Lord: Righteousness and Justice (Gen 18:19; Jer 9:22; 22:15-16; Amos 5:23; Ps 33:5; Prov 21:3)

    B. Heaven's justice (Gen 13:10; 19:24, 29) is operative when the cry of the oppressed, victims of atrocious wickedness, is heard, seen and recorded (Gen 18:20, 21; Ex 3:9; Isa 5:7; Ex 22:21-23, and elsewhere).

    C. God reveals that which He is going to do; "Surely the Lord God does nothing without revealing His secret to His servants and Prophets (Amos 3:7)

4. Colloquy between Abraham and *HaShem*

    A. Abraham's prayer before the Judge of all the earth (Gen 18:25), "Will You sweep away the innocent along with the guilty (suggesting the righteous in all nations)?" (Gen 18:22, 23; 20:4). Also, the survival of the righteous ought not be contaminated by the taint of the wicked. If so, then "the innocent and guilty fare alike" (Gen 18:25).

B.   Abraham's plea is not intercession for the wicked, but an appeal for the innocent, whose presence can save a city/society from perishing from the face of the earth.

C.   In Oriental fashion, *HaShem* and Abraham, on the heights of Hebron overlooking the lowest spot on earth, are represented as bargaining concerning the fate of Sodom. Alas, Abraham's *six* attempts (Gen 18:22-27: "Abraham stood yet before the Lord"; "Drew near and said"; "Will You sweep away and not forgive the place for the 50 righteous therein?"; "Far be it from You to slay the righteous with the wicked"; "Far be it from You, shall not the Judge of all the earth do justly"; "Here I venture to speak to my Lord, I am but dust and ashes") and five progressive petitions (Gen 18:28-32) are met with God's unyielding response. "And the Lord went His way, as soon as He had left off speaking to Abraham; And Abraham returned unto his place" (Gen 18:33).[1]

5. The Judgment of Sodom and Gomorrah

A.   *Mishnah Sanhedrin* 10.3: The men of Sodom have no share in the World-to-Come, for it is written, "Now the men of Sodom were wicked and sinners against the Lord exceedingly (Gen 13:13); "wicked" in this world and "sinners" in the World-to-Come.

R. Nehemiah says: Neither of them shall stand in judgment; for it is written: "Therefore the wicked shall not stand in judgment nor sinners in the congregation of the righteous" (Ps 1:5).

B.   *Ha'af tispeh ... rasha'* (Gen 18:23b). Read not, "will You indeed (*af afilu*) sweep away ... the guilty," but "Your anger (*af*) sweeps away ... the guilty." The Almighty does not desire to condemn any creature, "For You are not a God that has pleasure in condemnation" (Ps 5:5); "I have no pleasure in the death of him that dies, saith the Lord God" (Ezek 18:32); "As I live—declares the Lord God—it is not my desire that the wicked shall die, but that the wicked turn from his (wicked) ways and live" (Ezek 33:11); Jer 18:7-10 speaks in general terms of the criteria in which the destruction or preservation of a people depends, including if a nation turns from its wickedness it can be saved; Jonah 3,4 (see also Zeph 2) is concerned with the destruction and preservation of wicked Nineveh; In what does God delight? In vindicating His creatures, as it says, "The Lord is delighted in His vindication (of wrongdoers)" (Isa 42:21); How may sinners disappear from the earth and the wicked be no more" (Ps 104:35)? By ceasing sinful acts so that wickedness will be no more.

C.   "Far be it from You" (*halilah leka*), mentioned twice in Gen 18:25, suggests that the Divine Name is desecrated if righteousness is swept away with the wicked. "Men of understanding, listen to me; wickedness be far from God, wrongdoing, from *Shaddai*" (Job 34:10).

As long as the ungodly are in the world, the fierceness of His anger is in the world; after the ungodly are perished from the world, the fierceness of His anger will be replaced by mercy and compassion. What is "ungodly?" Criminal societies ruled by worthless scoundrels ("children of Belial"), who are abhorrent in word, thought and action. And what is right in the sight of the Lord God? "Put the inhabitants of that town to the sword and put its cattle to the sword. Doom it and all that is in it to destruction: gather all its spoil into the open square, and burn the town and all its spoil as a holocaust to the Lord your God. And it shall remain an everlasting ruin, never to be rebuilt" (Deut 13:16-17).

E.   The power of the righteous can restore civilization. "Run to and fro through the streets of Jerusalem, and see now, and know, and seek in the broad places thereof. If you can find a man, if there be any that does justly, that seeks the truth; I will pardon her" (Jer 5:1). The advocacy of the good and the virtuous must be public and broad sweeping if societal values are to be transformed. A city/place that sequesters its moral voice (thereby, no ethical change in the public arena) cannot claim salvation by virtue of the righteous who live within (Ezek 14:12-20). The pious and the not so ethical (Lot, for example) may survive as individuals, but their muted, private voice will not save the wicked society (Gen 19:14).

6. Justice by God

Gen 18:17-32 is an attempt to explain Gen 13:10, 13 ("The Lord had destroyed Sodom and Gomorrah ... (because) the inhabitants were wicked and sinners before the Lord exceedingly"), in which God had decided to destroy Sodom, then carried out His decision (Gen 19:13, 24, 25), but saved Lot (Gen 19:15, 16) because He remembered Abraham (Gen 19:29).

"Abraham's intercession for Sodom" is an attempt to explain God's participation in disaster. This episode is an argumentation directed at removing any possible doubts about God's righteousness that could arise as a result of the catastrophe. Further, Abraham's relationship to God is based on loyalty and fidelity, understood as doing what is just and right, corresponding to the righteousness of God. Thus, when justice is to be meted out God appoints an advocate (Abraham) for the wicked, who, in turn, receives divine assurance that justice has come forth without reasonable doubt.

II. *From Sodom to Shoah*

1. The Story

No story in Genesis is mentioned as frequently in the TaNaK as the destruction of Sodom (and Gomorrah, Admah, Zeboiim): Deut 29:23; Isa 1:9 ff; 13:19; Jer 49:18; 50:40; Ezek 16:46-50, 53-55; Amos 4:11; Zeph 2:9;

Lam 4:6; Ps 11:6; Admah and Zeboiim: Hos 11:8, Deut 29:22 (cf. Gen 10:19; 14:2, 8). Typical is Deut 29:23: "The whole land brimstone and salt, beyond sowing and producing, no grass growing in it, just like the upheaval of Sodom and Gomorrah, Admah and Zeboim, which the Lord overthrew in His fierce anger." [Note: In all references in the Hebrew Bible to Sodom and Gomorrah the ineffable Name YKWK, stressing God's revelation to mankind and acts of loving kindness and mercy (*middat ha-rahamin*), is found. Only in Amos 4:11 do we find *Elokim*, which teaches His divine justice and authority (*middat ha-din*).]

"Shall not the Judge of all the earth deal justly?" (Gen 18:28) is the peak of Abraham's defense. Justice is the main pillar of God's authority and man's society. "Justice, justice shall you pursue, that you may live" (Deut 16:20). The boldness of our Father Abraham's challenge, the universality of the phrase "all the earth," and the absolute conviction that the infinite might of God must be controlled by decrees of justice is the pinnacle of the Torah way. Indeed, ever since Sinai, justice and mercy are seen as the pillars supporting human society, and the former is the prerequisite for a world at peace. Alas, no event in Jewish and Christian collective memory is comparable to the Shoah that challenges the believability of *middot ha-din* and *rahamin*. Why so? Gen 18's emphatic distinction that *Heilsgeschichte* is based on merit of the just is diametrically opposed and directly adverse to the extinction of the suffering just in the Shoah. Are the events of the Shoah proclaiming an "unjust God," and if so, is this not a contradiction in terms?

2. The Silence of God

May not the fate of the murdered Jewish nation suggest that God's voice is silent:

Before Abraham, who declared, "Far be it from you to do such a thing" (Gen 18:25)

Before Moses, who pleaded, "Why are You angry against your people" (Ex 32:11)

Before Joshua, who cried, "Lord God why did You lead this people across the Jordan only to deliver them into the hands of the Amorites, to be destroyed by them" (Josh 7:7)

Before David, who queried, "Why, O' Lord, do You stand aloof, heedless in times of trouble?" (Ps 10:1)

And His way destructive:

Job 9:22: "It is all one ... He destroys the blameless and the guilty."

Job 12:4: "A just and blameless man proclaims, 'I have become a laughingstock."

Job 12:16: "Erring and causing to err are from Him."

Ezek 2:8: "Thus said the Lord: I am going to deal with you! I will draw my sword from its sheath, and I will wipe out from you both the righteous and the wicked."

3. The Anguish of Abraham, Our Parent

It is apparent that Abraham's heart is heavy when he rises early in the morning to gaze with pitiful eyes upon the fulfillment of the Divine decree: "And Abraham got up early in the morning to the place where he had stood before the Lord. And looking down toward Sodom and Gomorrah and all the land of the Plain, he saw the smoke of the land rising like the smoke of the furnace" (Gen 19:27-28).

This is a counterpart to "Abraham remained standing before the Lord" (Gen 18:22), one of the Eighteen *Tiqqune Soferim* (Scribal Emendations) attested in certain Masoretic lists. The original, "the Lord stood before Abraham," is a daring statement that boldly proclaims an unacceptable anthropomorphism; that is to say, the Sovereign of the universe stands accountable before mortal man. A careful read of the Abrahamic role in Gen 18, 19 suggests that Abraham's genetic and extended progeny are not the subject of blessing alone. Humanity is vulnerable to catastrophe and Divine judgment. Abraham looks down at the scene of the ancient disaster—as at the end of his bargaining with God—and is silent. But "God remembered Abraham and removed Lot from the midst of the upheaval" (Gen 19:29). Does this mean that the God who judges is also the God who remembers? Does this point anew to each generation since Sodom and Gomorrah the meaning of God's promise to Abraham: "I will be your God"?[2]

Or is the intent of Abraham gazing in silence over the calamity of old, a look beyond himself into the history of his people ending in the finality of Auschwitz? If so, then Abraham's proclamation, "I am but dust and ashes" (Gen 18:27), is not an expression of deepest humility but group-fulfilled prophecy.

4. Wicked Lot and the Lot of Humanity

In rabbinic tradition, Lot is generally described as lascivious, ungrateful to Abraham and he is accused in Gen 19 as being immoral and incestuous (Gen 19:8, 32-36). Also, he chose to sojourn in Sodom, a city whose inhabitants gave free reign to their wickedness. Before Divine judgment he managed to escape to a very small place, the cave of Adullam (Gen 19:20, 30). And his wife who heeded not the call, "escape for your life! Do not look back" (Gen 19:17), was smitten. Gen 19:29 makes clear that Lot owed his life to Abraham's intercessions; however, the Rabbis further maintained that he was rewarded for not exposing Abraham's identity in Egypt (Gen 12:10-20). Finally, as father of Moab and Ammon (Gen 19:30-38), he was the precursor of the House of David and the messianic line (via Ruth the Moabitess and Naamah the Ammonitess).

The meaning of the Lot story for the post-Shoah age is complex but straightforward: When catastrophic disaster hits, whether by Divine decree or not, there is neither bystander nor spectator, only the escapee or the smitten. So we ask; Do we honor the Torah injunction not to look back and observe

God's judgment of destruction or record His silence in the face of annihilation? Must we ponder the imponderable, as we must, and discover the victims' deepest degradation, that is to say, they are dust and ashes. "Dust" is the lowest form of matter upon which everyone steps and "ashes" the last remnant. Or does the lot of humanity face itself as human stalagmites formed on the floor of a cave by the memory of the Shoah and realize one truth: Sodom was destroyed. Shoah happened in history. The bad and the good were swept away together. Abraham's intercession did not help. The cry of the innocent did not deter the "Final Solution." The human-Divine colloquy demonstrated that the destruction of Sodom and Gomorrah was just. Nonetheless, can we say indisputably the same about the Shoah? Or is the Shoah a wake-up call not to cave in?

"And lo, the Lord passed by. There was a great and mighty wind, splitting mountains and shattering rocks by the power of the Lord; but the Lord was not in the wind. After the wind—an earthquake; but the Lord was not in the earthquake. After the earthquake fire—but the Lord was not in the fire. And after the fire—a still small voice" (I Kings 19:11b-12).

This then is the charge from Sodom to Shoah and in all generations between and after: Small humanity in a small cave hear and act on the murmuring sound and go forth from closure into life. Otherwise, consider the alternative.

Reimagining Jesus: The View from Tradition

III. What Kind of Jesus?

What sort of historical Jesus can traditional Judaism tolerate? The Jesus of different Christologies could never find support in Judaism, since the God-man of the "hypostatic union" is foreign to Judaism's teaching on absolute monotheism. As the promised Messiah,[3] he did not meet the conditions which the prophetic-rabbinic tradition associated with the coming of the Messiah. For example, there was no harmony, freedom, peace and unity in the Land and enmity and struggle abounded everywhere. As a unique teacher, his attitude towards the Torah[4] and his remarks about the great commandment[5] make him no more of an authority than any disciple of the contemporary schools of Hillel and Shammai. Moreover, a number of his legal decisions are contrary to Torah (Written and Oral) tradition. Case in point, Jesus on the Shabbat[6] and the Shabbat as developed in post-biblical Judaism. The Shabbat state is one of complete harmony between man and man and between man and nature. The Shabbat is a weekly 24-hour period devoted to joy and recreation, worship and learning, a total cessation from toil, sorrow and suffering. By not working, that is by not involving oneself creatively or destructively in the process of social and natural change which is what the Shabbat rules are all about, man is free from the chains of nature, progress and time.[7] Thus, in rabbinic jargon, Shabbat is a taste of the "world to come" which is wholly Shabbat, although only for one day a week.

As a moral and religious genius, we fail to see where Jesus bettered the ethical code of Judaism. For example, the distinction between the positive articulation of the Golden Rule as given by Jesus[8] and its negative form as given by Hillel.[9] Jesus' ethic is seen in Christianity as altruistic and denies the individual objective moral value and sacrifices him for the sake of the other. Hillel's moral code as understood within Judaism eliminates the subjective attitude entirely. It is objectively involved with abstract justice, which attaches moral value to the individual as such without prejudice to self or other.

Hillel's argument is that no man has a right to ruin another man's life for the sake of his own life, and similarly, he has no right to ruin his own life for the sake of another. Both are human beings and both lives have the same value before the heavenly throne of justice. The Torah teaching, "Love your neighbor as yourself,"[10] means for the Rabbis of the Talmud just that, neither more nor less; that is, the scales of justice must be in a state of equilibrium with no favorable leaning either toward self or neighbor. Self-love must not be a measuring rod to slant the scale on the side of self-advantage and concern for the other must not tip the scale of justice in his behalf.[11]

Jesus' message that socially unfortunate persons and groups are specially protected by God[12] is not a new idea. Why so? The Bible records a number of times that the God of Israel; a) despises the powerful and mighty who live by strength alone; b) favors by community legislation the protection of the poor, widowed, orphaned and lamed; and c) proclaims that "the meek shall inherit the earth,"[13] and "the pure in heart shall see God."[14] Also, the Essenes of Qumran fame, who were fond of their title, "poor in spirit," may have influenced a number of Beatitudes[15]; and the Beatitudes' hope for the future is remarkably paralleled to The Testaments of the Twelve Patriarchs on the eschatological future.[16]

Jewishly speaking, Jesus is not a prophet in the Torah sense, since he does not fulfill what "Moses truly said unto the fathers, a prophet shall the Lord your God raise up unto you of your brethren, like unto me"[17] The test of a true prophet was the fulfillment of the specific prediction that he announced as the credentials of his divine call and not the sum total of miracles and signs performed.[18]

The central unifying theme of Jesus' preaching was the immanent dawning of the Kingdom of God, which he interpreted to be the visible manifestation of the sovereign power of God ushering in the messianic days, bringing judgment on evil and divine blessing for the righteous.[19] Alas, the social, political and spiritual stability of Israel and the world did not take place. The state of complete harmony between man and man did not occur in the lifetime of Jesus. There did not evolve the prophetic view of the "ends of days": the earth fruitful again, man not having to live by the sweat of his brow, swords into plowshares, wolf and lamb dwelling together, war no more, but the reign of harmony, dignity, unity and free-dom. Furthermore, some New Testament accounts suggest that the authority of Jesus is divine as Torah; this seriously jeopardizes the claim that Jesus was a prophet since the prophet is bound by Torah, to which he may neither add nor subtract.[20]

My own approach to finding the historical Jesus in the text of the New Testament may appear to some as extreme. It seems to me that the canonical Mark contains authentic traces of the historical Jesus shrouded in repeated motifs of secrecy which are intended to obscure the role of Jesus as a political revolutionary sympathizer involved in the Jewish national struggle against Rome.[21] When the Gospel of Mark is analyzed in its own light, without recourse to the special status which tradition and canonicity confer, it becomes an astute polemic against the Mother Church in Jerusalem, whose influence diminished considerably following the fall of Jerusalem in 70 C.E., and a clever apology to make early Christianity palatable for Rome by not identifying Jesus with the national aspirations of the Jews. The Markan account on the trial of Jesus and his execution, along with the portrait of a pacifistic Christ, are for the most part historically questioned by S.G.F. Brandon, who sees in these narratives attempts by the Gentile Church to win Roman favor by exculpating Pontius Pilate from his share in the crucifixion of Jesus.

We agree. Regarding the Synoptic Gospels account of Jesus before the Sanhedrin,[22] the trial before Pilate,[23] and the sentence of death,[24] the question of historical fairness intrudes into these accounts. Were there two Sanhedrins, religious and secular, or one? If two, which court condemned Jesus? Where in the biblical-talmudic tradition is blasphemy defined by claiming that one is the "Messiah the Son of the Blessed?"[25] Lev 24:13-23 and Sanhedrin 7.5 proclaim that whoever curses God is guilty of blasphemy.[26] Rarely recorded are malediction and impious profanity by one who claims to be a messianic pretender. True, Josephus recorded many messianic pretenders between 6-70 C.E., but we have no record of any put to death. Bar-Kochba was called Messiah by Akiba but tradition does not speak ill of either second century hero. And no less a personality than Maimonides relegated the messianic doctrine to a secondary position among the articles of faith. Also, one guilty of blasphemy was stoned to death and not killed by crucifixion as recorded by Mark.[27]

IV. Jesus as Zealot

That Jesus was sympathetic to the zealot cause may explain why the charges of sedition were not overtly denied by Jesus when asked, "Are you the King of the Jews?"[28] Other references support this view. One of his trusted disciples was Simon the Zealot.[29] The Zealot Movement, rooted in the tradition of being "zealous for the Lord,"[30] arose in the Galilee in the first decade of the era. It may be assumed that the boy Jesus raised in Nazareth would have listened often to tales of zealot exploits against the hated Romans and how many of the former died martyrs' deaths in a futile attempt to replace the bondage of Rome with the yoke of the "kingdom of heaven."[31]

These childhood experiences listened to in earnestness and awe caused the adult Jesus to sympathize with the anti-Roman feelings of his people. Thus, the "cleansing of the Temple" pericope is not to be read as anti-Temple but a critique of the Temple functionaries who collaborated with Rome.[32] This episode appears to have coincided with an insurrection in Jerusalem during the period of Gaius Caligula (34-41) in which the zealots appear to have been involved.[33] The famous question concerning tribute to Caesar has Jesus saying, "render to Caesar the things that are Caesar's and to God the things that are God's,"[34] thereby implying Jewish support of Roman fiscal and political policy. This is an assimilationist position and it is very doubtful that the historical Jesus can be identified with it. Better to say, Mark, a Roman national, coined Jesus' answer for it guaranteed that Jesus was loyal to Rome and opposed to Jewish nationalism. A necessary survivor kit for Gentile Christians living in Rome during and after the zealot-inspired Jewish war against Rome.

The *ipsissima verba* of Jesus recorded in Matt 10:34, namely, "I have not come to bring peace, but a sword," supports the militancy by Jesus mentioned in the Gethsemane tradition: Luke 22:35-38 portrays Jesus asking his disciples if they are armed and they reply that they are doubly armed. The size and arming of the arresting party "from the chief priests and the scribes, and the elders"[35] can be cited as evidence of the intention of Jesus. The unknown disciple who draws a sword and cuts off the ear of the High Priest's slave is identified in John's Gospel as Peter.[36]

Others say, the question of Jesus, "Have you come out against a robber with swords and clubs to capture me?,"[37] separates him from the Zealots. But can the militant Jesus be hidden in the image of the Christ of Peace? We think not. Mark's anti-Jewish bias and pro-Roman sentiments inspired him to lay the guilt of the death of Jesus in the hands of Jewish authorities. Jesus was not an insurrectionist nor did he commit a crime deserving death by Roman Law.[38] Later Church narrative accepts this view without serious emendation and further represents him as the "Prince of Peace." An early source of this tradition is the editorial note in Matt 26:52. Here a post-70 C.E. Jewish Christian evaluating the ill-fated Jewish War declared in Jesus' name: "Put your sword back into its place; for all who take the sword will perish by the sword."[39]

A constant motif is the silence of the apostolic writings on matters pertaining to the political situation of the time. The Zealots of the period are essentially overlooked; episodes in which they were involved, as reported by Josephus and others, are not reported. Luke-Acts is silent about the identity and antecedents of James, Peter, and the other leaders of Jewish Christianity. Mark's theology makes it necessary to prejudice the historical situation and declare that Jesus could not have involved himself in political nationalism and other contemporary issues. Later apostolic writers submissively followed the Markan line. How far theology distorts history is further shown by denigrating the Pharisees as the bitter opponents of Jesus.[40]

In summation, according to Mark, the earliest canonical gospel on Jesus, the catastrophe of 70 C.E. and its aftermath was brought about by the Jewish leaders who plotted Jesus' death, the Jewish mob who had demanded it, and the Jew of the Land who refused to accept the Jesus way. Further, Mark is the source that Jewish disciples do not know Jesus,[41] and it is the Roman centurion at the crucifixion who recognizes Jesus as the Son of God.[42]

V. Messianic Thunder

Our thesis suggests that New Testament belief about "Who do the people say that I am?"[43] is more actuality than factuality. The traditions of the early Church in regard to the historical Jesus are shrouded in the idiom of Midrash. By Midrash, I mean an existential understanding by man of his environment, history and being. Its purpose is not to provide objective descriptions of the world or to relate objective facts, but to convey a particular cultural worldview. Its content is doctrinal and ethical and its form is mythic. The very nature of Midrash is to "demidrashize," i.e., to decode the original form and make the content more meaningful for different time and clime. Indeed, the New Testament shows evidence of this. For example:

> Given: Jesus returns in the clouds of Heaven.
> Pauline: Shifts the emphasis of the failure of Jesus' return to the believer's present life.
> Johanine: Achieves the same Pauline goal with its conception of eternal life here and now present to the faith, and of judgment as already accomplished in the world which Jesus brings.

Our cross-denominational exploration of Jesus puts him in history, not divinity, and conveys that he was a loyal son of Israel. Not a false Redeemer of the Jews but failed, as witnessed by the words at the cross: *"Eli, Eli, lama sabach-thani?"*[44] Nevertheless, can the words attributed to Jesus bear fruit on the different branches of Judaism and Christianity after the Shoah? We think so but on the road from Calvary to Auschwitz, with a pit stop in Sodom, we must leap beyond defects in Christ's teaching. To do so is an invitation to "remidrashize" the good and the bad, the beauty and the ugly. We begin by looking at the post-Shoah world as it is and by not being afraid of telling the truth.

After Auschwitz, not "Dinotobia" but "Jurasicphobia" is the real thing. In Edenic mythology, "the wolf shall dwell with the lamb, and the leopard shall lie down with the kid, and the wolf and the young lion and the fatling together" (Isa 11:6), but in the real world, cruel death (AIDS, Ebola virus, among the worst) is a functional inevitability of a natural system. To our way of thinking no social reform would take the exaltation of poverty and damnation of riches as an outline for an idyllic society; or the parables of the fowls of the air and the lilies of the field as an answer for anxiety[45]; or the multiplication of the bread and fish as an answer to the world's famine problem[46]; or setting up members of the household against one another as answer to the generation gap or conducive to *shalom bayit* (domestic tranquility) in our times[47]; or the prescriptions for healing the blind,[48] deaf,[49] epileptic,[50] paralytic,[51] dumb,[52] sick,[53] and infirm[54] as guides to cure disease endors-ed by the A.M.A.; or altruism which effaces "self" for "other." In short, it is incon-ceivable to take literally these teachings to be an adequate practical conduit to life and experience in a post-Shoah age. Nor do we take literally the condemnation of the "lost sheep of Israel," who do not heed Jesus' redemptive words: "Truly, I say to you, it shall be more tolerable on the day of judgment for the land Sodom and Gomorrah than for that town." (Matt 10:15)

In the long history of Christianity there exists no more tragic development than the treatment accorded the Jewish people by Christian believers based in part on Christian creed. The cornerstone of supersessionist Christology is the belief that Israel was spurned by divine fiat for first rejecting and then killing Jesus. This permitted the apostolic and patristic writers to attribute to Israel the evil of the Sodomites, and more, to assign the worst dire punishment on judgment day. These are not words, just words, but they are links in an uninterrupted chain of antisemitic diatribes that contributed to the murder of Jews in the heartland of Christianity and still exist in a number of Christian circles today. How to mend the cycle of pain and the legacy of shame? The key is a midrashic interpretation informed by a moral imperative.

An illustration is in order. Three times the Pentateuch mentions the legislation of *lex talionis* (law of retribution; "eye for eye"): the penalty for causing a pregnant bystander to miscarry when two individuals fight (Exod 21:23-25); the case of one maiming another (Lev 24:19-20); and punishment meted out to one who gives false testimony (Deut 19:18-21).

Though the law of "measure for measure" existed in the Ancient Near East and persists today in parts of the Muslim Middle East and elsewhere, there is little evidence that the Torah carried out this legislation literally except in the case of willful murder (e.g., Gen 9:8; Num 35:3, etc.). In the (M)Oral Torah, "Life for life" in cases of non-homicidal intention and "eye for eye" when physical injuries are not fatal are seen as a process for fair compensation. Thus, equitable monetary compensation is understood by the Oral Torah in the case of a pregnant woman who loses (fetal) life ("you shall give life for life," Exod 21:23b) and when animal life is forfeited ("And he that smites a beast mortally shall make it good: life for life," Lev 19:18). Indeed, the Written Torah casts aside all doubts as to the intent of the Hebrew *lex talionis*: "And he that kills a beast shall make it good; and he that kills a man shall be put to death" (Lev 24:21).

Rejecting the literal application of *lex talionis*, hopefully, puts an end to the mean-spirited charge in classical Christianity that Judaism is "strict justice." Rather it is advocacy of remedial justice for the guilty and just concern for the injured. Nonetheless, the severe language of the Written Torah's *ayin tahat ayin*, "eye for eye," may suggest the ideal in human behavior, which few moderns comprehend: there is no remuneration in the world that can compensate serious injury, death, or any act of victimization.

In the same spirit, we choose to see Jesus' condemnation (Matt 10:15) and militancy (Matt 10:34) neither as antisemitic nor anti-Judaism, but rather as "messianic thunder": a) this direct reproach of Jesus to his people evidenced his identity with and concern for them; and b) for God's Day of Retribution, war (sword) against evil by every available means to enable the messianic prophecies of Isa 2:4 and Mic 4:3 to become reality. Then, redemptive awakening and now, necessary awakening, this is the great comforter of the pains of Exile and Shoah. Once heeded, Jews and Christians can believe in the improvability of humankind. May their mutual Covenant in Blood[55] seize the day when Shoah will be no more.

1. Here and following my debt to the late Israel Orthodox scholar, Nechama Leibowitz, is evident. Her *Gilyonot le-Iyyun be-Farashat ha-Shavua* (early 1950s-1980s) has introduced a generation of Hebrew readers to the world of ancient and modern Jewish commentary on the Book of Books.

2. Claus Westermann, *Genesis 12-36, A Commentary*, trans.by John J. Schallion S.J. (Minneapolis: Augsburg Publishing House, 1985), p. 308.

3. Cf., among others, Matt 26:62-64; Mark 14:60-62; Luke 22:66-70.

4. Cf. Matt. 5:17-20.

5. Matt 22:37 = Mark 12:30 = Luke 10:27—Deut 6:5; Mark 12:29—Deut 6:4; Matt 23:39 = Mark 12:31 = Luke 10:27b—Lev 19:18; Mark 12:33- cf. I Sam 15:22.

6. E.g., Matt 12:1-8; Mark 2:23-28; Luke 6:1-5 and parallels in Deut 5:14, 23:25; Ex 20:10; I Sam 21:1-7; Lev 24:7-9.

7. The insertion of the Shabbat in the creation story of Genesis suggests that its sacredness is meant for universal man and not intended for Israel alone.

8. Cf. Matt 7:12; Luke 6:31.

9. The origin of the Golden Rule is Lev 19:18. Evidence of the Golden Rule as the essence of moral life is found in Jewish tradition long before the period of Hillel and Jesus. E.g., the second B.C.E. books of Ben Sira and Tobit expound: "Honor thy neighbor as thyself" (Ben Sira) and "What is displeasing to thyself, that do not unto any other" (Tobit). Similarly, the first century B.C.E. book, *Testaments of the Twelve Patriarchs*, warns: "A man should not do to his neighbor what a man does not desire for himself.'

10. Lev 19:18.

11. Cf. The Baraitha in *B. Mes.* 62a, which pits the view of the altruistic Ben P'tura against R. Akiba, and *Pesah* 25b where a man asks Raba (c. 280-352) what he should do if an official threatened to kill him unless he would kill another man.

12. See the Beatitudes, Matt 5:3-12 and a shorter version in Luke 6:20-23.

13. Cf. Ps 37:11.

14. Cf. Ps 24:4.

15. For example, the writer of the *Thanksgiving Scroll* 18:14-15 thanks God, "(F)or having appointed me in thy truth a messenger of the peace of goodness, to proclaim to the meek the multitude of thy mercies, and let them that are contrite of spirit hear salvation from an everlasting source, and for them that mourn everlasting joy."

16. *The Testaments of the Twelve Patriarchs*, a pseudepigraphical book modeled on the "Blessing of Jacob" (Gen 49), proclaims to relate in its twelve books the message that each of the twelve sons of Jacob gave to his descendants on his death bed. The bulk of the work was written by Jewish hands and dates from the Maccabean period (second century B.C.E.). There are a number of additions to the original, some clearly of Christian origin and some by the hand of an anti-Maccabean writer who lived before the Christian era. In the "Testament of Judah" (25:4-5) it is written: "Those who have died in grief shall arise in joy, and those who have been poor...shall be made rich, and those who were hungry shall be filled, and those who have been weak shall be strong, and those who were put to death for the Lord's sake shall awake to life. And the harts of Jacob shall run in joyfulness, and the eagles of Israel shall fly in gladness; but the ungodly shall lament and the sinners shall weep, and the peoples shall glorify the Lord forever." The possibility that the New Testament authors of the Beatitudes and Luke 6:24-25 drew from the "Testament of Judah" is a very real one and cannot be dismissed as coincidental.

17. Acts 3:22, 7:37. Cf. Deut 18-22.

18. Even a false prophet or dreamer is capable of signs and wonders (cf. Deut 13:2-6). Miracles in themselves cannot be used as conclusive support in matters of Jewish law is a talmudic dictum that characterizes all *Halachah*.

19. John the Baptist and Jesus began their ministries with the message that the heavenly kingdom was at hand (Matt 3:2, 4:17; Mark 1:5). In many parables beginning with words

such as "the kingdom of heaven is like," the nature of the kingdom is explained by Jesus as it "comes," is "given," "received," and "entered." That is to say, "kingdom" is not viewed as a product of human achievement but as divine salvation. More than proclaiming the kingdom as future or the kingdom as church, Jesus affirmed the kingdom as present. Such is the under-standing of the expression "is at hand" (Matt 3:2, 4:17; Mark 1:5); "the kingdom of God is upon you" (Matt 12:28; Luke 8:20); "the kingdom of God is within you" or "in the midst of you" (Luke 17:31) and the like. Jesus also promised that some of his hearers will not taste death and will live to see "the kingdom of God come with power" (Matt 16:28; Mark 9:1; Luke 9:27). Even the parables (e.g., the Tares, the Ten Virgins, etc.) that speak of a waiting period for the kingdom, its manifestation is definitely felt to be in the immediate future of the disciples. The early return of Jesus did not take place and aroused difficulties among the early Christians (cf. II Pet 3:4), which the orthodox thought cleverly avoided by associating the doctrines of Judgment, Eternal Life, and the Resurrection of the Body with the second coming of Jesus, however displayed. Nonetheless, a number of first and second century Christians maintained the continual present manifestation of the kingdom of God (e.g., Rom 14:17; Col 1:13; Rev 1:6, 9, 5:10).

20. Deut 4:2, 13:1, 17:11. See too Matt 5:17-20, which may contain *ipsissima verba* of Jesus on this point.

21. The writings of S.G.F. Brandon, the late professor of comparative religion at the University of Manchester, have influenced my thinking on Jesus as political revolutionary.

22. Matt 26:57-75; Mark 14:53-72; Luke 22:54-71.

23. Matt 27:11-14; Mark 15:2-5; Luke 2:3-5.

24. Matt 27:15-26; Mark 15:6-15; Luke 23:17-25.

25. Matt 26:63-65; Mark 14:61-65; Luke 22:67-70.

26. Cf. Acts 6 where Christian tradition records that Stephen was guilty of death since he spoke "blasphemous words against Moses and against God" (Acts 6:7). See too Ex 22:27; I Kgs 21:10, 13 ("you have reviled God and king").

27. A brief description of the crucifixion is found in Matt 27:33-44; Mark 15:22-32; Luke 23:33-43.

28. Matt 27:11; Mark 15:2; Luke 23:3. Cf. Also Mark 15:9, 12 and the charge against Jesus inscribed on the cross (Matt 27:37; Mark 15:26; John 19:19).

29. Cf. Matt 10:14; Mark 3:18; Luke 6:15; Acts 1:3. In Matthew and Mark it is written "Simon the Cananaean" (Zealot). Matthew's Jewish audience can understand the Aramaism, but Mark, who normally translates Aramaisms (e.g., Mark 7:34) into Greek, purposely does not here. The writer of Luke-Acts, writing a generation after Mark, no longer sees the taint of political sedition about Jesus or is simply unaware of Mark's dilemma and unashamedly identifies Simon as a Zealot.

30. Cf. The roles of Phineas (Num 25:7-10), Mattathias (I Macc 2:15ff), and Elijah (I Kgs 19:19 ff) as zealot types.

31. "Blessed be His Name, whose glorious kingdom is forever and ever," recited in the Temple during the Day of Atonement services, was added by the Rabbis to accompany the opening verse of the *Shema* (Deut 6:4). Since the period of Gaius Caligula (34-41), Roman emperors demanded from their subjects divine respect. The loyalist Jew who rejected did so at the penalty of death. He submitted to the rule of God alone whom he proclaimed in "Hear O Israel, the Lord our God, the Lord is one," and followed by the above doxology. In a similar fashion, the nationalist Jew took the yoke of the Kingdom of God.

32. Mark 11:15-19; Matt 21:12-13; Luke 19:45-48.

33. A reference to Pilate's ruthless suppression of the rebellion may be found in Luke 13:1.

34. Mark 12:17; Matt 22:21; Luke 20:25.

35. The episode of Jesus taken captive is found in Mark 14:43-52; Matt 26:47-56; Luke 22:47-53.

36. Mark 14:46; Matt 26:51; Luke 22:50; John 18:10.

37. Mark 14:48; Matt 26:55; Luke 22:52.

38. Matt 27:23; Mark 15:14; Luke 23:22.

39. Also, Luke 22:50. A similar message is associated with national restoration and rebuilding the Second Temple (515 B.C.E.) in Zech 4:6, which is later linked to the Synagogue service of Chanukah by the Old Rabbis in order to play down the militancy of the Maccabean victory and state.

40. The word Pharisees occurs over a hundred times in the New Testament (29 times in Matt; 12 times in Mark; 27 times in Luke; 19 times in John; 9 times in Acts; and one time in Phillipians). There is ample fodder in these references to portray Pharisaism as sanctimonious, self-righteous, hypocritical petrified formalism, and a degraded religious system corroded by casuistry. The bitterest tirade against the Pharisees in any first century Christian literature is Matt 23.

41. Cf. Mark 8:27-33; Matt 16:13-23; Luke 9:18-22. The Petrine blessing found in Matt 16:17-19 was added by a Jewish Christian to offset Mark's rebuke of Peter (The Jerusalem Church) as Satan by Jesus (Mark 8:33).

42. Matt 27:54; Mark 15:39; Luke 23:47.

43. Matt 16:13; Mark 8:27; Luke 9:18.

44. Matt 27:46; Mark 15:34.

45. Matt 6:25-34; Luke 12:22-34.

46. Matt 14:13-21; Mark 6:30-44; Luke 9:10-17. Cf., also, Matt 15:32-39; Mark 8:1-10.

47. Matt 10:34-37; Luke 12:51-53; Matt 10:37-39; Luke 14:26-27; Matt 19:29; Mark 10:29; Luke 18:29; Matt 16:24-25; Mark 8:34-35; Luke 9:23-24; John 12:25-26; Matt 8:22; Luke 9:59-62. See further my article, "Psalm 138:4, A Religious Polemic in the Hagaddah," *CCAR Journal*, 17:1 (January 1970), pp. 57-60.

48. Matt 9:27-31, 20:29-34; Mark 6:22-26; Luke 18:35-43.

49. Matt 15:29-31; Mark 7:31-37.

50. Matt 17:14-21; Mark 9:14-29; Luke 9:37-43.

51. Matt 9:1-8; Mark 2:1-12; Luke 5:17-26.

52. Matt 9:32-34, 12:22-23; Mark 3:22; Luke 11:14-15.

53. Matt 8:14-17.

54. Matt 12:11-12; Mark 3:1-6; Luke 13:10-17, 14:1-6.

55. Matt 26:28; Mark 14:24. On blood and covenant in the Jewish tradition, see Zev Garber, *Shoah, The Paradigmatic Genocide* (Lanham/New York/London: UPA, 1994), pp. 72; 141-143.

Going Down to Sodom
Re-Thinking the Tradition in Dialogue
James F. Moore

This essay was written as part of a panel discussion in dialogue on scriptural texts held in Provo, Utah, for the Scholars' Conference on the Holocaust and the Church Struggle in March of 1995. The group that participated in that panel has now produced three more panel discussions for subsequent Scholars' Conferences, the first of which was published as a set for a special edition of **Shofar** *in 1997. I mention the history of this discussion because this activity, which continues now as a regular part of each Scholars' Conference, is especially in keeping with the interests and lifelong desire of Harry James Cargas. As an original member of the group that began those conferences, he has long sought for ways to re-think Christian tradition so as to take account of the impact of the Shoah on Christian thinking. When I first taught my course on the Holocaust, more than a decade ago, I used Harry's book, a copy of which still has his note to me on the inside cover, and found that his challenge to Western Christian tradition and Christian complicity in the Holocaust is among the most profound statements that my students have encountered. They could hardly ignore the direct, hard-hitting way that Harry laid out the story and the questions. I hope that the dialogue, represented by this essay, can be seen as one legacy of the work that Harry James Cargas has done for all of us.*

We return to our project begun two years ago in Tulsa with a second installment of our dialogue on texts. We have chosen to link two texts that are far too rich in possibilities for conversation to ignore—Genesis 18 and Matthew 10. In particular, we focus on the latter part of Genesis 18 and the former part of Matthew 10. Even in this narrowing we have introduced a startling number of possible topics for dialogue, which will be enumerated below, any one of which might deserve our attention. Before moving to a general setting of topics and a discussion of the texts, let me set out the basic criteria that shape our discussion together.

We decided to set three essential criteria for our dialogue that make our conversation unique. First, our dialogue requires a commitment to take our individual traditions seriously, thus the linking of texts from Hebrew and Christian scriptures. We commit ourselves, therefore, to look again at these texts, considering them afresh with the intent of allowing the texts to speak again. The aim is to fight any tendency to assume we know each other and to open ourselves to be surprised and informed. Second, our conversation requires legitimate dialogue. Thus, we aim not only to make use of the gains of dialogue over the last four decades but also to assure that our reading of texts opens doors for conversation, recognizing above all what clues would lead us to more—not less—conversation. With this commitment, we realize from the outset that our panel discussion is open-ended, admitting that wider participation is needed and further conversation assumed. Third, our dialogue must be post-Shoah, meaning that what we say must ask the question whether our theology can fit, can be said after the events of the Shoah. This commitment implies at least two things. First, we take on Irving Greenberg's challenge that no theology can be genuine today unless it could be said in the presence of the burning children.[1] Whatever that might mean to the many interpreters of Greenberg, it at least introduces a strong hermeneutic of suspicion about our normal ways of doing theology. Second, we assume that our theologies today somehow do the impossible, incorporate the story of the Shoah as an ingredient of how we, individually, now understand ourselves.[2] Each of us has spent a number of years trying to do this in our own styles. We have purposely chosen not to limit the wide variety of what this might mean including always being sensitive to those, especially the survivors, who are dubious that we can do this. We are, after all, second generation believers and scholars. We must approach what we say from this perspective; however, we continue to do this with an openness to other perspectives, knowing that we cannot assume that what we say is "the" genuine post-Shoah theology but rather a contribution to what must be an ever evolving discussion. Thus, our conversation guided by the three criteria is a model for how theology is to be done and a contribution to the doing of post-Shoah theology.

The Possible Themes

While our concentration in Genesis is upon the dialogue between Abraham and the Lord about the fate of Sodom and upon the specific reference to Sodom and Gomorrah in Jesus' commissioning of the disciples in Matthew 10, we still face a rich diversity of possible themes for our reflection. The Genesis text is familiar, in which one of the strangers seeking hospitality with Abraham remains behind with Abraham after it is made clear that their intent was to go to Sodom to discover whether what had been heard was in fact true. That the text clearly identifies this lingering stranger as the Lord leaves us with much to talk about. The text obviously is a theodicy, speaking of God's relation to evil in the world. Just what that evil is, is not clear here and is only ambiguously represented in Genesis 19. The point is that Genesis 18 becomes an occasion to dialogue about God's relation to evil in the context of our texts. Insofar as the Matthew text is also such an occasion, the texts can become a fruitful context for our dialogue. The Genesis text is obviously also a source for thinking about God's justice and human involvement in both suffering and challenging God's justice. The text offers a particularly valuable context for this discussion because the story not only talks about God's justice but also incorporates a specific wielding of God's justice in the world. The reference in Matthew to the Genesis story also becomes a source for discussion of God's justice, but the terms are apparently changed and the emphasis placed upon God's judgment and not on God's justice. Even more, the implication of the text seems eschatological, pointing not to an immediate effect but to the messianic age.

We would likely have quite a lot to discuss just in tackling these two sets of issues in the framework of our three criteria, but two additional sets of issues should also be drawn in. The Genesis text speaks of redemption as well as justice. Even more, the text seems to equate justice with the fair treatment of the righteous more than with just treatment of the wicked. Using these terms makes our discussion ambiguous from the start since we have no clear measuring stick for speaking of righteousness at this point. Abraham's obedience to God's word was said to be granted as righteousness, but there is no clear set of principles that allow for judging the righteousness of anyone else, even by the standard used for Abraham. Thus, we will need to explore what this word can mean, not to mention what it can mean for us today, post-Shoah. Connected to this discussion, however, is also the historical description of God's redemption of the righteous, and Lot's actions allow for a fairly loose understanding of what counts for righteousness. We can gain this perspective fully only by linking the one story with the next, the story in Genesis 19.

The drama of Genesis is not the same as the drama portrayed in Matthew. We do not know if the judgment of the disciples upon a town is to be considered divine judgment, but the latter context, the road to redemption, is clearly present in this text. Even more, in Matthew we do have a framework for understanding righteousness and the issue may be what that framework is to be, given the teaching of Jesus and the commissioning of the disciples. The fact is that almost all Christian biblical scholars into this century have read this text as a replacement theology; as Norman Perrin argued, Jesus as the new Torah.[3] We can hardly miss this dimension of the Matthean text that leads us back into a critical issue for Jewish-Christian dialogue, especially post-Shoah dialogue. We may find that reading this possible theme as part of a midrashic interpretation of Genesis 18-19 will lead us further into a quagmire or possibly into new insight and direction. I propose that direction at least.

We cannot escape the final set of issues that surely stand outside of both of our texts but are part of the interpretive tradition, the issues related to traditional Christian and Jewish understandings of homosexuality. We ought to be encouraged to take up this issue partly because so little has been done to reflect on the place of homosexuals in the Nazi list of targeted people. Since our texts place this discussion (and I am fully aware of the likelihood that the Genesis text, at least, is ambiguous about the issue of homosexuality) in the context of God's justice and human righteousness, we are all the more challenged to take on this issue directly.

Thus, I have identified four sets of themes that this paper will try to address in the effort to think again about Genesis 18 and Matthew 10. The richness of the texts suggests that there are other themes that my colleagues may see. And I admit the futility of thinking that I can give adequate treatment to each of these issues as well as the texts themselves, not to mention the effort to fit our discussion into the confines of the criteria set for our discussion. My effort is suggestive, not attempting to find final conclusions; in fact, we are likely better served by talking in terms of suggested paths and directions of interpretation rather than to close off any discussion prematurely. On the other hand, we need to know that the criteria we have brought to this discussion will allow us to judge whether some ways of thinking are not viable for us. Not every possible reading is valid or even equal. Even so, those judgments must also be set as topics for dialogue, for an ever-widening conversation and sharing of ideas between those of us committed to this topic and to each other.

Genesis 18

The focus of our attention is upon the second half of Genesis 18, beginning with verse 16; however, this narrative section requires a link to the earlier section of chapter 18 and forward to chapter 19 in order for the full meaning to be understood. In addition, the previous section of chapter 18 provides a striking contrast with the conversation beginning at verse 16. What seems striking is that the previous story seems to represent the opposite story line from what is to come in the next section. In the earlier narrative, the Lord comes to Abraham and Sarah to give a blessing, the news that there shall be a son even at their advanced ages. This blessing comes in the context of the visit of the three strangers who receive hospitality from Abraham. The subsequent story has the Lord coming to Sodom to render judgment and bring a curse, the destruction of the city for grave sin. The section we are discussing appears to be an interlude between these two narratives that mirror opposites, even to the point of noting that the people of Sodom refuse hospitality—except for Lot and his family. This parallel will become interesting for us as we proceed.

I call our section an interlude, but it obviously stands out as an odd interlude in that, on the one hand, it appears to be a bridge between narratives but, on the other hand, clearly introduces a debate with implications beyond the particulars of these stories. Thus, our text is more than an interlude and takes on importance beyond its narrative place, that is, if we assume that the text has a meaning for Israel beyond the resolution of that particular situation. Indeed, we see in this text the appearance of the themes of justice and righteousness, *mishpat* and *tzedakah*. In this text the former is applied to God and the latter to humans; that is, God's actions are not measured, apparently, in the same way and are not referred to as righteous.

This distinction appears to be critical for the text as the story of Abraham pre-dates the Exodus-Sinai experience and the details of the covenant of Sinai, even though the text was surely written with the Sinai covenant in mind. The text must be read as if the covenant code was not assumed background and the justice of God must be seen as measured by God's own standards—those made evident in God's dealings with Abraham. When Abraham challenges the Lord, saying that surely the judge of all the earth must do what is just, we must assume that Abraham means that the Lord should act consistently with what has previously been the case. What comes to mind is the immediately preceding story about Abraham and Sarah and the request for hospitality. If God would give Abraham a blessing for hospitality, then surely God would be bound to give the righteous elsewhere a blessing. The story that comes before our own is transformed by our text into a principle of justice in this way, giving a basis for understanding divine justice by limiting divine action to the principle of equal treatment, the Lord being consistent in action.

To be sure, this principle cannot be simply and rigidly applied since hospitality is not the only measure of human righteousness (more on this below), but this standard of divine action does become a central feature of biblical theodicies. If God's actions do vary with circumstances, the standard of equal treatment based on the demand that God be consistent (that is, be just) does not vary. It is this principle that can form the basis of the typical questions that confront us in talking about divine action in relation to evil and also of the reasons why humans suffer. If God is consistently bound to this principle of justice, then naturally the difference in treatment of humans (why differences occur among humans in their suffering) must be understood on the basis of the human condition. Humans suffer differently because their situations differ and not because God arbitrarily uses different standards for different people.

Of course, what is implied by this way of thinking toward a theodicy is that God will be just by treating the righteous differently than the unrighteous. The problems that emerge from this assumption, of course, are already evident in our text, one of which is the treatment of the righteous and the unrighteous if their fate is intertwined. Would it be fair, for instance, to sink a boat full of the enemy if a number of our friends are on the same boat? We can ask whether this principle of morality is implied in our text—indeed, that is Abraham's challenging question. It is not clear that this principle works all the time for divine action, even if it might be basic to human morality. At the very least, this story presents a text for thinking about this question which would extend the principle of equal treatment even to those who are inextricably tied to the fate of the unrighteous. The answer in the text offered as God's reply suggests that the righteous will be protected even if they are living among the wicked.

What this text does not consider—but we must—is whether the Lord is indeed judge of all the earth. That is, we must ask whether every case of human suffering is also an instance of theodicy—God's involvement. The apparent meaning of this text—if it is universalized—is that justice in our world is directly connected with divine justice and action. Our text does not consider the other option that God, having heard the outcry about Sodom, would ignore the cries and not act. The issue is far more the question of the basis on which God acts and not under what conditions might God not act. Abraham's plea is not that God would fail to act but rather that the righteous be saved. Our text does not know a God who would ignore the cries of the righteous, even if other theodicies had begun to emerge by the time the texts were written and even more by the time of the final edited version. There is already a theme of God delaying action or of the hidden purposes of God or of human ignorance of the larger divine purposes that we cannot understand. All of this still presumes a God who acts, who hears the cries and responds. This is essential to biblical theodicies. Our question is whether such theodicies can work for us in a post-Shoah world.

The Possibility of a New Theodicy

I am aware that the interpretive tradition represented by the Midrashic literature often turns texts toward meanings that are completely different from the original intent of a text, even to a subject that appears quite removed from the Torah text itself. In our search for a new theodicy that considers the questions we are raising, it makes sense to look at this literature for beginning clues. A limited search of this literature shows that something like that did happen. The focus of the application of this text often seems to be on human boldness in addressing God. That is, the text is perceived not centrally, as a reading of God's involvement, but rather as a reading of human prerogatives in relation to God. The precedent set by Abraham is a powerful one, indicating the degree of privilege that humans possess in that they can challenge and even dictate to God what is justice and how God should act. This text becomes a rationale for affirming the rebellious spirit of humanity in decrying the ineptitude of God or the indifference of God. Never mind that the Genesis text seems to say that God initiates the matter and that Abraham considers Sodom sort of as an afterthought to God's inquiry. The Rabbis turn the text around and envision a humanity that approaches God in order to inquire whether what we think about God is in fact true. This is a text, in that way, of God's accountability rather than of human accountability.

Indeed, there might be considerable justification for this turning of the text that did not occur to the minds of those who first heard and recorded this story. Still, the audacity of Abraham in bargaining with God as to the very nature of divine justice gives ample room for the creative mind to turn the text toward emphasizing that very audacity. We have here a holy audacity, the sort of approach to God that Elie Wiesel recalls as he speaks of the tradition of contention, of open argument with God, that is more in keeping with Elie's own struggles than some deterministic picture of passive acceptance. Surely, this is a far cry from the image often given of "sheep led to the slaughter." The challenge is that the people will not merely be led—even by God—to such slaughter. But, of course, that is the challenge that lies within the ambiguous sense of theodicy that emerges from this turn of the text—How do we know when God is leading even in ways for us to contend with God?

What the Shoah brings us is the unholy monster that humanity can be, a monster hardly envisioned by either the first editors or the Rabbinic interpreters. There are those, we now know, who contend with God and force a definition of justice on God that can only be seen as evil, those who would do away with God so that there is no longer a conversation, a mutuality, a God. There is perhaps a covenant fashioned, but this is the demonic that turns every sense of justice and value on its head. This is a different kind of contention, a different kind of humanity that is more than audacious. It is what we would hope to call an inhumanity. Can we imagine an Abraham who would not only contend with God but would say that, of course, while you are looking at Sodom to find the wicked, why not find all the Sodomites and any others who are connected to them and wipe them all from the face of the earth? And then we can say that this is divine justice, the way things ought to be. And what would we say of the righteous in their midst? Such visions of justice would have to imply that the righteous are just part of that evil conspiracy and must also pay the penalty. But we cannot imagine such an Abraham, for Abraham's contention was in behalf of the righteous. Never mind that we have so little to measure what it means to be righteous; Abraham contends for the righteous in such a way as to understand justice even saving, rescuing the guilty for the sake of the righteous. So we cannot imagine an Abraham who would say, let us wipe them all from the face of the earth, but now we can imagine a human who would say that and call it justice. Can we read this text any more without knowing this? Can we hear the Rabbis lifting up the arrogance of human contention with God any more without now knowing what humans can do with their arrogance?

On either side we find ourselves driven to silence, baffled about whether either reading can be retrieved for us as meaningful. We wonder about ourselves thinking that we could be either; (1) an Abraham, who cannot believe what he hears from God and challenges God for insensitivity to the righteous, maybe not ever again able to accept God's justice without question or (2) a human who contends with God by seeing divine justice as revenge against a people we see as evil and now can arrogantly seek to wipe from our midst. What sort of human am I? Which of these can I be sure to be and am I not left with the feeling that both—finally, in the face of the Shoah—render both readings of the story meaningless?

We people of our texts cannot allow ourselves to sink to the level of meaninglessness, even if we know for some moments of the truth that lurks in that very meaninglessness. And we know of the truth, of that which we cannot deny, that in the face of the unholy monster, the arrogance of humanity turned demonic, either the just God or the just human can appear to mean nothing, for both died at Auschwitz. The demon won, and this is our justice. Surely this is always a possibility that only leaves the challenging questions of Abraham empty in the process. But this is not all for us because we cannot let it be all for us or for God.

In fact, what this text must mean for us, at least in part, is that Abraham's brashness in confronting God became a principle in a way like Wiesel and others have suggested—that we seek justice even if and when God fails to seek justice. The Abraham text breaks us free from the notion that obedience and trust, while still significant, cannot define our whole relationship with God and with one another. Not even God warrants that kind of absolute trust. Thus, we cry out "Isn't the Lord of the universe also required to be just?" And when we cry out, we echo the voice of Abraham. Now also when we cry out we join the voices of the Shoah. Isn't the Lord of the universe also required to be just? And in our cries we set in motion our actions that move ahead as if such justice still prevails, in the face of all that might show that it does not.

But this is not and cannot be merely a theological debate. We do not get the message, if we only perceive this exercise as a shaping of a new theodicy. Our calling God to justice in our anger (yes, in our anger) is not enough, for the Lord says that He will go down to Sodom and inquire as to whether what we have heard is true. And is it the case that Abraham remains behind? This is the story and we are certainly puzzled by this, on the surface. With all the arrogance that Abraham exhibits and with the other occasions when Abraham picks up and goes, we have in this story an Abraham who stays behind. Isn't he the least bit curious about whether the rumors are true? In spite of the apparent concern for his nephew, Lot, he does not go himself to see and to act. Here, Abraham remains behind.

Our sensitivities are now heightened. Whatever we might say practically about situations or whatever we might argue in defense of Abraham—after all, has he not done enough just by challenging God's justice?—we cannot easily tolerate the one who knows the threat but does not go down to Sodom to find out if the rumors are true. Surely it is evident from the beginning of the discussion that Abraham knew the seriousness of all that was going on. If evil was rampant in Sodom, evil that threatened to obliterate righteousness, then somehow Abraham would have gone with the Lord. Abraham would have gone down to Sodom, to see on site if the rumors were true.

Naturally, we are uneasy about quick moral judgments, but this story must confront us this way, not as a means for pointing fingers at those who did not go down or did not follow through, whose moral indignation somehow did not translate into personal action. But is it righteous indignation if it is not also righteous action? And so our Abraham must not only challenge God's justice but must also go with the Lord to Sodom. And this journey is not merely a curiosity, for Abraham in his brashness has already called God to righteous action. This going down is a call to righteous action for Abraham as well. For the sake of 10 would we act to save, or 100 or 1,000? How many does it take before our calls for justice move us to act justly? Notice the irony that God, already planning to act, must decide whether the presence of smaller and smaller groups of believers would cause Him to save the whole. Now we speak of our actions and the question for us reverses. How large must the group be before we finally take notice of the terror and the suffering and choose to go down to Sodom? And now that we have seen what can happen, what assures us that we will go down to Sodom at our opportunity? Will we settle for arguing with God about divine justice?

There is yet one more point to make. Surely the call for divine justice cannot mean that God merely tolerates evil for the sake of the righteous. What redemption is there in allowing all to remain for the sake of a small group? Will not those righteous suffer all the more, knowing that God will not act against the evil that is present? Won't those who perpetrate evil gain in arrogance, knowing that the righteous are vulnerable targets? This is not justice but insanity. Justice cannot mean tolerance and Abraham could not have really intended his challenge to lead to that. Whatever we might perceive as appropriate divine justice (and we are likely to harbor views that work for our benefit), God cannot merely go down to Sodom. If justice is the goal, God must remain in Sodom. Now that notion is novel, requiring something different in our understanding of God. If God acts to save all for the sake of the few, what does it mean for God to remain in Sodom, that is, to dwell in the midst of evil? I have a sense that we draw close to what our traditions understand as God's righteousness and not merely God's justice. Isn't this question a central question for our dialogue? Isn't this issue at the heart of how we can, individually and together, move forward toward a new theology? I do not pretend to resolve this question but rather openly implore us to work on it together. In the end, we are likely to discover what we, individually and together, understand to be human righteousness as well, that which we—as part of our communities, that is—take to be our call before God, a God who now has to be challenged to be just.

Matthew 10

The narrative discourse in Matthew 10 speaks of another going out and includes within it a reference to the destruction of Sodom and Gomorrah. The reference seems to imply that the story of Genesis 19 is already part of a standard interpretation of texts which presume that the destruction is symbolic of the worst punishment that can come from God. That is to say, the theme has already moved from justice to judgment. There appears to be no further interpretation of the Torah text, but a simple symbolic application that rests on an already assumed judgment. To this judgment is compared the fate of those who do not receive the messengers of Jesus, those sent out to proclaim that the kingdom of God is at hand.

The reference is clearly broadened if the larger context is seen not merely as instructions to Jesus' disciples but generally the followers of Jesus after Jesus' death. While the original context does not seem to warrant that expansion of the reference, the rest of the discourse does broaden the meaning by referring to the way that the disciples will be arrested and flogged in "their synagogues." Since such a scenario would have been odd in the original setting, the text appears to extend Jesus' words and meaning into a more general judgment upon the Jews, particularly the Jews who refuse to listen to the messengers from Jesus. Such a reference is surely not surprising for the gospel of Matthew even though we are led to say that the extension reflects not Jesus' intention but that of the gospel writer, not Jesus' perspective but the perspective of the post-resurrection church.

Such a comment may not be that significant since our history shows that followers of Jesus have often read Jesus' words as bearing that intent. The apparent expansion of meaning by the editor of this gospel is, thus, in keeping with much of Christian history in terms of Christian views of the Jews. Even in Matthew's time, this justification of a summary judgment of the Jews by Matthew's group must be seen as a frustrated response to "other" Jews since the early church included converted Jews and may have continued to see itself as an extension of Judaism (thus, the strong emphasis on observance of the law in Matthew 5). Still, the gospel probably was fully completed after the destruction of the Temple in Jerusalem and these words attach to a growing sentiment among these Christians that the destruction was a sign of final judgment on Judaism, a judgment even worse than that given to Sodom and Gomorrah.

But, if this is the interpretation given to Genesis 19, even in a superficial, symbolic reference to the destruction of Sodom and Gomorrah, then the implication is more than just a reflection of early Christian attitudes toward Jews. That the words are reported as words of Jesus suggests that they are given additional authority and the interpretation carries with it a picture of God that connects with the judgment, presumed, on those who refuse Jesus' messengers.

This picture of God is one of a harsh judge who is not patient with rejection but treats rejection with vengeance. Even more, the picture is traced to Jesus' words about the messengers sent out, as if Jesus endorses this view as a way of encouraging his disciples, his followers. Such a reading of Jesus' teaching, especially in relation to the Jews, must be thought through seriously, with a probing inquiry as to whether such an understanding of this text even fits appropriately for standard Christian theology, not to mention our judgments about what can be genuine Christian theology after the Shoah.

Where Is God Now?

In our narrative, we have no human voice, no match for Abraham's plea, which stands ready to confront God about God's justice. We have no sense that God's view is ambiguous, always waiting to learn whether what God has heard is, in fact, true. Instead, the human voice is the messenger who is left with asserting the judgment and, thereby, bringing on the devastation wrought by God. They are simply to shake the dust from their feet and God will respond without question. But can this possibly be the correct reading? If we look at the history of reading this text together with interpreters of the text, we find near unanimity, as if the meaning were self-evident. How is it possible that this reading has emerged as the way to understand Jesus' instructions without question? Perhaps the clues of the text itself are undeniable, at least as the editor expands Jesus' meaning in the summary judgment on Judaism. Perhaps we are driven to read Jesus' words as consonant with the view of the editor/author of the gospel because the clues of the text are so strong. But such a reading in isolation fails as a theological reading of the text since the implied image of God is utterly out of place for general Christian theodicy.

But we can see that even my critique can be challenged, since the early Christian texts so thoroughly embodied a prophetic perspective that carried apocalyptic tones. That is, this prophetic picture of the judging God appears to be quite in line with apocalyptic literature and Matthew includes significant elements of apocalyptic literature. The whole tenor of the passage is reinforced at the end of the full narrative with a reference to Micah 7:6, clearly a prophetic view of God's judgment. The irony of this match, though, is that Micah speaks of the terror of the remnant of Israel before the nations which leads to a sense of internal fear that no one can be trusted. Instead of a judgment on Israel, Micah's point is to encourage Israel to stay with the Lord who will ultimately reward the faithful. The standard Christian reading tends to reverse Micah's message, turning it into an encouragement of the church and a judgment on Israel.

It is shortsighted, though, to say that the judging God of Matthew 10 is a product of the mood of the time. Surely, the text has been read this way precisely because Israel was and has been a symbol of opposition to the church. The prophetic perspective is used not as a sign of the truth, really, but as a justification for anti-Judaism that was seen as a direct affirmation of the truth of Jesus and Jesus' followers. The message that the kingdom of God is at hand is a marker that shows what is at stake is the very truth or legitimization of the church and the Jews have always represented a challenge to the legitimacy of the church. It is a typical maneuver to claim that God's judgment, God's word, justifies this anti-Judaism. This is typical of the church, but it is dubious that such a view could be attributed to Jesus. Thus, many would dismiss this passage as later Christian propaganda, having little to do with Jesus' central message and much to do with later Christian anti-Judaism and self-justification.

To say this, however, leads us nowhere. As true as this may be, we are still left with a text and no closer to an alternative reading of Christian scripture, no closer to what might have been Jesus' message. We could simply dismiss the text on these terms, but we would do nothing for our project otherwise, nor would we push dialogue along. Our only path toward a constructive discussion is to assume that the discourse is, in fact, an interpretation of Genesis 19, probably relating to Genesis 18, and not merely a symbolic reference that presumed the judgment of Sodom and Gomorrah. Even more, we could see the reference to Micah not as a reinforcement of an apocalyptic perspective leading toward pictures of God as harsh judge and the image of the condemnation of the Jews. We could ask if there is a reading of Genesis 18-19 and Micah 7 that emerges from this discourse that leads us toward real dialogue and toward genuine insight for a post-Shoah Christian theology.

Toward A Christian Midrash

If we assume that our text is a midrash on Genesis 18-19, a picture emerges for us other than what has been the more typical traditional view. The fact is that the text of Matthew 10 does not speak of judgment as if it has already been given. That is to say, the judgment that looms in the text is one that lies ahead and not behind. Only if we assume the precarious vantage point of the editor of Matthew do we think of the judgment as one that lies behind. Since we are not privy to the mind of the author, we can only speak of the text that we have been given. In this text, the judgment lies ahead and, thus, our text compares more directly with Genesis 18 than it does with Genesis 19, to the dialogue about what God should do about what has been reported. In this regard, it is noteworthy that Matthew 10 does not picture God going ahead but, rather, pictures disciples being sent. That is to say, our text changes the whole arena of the making of moral judgments. The disciples are not led like Abraham to ask whether God is just, but are themselves challenged to be just.

In fact, this personal involvement in judgment seems to be what is missing from our reading of Genesis 18. Abraham questions God's justice but does not look at his own. We are told by the text that Abraham is righteous—at least, accounted as righteous—for his actions, but in the case of Sodom and

Gomorrah, Abraham only intervenes before God. Abraham does not go down to Sodom in order to see for himself, let alone to act to persuade others of what is right and just. Indeed, both the intervention before God and the choice to go down ourselves are vital aspects of a single truth about justice, but surely the prayer before God is not completed until we choose to go down to Sodom. Aren't we just a bit surprised that, having heard of the evil there and God's intent, Abraham does not go along? Aren't we surprised that Abraham does not go to check on his kinsman, Lot? Abraham's accusing approach to God is not turned upon Abraham; should not the chosen one of God also act justly?

On this level, the Matthew 10 text is a valuable broadening of the Genesis 18-19 text. Justice cannot be merely the prerogative of God, as if we can trust that God will not only act justly but also counteract the effects of evil. In fact, the effects of evil are not counteracted in Sodom; Lot must finally flee for his own life after his guests are terrorized. And if the guests in Sodom are symbolically the very presence of the Lord, then God is terrorized even before acting with judgment. The text in Matthew comes as a message to the disciples to go out even to those places of evil, so that justice might prevail. There is no haven to be found under Jesus' wing. There is no discipleship possible that does not include acting as the one sent. In this re-write of Genesis 18, Abraham goes down to Sodom to speak to the "lost sheep of the house of Israel."

Of course, this reading of theodicy is all the more necessary in a post-Shoah world in which the justice of God is fragile indeed; not that the Lord of creation will not act justly but that the Lord of creation does not act to thwart the full force of evil. The judgment and its effect lay ahead of us and there is no real guarantee that the righteous will be saved in time. Thus, our plea to God through Abraham is itself righteous, but then we go down because we are sent, even into the places of evil. Naturally, this means that the option of the bystander no longer is viable for disciples of Jesus, if it ever was. Of course, the message can be viewed as a word for all the chosen of God, but this word for Christians is especially loud sounding after Auschwitz.

There is more, of course. The words that I repeated just above—go only to the lost sheep of the House of Israel—speak much in this transformed look at this Christian midrash. Why the instruction to go only to the lost sheep of the House of Israel? On traditional terms, the meaning is clear. The initial witness is to Jews, and the most insidious reading of this passage is that their refusal is proof that they are lost. But this is insidious, for how can we read these words as if the sending is only a game to prove the contemptuous teaching that Judaism is lost? Surely the sending must be genuine. Surely, there is a meaning more than judgment declared of this text. Thus, the sending is more than just a portent of final judgment. It must be.

If we have a midrash here on Genesis 18, then perhaps a window can open for us. Who is the lost sheep in Sodom? Doesn't the traditional reading of this text make the distorted misreading of comparing the Jews who reject the disciples with the evil of Sodom? But the lost sheep of Sodom are the righteous for whom Abraham pleas. That is, the lost sheep are truly lost because they are caught in the web of an evil place without anyone to stand by them, to come to their aid. And this is the core of a new reading of Abraham's plea, isn't it? Isn't the center of our attention in Genesis 18 the lost ones and not the justice of God, for of what value is the righteousness of God if the righteous of Sodom are still in peril? Why make arguments that absolve God if the righteous in an evil world are all the while ground under and lost without a trace?

And so God goes down to Sodom not to bring judgment on the evil ones but to go to the lost ones of Israel. I have my eye on the image in *Night*, of the boy hanging on the gallows. I have my eye there because there is where God must be. I have no idea what that means to confess that belief because it is terrifying to think that God is terrorized by evil in order to be with those who are truly lost and vulnerable. Still, I have no choice but to think this, now that the unthinkable has happened. God goes down to be with the lost. But Matthew 10 is a different picture. For in this text the disciples go down to the evil place to be with the lost sheep of the House of Israel. As Abraham surely did go to be with Lot, we go to be with our kinspeople. We go alongside God.

Does it so challenge the normal understanding of mission to read this text in this way? Do we shout out that the text says it differently? But the text leaves more room than we think, for the judgment in the text does not lie behind us but before us. The people of Israel are not perceived to be lost by Jesus because they are irredeemable. That is the chosen teaching of generations of Christians who could not bear to look upon Jews as their kinspeople. Oh, what shout and cry this is that I hear, that mistakes mission for hatred. Aren't we more likely disciples of Jesus if we read this text as a mission of compassion? We go down to Sodom to be with our kinspeople who are lost in a web of evil, for to stand to the side is anathema to what it means to be a disciple.

Surely Christians are sent not merely to the people of Israel in this sending, but they are sent at least to them. In the Shoah story that now rides over us like a cloud of darkness, that makes us say I must go down to Sodom to see whether what I have heard is true, we see our story tied to those who did act, to go into the midst of evil as rescuers of precisely the lost sheep of the House of Israel. In this story, we were called and sent precisely to them, and so many failed to go, partly because they could not bear to see this mission of compassion as their mission. If Abraham could not be called to this mission to his kinsman, then how can we imagine that we can be trusted to show compassion to others? So we now know, that we are sent to the lost sheep of the House of Israel because our very sense of mission, our part in *tikkun olam*, is tested in that moment of call that is neither a ponderous decision nor a planned strategy but a spontaneous expression of being a disciple.

There is more in this Christian midrash, an extension already suggested by the reference to Micah 7. How is Micah 7 both a link to discipleship of Jesus and to Abraham's plea before God? In fact, the reference to Micah 7 seems to rub harshly against the reading of Matthew 10 I have just offered, the compassion toward our kinspeople. There is in Micah this underlying sense of betrayal from within that pervades part of the message so that our instincts of compassion for family may only lead us further into betrayal. This message stands out starkly against the instinctive act to stand with our family in times of greatest threat. The paradox of the text may need to be left as the dynamics of any historical situation, especially that of the Shoah, cannot be so easily resolved by simple directives, even to rescue. The moral ambiguity that runs through the stories of the Shoah does not permit us to speak easily of betrayal or of our own actions "if we were there." Thus the harsh, dissonant sound of the reference to Micah 7 should stand without further comment in this way, at least.

But our midrash cannot let this harshness stand as the traditional Christian reading also leads to another, far too simplistic, reading if we are to take the simple text as judgment and not as midrash. Once again, though, the judgment lies ahead of us and not behind. We do not know beforehand if family betrays. There is no necessary connection between the family relation and inevitable betrayal, not even an inevitable betrayal. Even more, the moral ambiguity of our world on normal terms, not to mention within the chaos of the terror of the Shoah, does not allow us to see betrayal so easily as we would like to see. Thus, we cannot read this text as so many have, that our family, the Jewish people, are collaborators with evil. We cannot read this reference as an admonition to give up on family and seek only relation to God and Jesus. We cannot do this because we cannot even know for sure what our connection to God and Jesus is at any point along the way.

Thus, I choose to read this reference as midrash that calls us to look at the whole text of Micah 7 as a link between Matthew 10 and Genesis 18. Micah and Jesus worry about the possibility that family ties will draw us into betraying our best moral instincts. Indeed, we see this within the Shoah story as well. What better example do we need of this kind of betrayal except that the Shoah story reverses things, showing Christians as the ones who betray. But this fear of betrayal from within is not the full meaning of Micah 7, even if it is a significant point. That fear is set within a larger context of God's mercy in which God, at least, is portrayed as one who overlooks our iniquity. The rabbis tended to see this text as a special example of God's mercy, especially toward those who "pass by the sins of others." Don't we have, here, an expression of a petition of our Lord's prayer that leaves us with the paradox of "Forgive us our sins as we forgive the sins of others?" Surely this is the whole context of the meaning of mercy for Christians and for Jews.

But this view of God is also what Christians have meant by God's justice. Perhaps the issue was at stake in Jesus' time between various groups of rabbis. Whatever, there seems to be a strong strain within Rabbinic Judaism as well of viewing God's justice as God's mercy. The view is set within the same paradox that I have pointed to in the Christian version of Jesus' prayer, mercy for mercy. But am I wrong in seeing this in a gospel that speaks both of the blessedness of the merciful (for they shall see mercy) and of love of enemies? Surely, we cannot read Jesus' message to the disciples in a way that denies the larger sense of mercy that Jesus' teaching implies, especially toward those we love, our family.

So, how shall we read this text that speaks so harshly of betrayal and moral ambiguity? Perhaps, we read the text as an extension of Genesis 18 and the discussion there of God's justice. What is it that Abraham implies by saying that the Lord of the universe must surely be just? Are we not led to understand this passage now as meaning that the Lord of the universe surely must be merciful? I am God and not humanity, says the voice of Hosea, a text that rings consonant with Micah 7. The prophetic commentary on Torah transformed the question of justice into a question of mercy and the Rabbis extended that teaching even more. It was this Rabbinic teaching that so thoroughly captured the message of Jesus.

Now we can return to the harsh words about family in Matthew 10, reading things differently. Instead of seeing this as an admonition to the disciples to turn away from family, from the Jews, didn't we already see in this text the plea to go to the lost sheep of the House of Israel? We see this as a specific opening of a discussion on the power of God's mercy. And are we to be less than God in this way? For God even lays aside His justice for those who also pass by those who offend. And what does family mean, but the moral ambiguity we have spoken of? We are tied not only by compassion but also by enmity in family, seeking all the more justice with those closest to us. In those relationships we can very easily lose sight of another way, the way of divine justice, which is mercy. Not even this powerful need to be justified, that has led so often to Christian teaching of contempt for our brothers and sisters in Judaism, should have stood in the way of our going down to Sodom. And if we put it even more harshly, we hear Jesus saying that we should love our enemies and do good to those who hate us. In this we hear the echo of the Rabbis, for we are called to be ones who let the sins of others pass by. So we go down to Sodom to be with those who are of the House of Israel; there we shall find God.

Judgment Nevertheless

There is still the destruction of Sodom which the midrash in Matthew 10 does not eliminate. The midrash only transforms the notion of judgment and leaves the judgment ahead of us. Yet the Shoah story cannot quite allow that, for judgment was rendered quite apart from God's justice or human intervention. In fact, both were made helpless in the face of the judgment so coolly handed down by the Nazis that surely we cannot now say there is no present judgment. We cannot read this story only as a plea for the righteous or only as a call to the mission of *tikkun olam*. Both the plea and the call seemed silent in the face of the sounds that were heard in the Kingdom of Night.

But, you say, must we continue to hear those sounds while we read our traditions now? Isn't this only to give in and surrender a victory to the evil one? Indeed, it seems just that, as I hear Elie Wiesel's words echo—"It is impossible for a Jew to hate."[4] And I hear the words of Etty Hillesum echo as well—"there is good in all human beings and we must seek to find that good"—a view that is said to be Christian by one of her friends.[5] To read our texts in such a way so as to justify once again a reason to hate seems out of place, as if we are not listening even to the survivors. Surely, there is still judgment, but not that which is born of hate.

Even so, there is judgment and that judgment, in terms of the Matthew text, is reserved for those who do not accept the bearers of the message. And who is this from whom we now turn, ready to shake the dust from our feet? We know who this is, don't we? These are the ones we cannot face now because they were the teachers of hatred, the ones who practiced hatred, the ones who murdered and ignored out of hatred. We know that these must be exposed, especially those who did these things out of a sense of Christian obligation. We must judge the notion that Christianity means hatred of Jews and we must be prepared to act openly, to confront those who would teach that.

Our problem is that we would much rather turn away and shake the dust from our feet. We are embarrassed, perhaps ashamed to face these, to face our story. Thus the Matthew text must also be transformed. If we go down to Sodom, then we go down with both the purpose to stand with those who are singled out for persecution and to come face to face in confrontation with those who would persecute in the name of Christ. We do not go down merely to suffer, for there is no real redemption in mere suffering and **now** to think that is an obscenity. If we are sent out with a purpose, a mission, that mission has now been transformed and specifically defined by the Shoah. Our mission is to confront the sources of hatred and to expose the hideous lie that hatred is a Christian's obligation.

But this is a sneaky mission we have, for we then expose ourselves; or, at least, we expose the thin edge between healing and hatred. Surely we long to seek vengeance, perhaps even more than those who were targeted for Nazi hatred. We have this burning need to root out the evil from within and cleanse the soul of Christianity. And if we take a look in the mirror at our zeal, we will see hatred also staring back at us. There is judgment, of course, but not judgment wrought in hatred. This is judgment arising from justice, for we need this moment of healing that would take us down to Sodom, so that we might hear (that is, bring to trial) those things that we have heard to see if they are true. This is a judgment wrought in justice, for only then will healing be the result, rather than more hatred.

I am hearing the words of Wiesel again, ones that he spoke to this conference back at its inception; these are the words I hear and now I offer again. Wiesel reflects on the story of Rabbi Ishmael who, upon facing his death, did not weep. Why did Rabbi Ishmael not weep? Wiesel argues because he was a martyr, because he obeyed and because he wanted to teach a lesson to Judaism. That lesson was:

> To be a Jew is to have all the reasons in the world to destroy and not to destroy! To be a Jew is to have all the reasons in the world to hate the Germans and not to hate them! To be a Jew is to have all the reasons in the world to mistrust the church and not to hate it! To be a Jew is to have all the reasons in the world not to have faith in language, in singing, in prayers, and in God, but to go on telling the tale, to go on carrying on the dialogue, and to have my own silent prayers and quarrels with God.[6]

Can I be so bold as to say that after the Shoah, it is our calling to join Elie in the midst of this precarious balance between our reasons and our identity? Thus in the face of this witness, we go down to Sodom and we stay; not turning to shake the dust from our feet, we stay until we dispel all the reasons for hate, no matter how long that takes. And thus we Christians have transformed our sacred text and given it new meaning, shaping it into a new tale.

1. Irving Greenberg, "Cloud of Smoke, Pillar of Fire: Judaism, Christianity, and Modernity after the Holocaust," in Eva Fleischner, ed., *Auschwitz: Beginning of a New Era?* (New York: KTAV, 1974), pp. 7ff.

2. Note the challenge specifically given be Elie Wiesel in "Jewish Values in the Post-Holocaust Future: A Symposium," *Judaism* 16:3 (Summer 1967), p. 281.

3. Norman Perrin, *The New Testament: An Introduction* (New York: Harcourt, Jovanovich and Brace, 1974), pp. 173ff.

4. Elie Wiesel, "An Exchange," in *Holocaust: Religious and Philosophical Implications*, John Roth and Michael Berenbaum, eds. (St.Paul: Paragon House, 1989), p. 364.

5. Etty Hillesum, *An Interrupted Life* (New York: Washington Square Press, 1981)

6. Wiesel in Roth and Berenbaum, p. 369.

Job
Elie Wiesel

Once upon a time—long ago—in a land faraway, there lived a man both unusually simple and unusually complex, who is both hero and victim in a tale whose reverberations have been heard—and felt—for centuries. We intend to visit him once again.

His name—*Iyov* or Job—may serve as description of his tragic destiny. It means: *I-yov*, or: *ai-av*, which means: where is father—where is our father—where is He when people need Him to overcome—or at least: to understand—the misfortune and the injustice that have befallen them?

Why was *he* chosen to be tested by God? Why was *he* driven to curse his own life? What could *he* possibly have done to deserve such pain, such agony? All that he had amassed in the course of many decades—his possessions and acquisitions—were taken from him; his children were killed. He was alive, but all that was left him was overwhelming disorientation and disgust. And then...

Surely you remember the story and its magnificent rendering in Scripture. God's casual conversation with a tireless tourist named Satan; the succession of messengers and their similar, indeed almost identical reports; Job's unfathomable silence and then that of his friends; their sterile almost pointless dialogues; Job's ways of challenging God and God's way of challenging Job; and then, at last, the curious and puzzlingly reassuring happy-end.

The conclusion of the story leaves us dissatisfied. Our thirst has not been quenched. After reading the book, we know as much about Job as we did before—but nothing more. We understand God's ways as much—or as little—as before: no less but no more. We still fail to comprehend the behavior of any of the characters in the cast: God's apparent indifference to job's suffering, Job's apparent resignation when he yields to God's logic, his friends' deceptive compassion for his trials...

What is this book about? Suffering? Faith? Rebellion? Justice? The perversion of ideas? The decline of families?

These questions and many others have never been fully answered. Talmudic sages and modern scholars have tried to elucidate Job's pathetic options ranging from total rebellion to total submission.

Job: a fleeting yet obsessive image of a man turned symbol, or perhaps a symbol in quest of a man. Indeed, was there such a man? No, says a talmudic sage. *Mashal haya*: he was only a parable. Commented Rebbenu Shem-Tov: he lived, but only to serve as a parable.

Job: the eternal story of man's weakness and man's right and possibility to overcome his weakness. Job: an awesome legend. Job: a moment of fear and trembling. Job: a question mark. For years, he would not leave me; he kept on haunting me. His file remained open, the questions unanswered. And so I continued to search for new and new-old sources. I went back to Talmud *Bavli* and *Yerushalmi*. Back to Midrash *Iyov*. To modern literature. Jung's Answer to Job. Kierkegaard's and Kafka's. Why did Voltaire hate Job? Only because "he complained too much?" Why have both Islam and Christianity exaggerated Satan's role, especially in relation to Job's wife?

In my research I stumbled upon new commentaries. I gathered a word here, a surprise there, a point of reference, an omission, a repetition, and gradually I became convinced that one may—indeed, one must—examine new evidence in this astonishing case and see where it leads.

He was a good father but not a good Jewish father: read the text, it says so implicitly. His sons and daughters were never home; always attending. . . parties. Did they ever open a book? Study? Acquire knowledge? If yes—their grades are nowhere mentioned. That their behavior was not the best is clear from the story itself: Job, we are told, brought offerings to God for he was afraid: he suspected his children of having sinned in their hearts against God. But—if he was suspicious—why didn't he do something about it? Why didn't he speak to them? Why didn't he educate them? Why was he so indulgent, so kind, so uncritical towards them? Did he believe that they were always right?

Job: a source of constant surprise. Though removed in time and almost rendered fictional by legend, he never fails to touch anyone who approaches him. Rabbi Akiba preached the story of the Floods and nothing happened; then he taught the story of Job and he began to cry—and so did his listeners.

What did the High Priest read on the night of Yom Kippur? The Book of Job. The story and the lesson of Job helped him get ready for next day when he would enter the sacred sanctuary and utter the ineffable Name of God—thanks to Job and his anguish, and his pain, and his questions, the High Priest could better serve his people.

This is all very strange. *God* surely was Job's problem. But Job is not only God's problem. He is ours as well.

Ish haya beeretz Outz, Iyov shmo. There was a man in the land of Outz and his name was *Iyov*. And he was perfect and upright and God-fearing and he avoided evil.

This is the beginning of the story which already contains more intriguing questions than reassuring answers.

The country is named Outz—and no one knows where it is. As for the principal character himself, what do we know about him? Usually we are given a character's name and that of his father. Not here. Why not? Who were his parents? The text is so busy describing his qualities that his biography is lost in the process. But even the qualities are puzzling: they are listed in the wrong order. Traditionally one starts with the unimportant and one goes to the most important. Not here. *Tam* is the highest virtue whereas *Sar-mera* is the lowest. The sentence should have read as follows: *vehaya haish*, and that man was avoiding evil, fearing God, upright and perfect. Could it be that the author went to the wrong school of creative writing? No: as a literary composition it remains unequalled. Could it be, then, that he had a purpose in changing the logic of the sentence and the sequence of the listing? Is it possible that the author intended to offer us a clue about his hesitations with regard to his character? *"Vehaya haish hahu,"* and that man was perfect, upright, evil-avoiding BECAUSE he was fearing God?" In that case, the prologue of the prologue could be read to indicate a warning: *Iyov* was not such a *tzaddik* as he wanted to appear; granted, he had done many good things—but do you know why? Because he was afraid of God.

Call it *"Yirat shamayim,"* fear of heaven, which has been encouraged in our tradition. But there is another form, another mode of fear which implies a lower level of feeling and commitment: *"Yirat khet,"* fear of sin.

And the next passage, still inside the prologue, deals precisely with that. Job had seven sons and three daughters. He possessed a vast fortune—could he have been so busy taking care of his holdings that he neglected the education of his children? What *were* they doing? They were having a good time—so much so that Job was afraid. Afraid of what? Of punishment. In other words: right from the outset we are shown the decadence of a situation and its components. *Yirat shamayim* became *yirat khet* which became *yirat onesh*: the sublime concept of fear of heaven had now found its simplistic expression in fear of retribution. In other words: the text warns us not to be misled into treating Job as a truly Just Man; he is simply another complex and complicated human being who, like any of us, is capable of greatness and self-delusion, forever oscillating between total anguish and ultimate hope, between tragic quest and tragic truth.

Why tragic? Because of the next sequence in the narrative that takes the reader up to heaven where we listen in on a strange dialogue between God and Satan: on the surface the dialogue is banal, inconsequential, almost gossip. . . Did you happen to meet my friend Job? Yes? Is he well? Isn't he marvelous? Read the exchange of words and you realize that they lay the foundation for Job's trial and punishment: what begins with a harmless dialogue ends in intolerable pain and mourning. God praises Job only to force Satan to oppose him. That is the impression one gets from the text: God's compliments are meant to arouse Satan's criticism. And Satan understood it—otherwise he would not have dared to go on contradicting God! Which means: *the whole operation was God's doing, not Satan's.* In fact—who set the story in motion? Satan? No. It was God. It was God who opened the dialogue; Satan only answered. Satan was only an instrument. And Job knew it. That is why he felt that his argument had to be not with Satan but with God. And what an argument it was. . .

All of a sudden, Job's quiet and serene family-life is shattered. A messenger arrives with bad news; he has hardly finished, when a second one arrives with worse news; and a third—with much worse news. Destruction, catastrophe, death and murder: each time, each messenger ends his report saying: "And I alone escaped to come here and tell the tale."

Question: why did Job choose to believe them? From experience we know that a person's natural response to extreme situations is one of disbelief. Patients reject the bad medical verdict—and their relatives likewise. "It cannot be," is the natural reaction of the person exposed to sudden tragedy. Job is different. Instead of doubting the veracity of the messengers, he accepts their testimony without asking for proof or corroboration. Instead of saying: "This must be a bad dream—for only in a dream would so many terrible things happen the same way, to the same family, only in a dream would all the surviving witnesses repeat the same lines!" Instead of doubting the reality of his experience, he submits to it and acts accordingly, namely: he performs the ritual of mourning as stipulated by Jewish Law. Even though he is not Jewish!

And it is because he is not Jewish that he believes the messengers and their tales. Had he been Jewish, he would not have believed them. Remember: Jeremiah's warnings were not taken seriously. Remember: Jewish men and women escaped from ghettos hoping to warn communities on the other side of the approaching menace; they tried to tell the tale; in vain. Jews simply refused to believe that humanity could be so ugly, so vicious, so murderous. . .

No: Job was not Jewish—but his suffering was. That he was not Jewish is clear from most indications in the talmudic and midrashic sources about him. They all see in him a Just man, a Saint, a kind of Messiah for the Gentiles. The most common theory about him was that he was one of Pharoah's three advisors. His involvement with Jewish history? When Pharoah was faced with the question whether to allow the Jews to leave Egypt, Yethro said yes, Bileam said no, and Job said nothing: he remained silent, neutral. That was his sin. Neutrality is always sinful for it helps the oppressor, never his victims. That is why he was punished. But why should a Gentile politician be punished for not helping Jews? The answer is: powers means responsibility; one must use it wisely, ethically. In choosing to remain neutral, Job hurt both sides: Pharoah *and* the Jews. He is universal; upon rereading his story, I discovered that we Jews have taken from him much more than I thought. Upon rereading the book, I made other discoveries as well. For instance: two principal characters appear and disappear right away: Satan and Job's wife. Having played his role, having spoken to God, and having inflicted the expected series of blows upon Job, Satan withdraws from the stage never to be heard of again.

As for Job's wife—her role, in the beginning, is that of an antagonist—even of an irritant. There the text is unfair towards her. She is present but mute. Her only contribution is one line: "Curse God and die." Having added to her husband's despair, she withdraws to backstage and stays there—observing but unobserved—until the end: an object rather than a subject in her own story. Why such injustice? After all, whatever happened to Job also happened to her. Granted, when God talked to Satan he inquired about Job and not his wife—but is that a reason to ignore her altogether? Weren't they part of a family unit? Weren't they joined in marriage? When Job lost his wealth—she too was left with nothing. When Job lost his children, weren't they her children as well? The ordeal intended for Job affected them both. But then, why is the entire book about Job and not about his wife? Let us imagine a book written by her or about her: would she be as ungenerous towards him as he seems to have been towards her? "*Keakhat hanevelot tedabri*," he snapped at her. "Do not speak foolishly," said he, and the term he used is even stronger. Dismissing her plea to curse God and die—in other words: to put an end to their misery—he said: "We accept the good from God, why shouldn't we accept the bad as well?" Clearly it is he who is given the good part, the attractive role: he always knows what to say, what to do, when to keep quiet and when to rebel: if ever there exists a male-oriented book in Scripture, it is Job.

And yet, the book has been included in the canon. Its lesson has become part of our collective consciousness. Only now, having explored it in depth, do I realize how much we have taken from it for various circumstances.

Take, for instance, the Laws of mourning: they all derive from Job. He put ash on his forehead; he tore up his clothes; he sat on the floor; he used the ritual expression "*adoshem natan, adoshem lakach, yehi shem adoshem mevorakh,*"—God has given, God has taken back: may His name be blessed. Then he withdraws into himself, delving into his own anguished memory. And the three friends who came to visit him remained at a certain distance. At first, they looked and looked. Then, they listened. That's the Law: the mourner takes the initiative; the mourner decides when to speak and when to keep silent; the visitor must only react to his or her behavior so as not to be indiscreet, so as not to hurt the mourner's feelings inadvertently.

The Laws of Mourning, in the Jewish tradition, are the most human in recorded history: there is no area of human behavior in which our sages have invested so much knowledge, sensitivity and compassion. All this we owe Job.

He gave us a magnificent lesson in silence. His silence was both response and challenge: For seven days and seven nights he was silent—so great was his pain that no words could express or contain it. He reminds us of Aaron the High Priest: when his two sons, Nadav and Avihou, perished inside the sanctuary, what did he do or say? *Vayidom Aharon.* And Aaron kept silent.

Job lost seven sons. And three daughters. And his position. And his illusions about life and about justice.

And so he chose silence. (Often I envy him for a silence that generated and inspired more silence. I belong to a generation that was not as lucky: our tragedy and its memories are drowning in noise.) Still, in a way, the same thing happened to Job: it took seven days for his so-called "friends" to open their verbal assault against him. In our case, it took a bit longer—but the assault is still going on. Theologians and psychiatrists, filmmakers and television producers, novelists and critics. Poor Job: he suffered and they proceeded to explain his suffering to him.

And so we are given to understand that—as God states subsequently—the three friends are anything but friends. There are three terms, in Hebrew, to describe a friend: *Yadid*, *Khaver* and *Rea*. *Yadid* means: *Yad* and *yad*—hand in hand. *Rea*—*resh-ayin*—is close to *ra*: evil. And, in the text, they are called "*reim*"—they represent evil: they had come to console Job and instead had added to his pain, and even more to his sense of isolation, alienation and solitude.

What do they tell him? That he is guilty. The proof? His suffering. "If you don't know why you are punished, God does." They are constantly pounding him with their arguments. They are not with him in his time of need; they are against him. They seem to follow a kind of script, to have divided the task among themselves. With each discourse the attack gains strength, eventually penetrating his innermost defenses. They alternately use logic, emotion, passion to convince him, meaning: to deprive him of his own deep and personal convictions. They are on the side of the winner—on the side of the Almighty God. Their insolence and insensitivity are most shocking when they blame his dead children: surely, they must have sinned, otherwise God would not have punished them. How unnecessary. How cruel and gratuitous. There could have been no other purpose than to bring him to his knees; to defeat him; to crush him.

Well now—who sent them? What motivated them? Who were they? They pretended to speak for God but spoke against him; they may have thought that they were God's friends; they were only his defenders. They were Satan's friends. For they did to Job psychologically, mentally, what Satan had done physically. They tormented him. They tortured him. And because of them, I felt more and more empathy with Job. Their words ring false; they were deceitful. At best, they allowed themselves to be used as instruments of victimization. Of the worst kind.

I understood this better now than when I first studied Job. There are degrees in suffering. To suffer from actual causes is one thing, from human beings is another. To suffer from strangers is less cruel than to suffer from friends. Job's real tragedy—I mean: his ultimate tragedy—began when he felt misunderstood, worse: judged, condemned, betrayed by his own friends.

At this point let us stop the action and share with you a remarkable discovery I made while teaching the subject at Yale some years ago. Thanks to Professor Bill Hallo I came across an ancient text of some 800 before the common era from the late Babylonian period: though written much before the Book of Job, it sounds like Job.

It is an Akkadian dialogue of the unrighteousness of the world and it is conducted between a righteous sufferer and his friend.

Sufferer:
O wise man,. . .let me speak to you.
Then will I, the sufferer, not cease to reverence you.
For where is a wise man like you,
Where is a scholar who can compete with you.
Where is a counselor to whom I can unfold my grief?
I am devastated, am in the depths of distress.
When I was still a child, fate took my father from me.
My mother who bore me departed to the 'land without return,'
My father and my mother left me unprotected.
The cripple is my superior, the fool has an advantage,
The rogue has been promoted, but I have been brought low. . .
I looked around among men in the world, but the signs were full of contradictions.

Friend:
O wise and knowing man, rich in knowledge—
Your heart is evil and you blaspheme God.
The heart of the god is unfathomable, like the middle of heaven,
What he can do is hard to understand, and incomprehensible to men.
Give heed, my friend, understand my views,
Hear the careful expression of my speech.
They praise loudly the way of the famous man who knows how to murder, but oppress the lowly.
They assent to the evildoer to whom righteousness is an abomination, but drive away the honest man who heeds God's word.

Sufferer:
You are kind, my friend, behold my grief.
Help me, look on my distress, understand it.
I am a fearful slave who begs in humility.
I have not seen help and support for one moment.
I modestly go through the squares of my city,
My voice was not loud and my speech was gentle.
I do not go about with head upraised, but look at the ground,
like a slave I do not praise my God in the assembly of my associates.
May the god who has abandoned me help me,
may the goddess who has betrayed me show me mercy,
the shepherd, the sun of the people, be gracious to me like a god!

Thus we learn that the painful problem—or rather: the problem of pain involving theodicy—had preoccupied scholars and writers much before the

Book of Job was written. The difference between the two situations? In Akkadian and Babylonian texts, the sufferer speaks only to his friend—never to God; in our text, Job speaks always to God. Even when he addresses himself to his friend—or to his friends—his remarks are aimed at God: they serve only as vehicles or instruments of communication. His quarrel is not with them but with Him.

They often fail to understand him altogether. They comprehend only his silence which to them reflects his pain, nothing else. When they arrived they could not speak to him—*ein dover elav—ki rau*—for they had seen—*ki gadal hak'ev meod*: they had seen that the pain kept on growing. Yes, they too—even they—were sensitive to his pain; even they were touched by its intensity; even they had to recognize that it was genuine, impenetrable, irreversible. But when he began to speak, they turned against him. Why? What did he say that made them show their hostility? Did he blaspheme? Did he accuse the Almighty God? No: all he did or said was "*Arur yom Ivaled bo*"—cursed be the day I was born. He did not curse God—he cursed himself: his own life, his own past, his own entrance into history. What's wrong with that? What's wrong with a man who shouts his anguish when he suffers? His outburst is only natural and psychologically therapeutic: better speak up than keep your pain inside; better let go than withdraw into your shelter. Any psychoanalyst will tell us *that*. The passage would appear to be in praise of non-existence, of the talmudic affirmation that "*Noah lo leadam shelo nivra mishenivra*":—that it is better for man not to have been born. "To live is to suffer," he cries out. To live is to wait for death—and wait for it with anticipation and joy. He ends his opening address as follows: "For the thing which I greatly feared is come upon me, and that which I was afraid of is come onto me. I was not in safety, neither had I rest, neither was I quiet; *vayavo rogez*, yet trouble came". . . In other words: the story of Job is not about suffering nor is it about sadness; it is a story—a powerful story—about fear and anguish.

What did they expect him to do? Accept the series of tragedies passively—meekly—without responding? To submit and abdicate forever? And stay numb until death came? Numb and mute? Did they want him to be superhuman? Didn't they know that it is human to weep, to shout, to curse, to protest, to despair? Job was more human than they—and that is why we feel close to him, not to them. They should have kept quiet even after his speech.

His wife appears in a somewhat better role. What does she say? *Barekh et elohim*—curse God and get it over with. Perceptive, courageous, strong willed, she spoke her mind: she knew that man can never defeat God—not even in theological argumentation. Her purpose was to spare her husband from further disillusionment: she wanted him to die *before* the three friends had a chance to speak up! Maybe she meant *Barekh*—literally: bless God and die. Die while blessing Him. Let us see what He will say then. . . Therefore Job's answer to her is unwarranted. If there is one moment in this entire drama which fills me

[margin handwritten note: fear and anguish - not suffering]

with malaise—which draws me away from our revered Job it is when he admonishes her with quasi-brutality. He is too harsh with his wife; he shows no respect for her feelings, for her sorrow, for her identity; he shows no compassion towards her—and no appreciation for her advice and assistance. She is hurt, and offended, and withdraws and stays away from public scrutiny until the last phase when husband and wife are ordered to make up and rebuild their home. She is brooding and she is right: in a way, she is the only good person in the entire play. But then, we must be tolerant of Job's impatience, his restlessness: his entire being is one open wound—no wonder that he is quick to insult! Her solution was radical but too easy: you don't solve such important all pervasive questions with sweeping generalizations.

But, in the process, we come to discern the different attitudes that exist toward human suffering and its ethical and/or theological implications, for example:

One: intellectual surgery: you curse God and die—and the play ends before it has a chance to develop into a philosophical drama.

Two: you formulate questions in a way that makes all answers impossible, or implausible.

Three: you accept the answers in advance and in so doing you reject all questions. For Job there are no answers, for his friends there are no questions, and for Job's wife neither are valid, for her there is only one option: death—which is both.

But the Book is not only about attitudes to suffering—it is also about injustice. Clearly, the Book approves of its hero: Job is described as honest, pious and hospitable, and yet he is made to suffer agony—why?

Because of a deal—or a wager—made in heaven between God and Satan? On the surface the answer appears to be yes. But beneath the surface a puzzling factor is waiting for us: Satan is less guilty than God. Usually Satan prods man, here God prods Satan who, at one point, tries to prod God. As for Job, he remains totally outside the picture. What God and Satan speak and do and decide. . . only heaven knows. Not Job. Job is the true victim—both Satan's and God's. Is he aware of it? No. As far as he is concerned, he faces only one antagonist: God. Satan's role remains shrouded in secrecy: how would Job react if he were to learn of the initial wager? Why doesn't God reveal to him the origins of the story? Isn't Job entitled to know the truth about his own misfortune? Of all the injustices done to Job, this is probably the most subtle one: *he never learns the full truth.* At no point does God—or Satan—tell him: listen, friend; it all began with a casual chat we had about people—it all began with gossip. . . Job will live, survive, repent and die—without ever knowing the full extent, the real truth, of his own story.

Throughout his journey from despair to despair he gropes in darkness. He experiences the nostalgia and melancholy of a man in jail waiting for a door to open, for a sound to break the silence, for dawn to disperse the shadows. Read his discourses and you will marvel at his striking imagery: the metaphors he uses, and uses frequently, often refer to imprisonment: there is a person lying in his room, riveted to his pain, or: there is a person—a fetus really—closed inside its mother's womb. Job is alone and he knows it. He also realizes that as a human being he is mortal, thus vulnerable, thus easily reduced to dust: hence his humility. Even when he is angry, he speaks without arrogance. So humble is his language that many of his lines are being used in our liturgy for Yom Kippur, the holiest day of the year, the Day of Atonement. What is man? Only a shadow. What is life? A passing whim. What is human ambition? An illusion in the desert. "Our days are those of a hireling," says Job—and we repeat it after him. "What is man that you should magnify him?" What is man that you should as much as notice him? Listen further: "*Adam yelud isha katzar yamin us'va roguez. . . K'tzitz yatza, Vayivrakh katzel.* Man's days are short and his troubles—or his angers—are many; he comes like a flower and leaves like a shadow. . ." One is reminded of the awesome prayer we sing on Yom Kippur eve*: Ki hine kakhomer beyad hayotzer*—we are like pottery in the hands of the potter. . . like a ship in the hands of the captain. . . we are instruments in the hands of the artist, the worker, the creator. . . Note one omission in the many examples: never is it said—or even as much as hinted—that we are like toys in the hands of the toy-maker. . . Human beings are not toys, says the Jewish tradition. Man is the heart of the universe, his humanity is at the center of God's preoccupation and occupation. Not even God Himself treats man as a toy. How did Einstein put it? God does not play dice with His creation. Toys are manufactured for entertainment purposes; they last while they last, then they are thrown out—not so human beings. Every one is singular, exceptional, unique: irreplaceable. But then. . . what about Job? Isn't he a toy in the hands of God and Satan? Aren't they playing a game with him, a game whose rules are hidden from him? Is this why he uses all other images except this one—is this why he is never told the whole truth?

The Midrash does allow Job to guess at the possibility of a game—but of an involuntary one. There comes a time when Job wonders aloud whether God has not committed an error, an oversight. Perhaps mine is a tragic yet not unusual case of mistaken identity, he asks God: "Maybe you confused *Iyov* with *Oyev*—maybe you have mistaken me, Job, with *Oyev*—the enemy?

A legend: More in bewilderment than in sorrow, Job turned to God: Master of the Universe, is it possible that a storm passed before You causing You to confuse *Iyov* (Job) with *Oyev* (Enemy)?

Strange as it may seem, of all the questions raised by Job, only this one was answered. And God's voice roared in the tempest: Pull yourself together, man, and listen! Many hairs have I created on the human head, and every single hair has its root; I don't confuse roots, how could I confuse *Iyov* and *Oyev*? Many drops have I created in the clouds, and every single drop has its own source; I confuse neither drops nor clouds, how could I confuse *Iyov* and *Oyev*?

Many thunderbolts have I created and for each bolt a path of its own; I don't mistake one bolt for another, how could I confuse *Iyov* and *Oyev*? Know also that the wild goat is cruel with its young. As they are about to be born she climbs to the top of a very high rock and lets the little ones drop from the precipice. So I prepared an eagle to catch them on his wings, but were the eagle to arrive one moment too early or too late, they would fall to the ground and be crushed. I don't confuse moments, or lightning bolts, or drops, or roots—and you are asking Me if I am confusing *Iyov* and *Oyev*, Job and Enemy!

What did God tell him in this story? That there is no accident in creation. Everything has a purpose, all events are endowed with meaning. Though God is above time, He is also in time. Though He is against evil, He is responsible for both good and evil. The mystery of suffering implies God but indicts man—and man alone. Job's mistake, according to the Talmud, was not that he asked the question but that he dared to formulate answers. From his own individual case, Job wanted to build an original universal theory. Because he suffered unfairly, all suffering was unjust—which means: the whole world is unjust. In which case nothing matters: if both the Just and the unjust get what they do not deserve, then the principle of justice has no meaning. Comments the Talmud: Job's theory had but one aim: to remove the idea of justice and fairness from human existence. The Just was born just and the wicked was born wicked: you, God, made them what they became. In that case—everything is Your doing, Master of the Universe! But then—why is the one rewarded and the other punished?

God's answer is powerful and crushing: it questions not Job's ideas but the perception on which they are based. "Where were you when I laid the foundation of the earth? Speak up if you have understanding."

Actually, at this point, Job could have turned to the Presiding Judge with a request to rule God's question out of order: it is irrelevant, it is unrelated to his accusation, to his torment, to his life. After all, the question is not where Job had been when God created heaven and earth, but where *God* had been when Job underwent agony! If Job chose to remain silent and listen, it is because God had criticized him for using "words without knowing what they mean." From the moment Job doubted his own language, he knew that his case was lost.

Said the Midrash: when God addressed Job out of the whirlwind, he spoke as a pupil addressing his teacher. A strange role for God, isn't it? He chose it for one purpose only: to confuse Job. Job had expected God to speak to him as Judge, King, or even Father: not as pupil. "Pull yourself together, said God. I am going to ask you certain things, and you better answer me."

To increase his sense of bewilderment, God directed his attention to the greatest mystery of all, that of "*Maasse bereshit*," the mystery of the beginning, saying: "Did I ask you for advice on how to create being out of nothingness? Do you *know* the laws that govern nature and the universe? On what does the universe repose? You don't know—does it mean that it doesn't exist? But there are innumerable things that you cannot see—does it mean that you should not have faith in them, or in me? What about your soul: can you see it? And yet, it exists!"

God did not deny Job's right to question the validity of his own tragedy, only his determination to generalize it and thus turn human pain and divine intent into abstraction. In doing so, Job, unwittingly, echoed his friends' arguments.

His so-called friends were wrong because they claimed that his suffering was justified, that *all* suffering is justified. Then they went so far as to suggest that even his children had sinned. And that he exaggerated his own pain. . . for "publicity" purposes. They accused him of all but inventing it. And then: having failed to assume responsibility for what happened to him, rejecting it and placing the blame on God who, as everyone knows, is blameless.

They were guilty of refusing to understand someone who is suffering; and *Job* was guilty of not understanding someone who witnesses suffering.

But, in fact, they were all guilty of reducing human anguish and torture to abstract notions and theories. Therefore they were all rebuked by God—the friends more so, because they had *no* excuse: Job had. Also, he needed God—whereas they invoked Him only as pretext. Job needed God to convince himself that although he himself didn't know the answer, God did. Job was ready to accept divine injustice but not divine indifference. If God is not present in history, then history is absent from mankind. If God is God, God is at the beginning and at the outcome of all our endeavors. How did Rabbi Zusia put it? I don't mind suffering as long as I know that I am suffering for the sake of God. Job's attitude was somewhat different: he didn't mind suffering as long as he knew that his suffering came *from* God. Did he acquire such a conviction during his two dialogues with God? No. Never did God tell him that He was the one who made him suffer—and for what reason.

All he did was to counter his questions with OTHER questions: "Do you know the place where darkness is dwelling? Have you ever seen the gates of death? Have you ever perceived the breath of the earth? Has the rain a father? Out of whose womb came the ice? Who can number the clouds in wisdom? Who provides food for the raven?"

Questions, questions, nothing but questions—one more intriguing, more mysterious than the other. It is as though God has decided to teach Job a course in cross-examination procedures: You, a human being think YOU have questions? Listen to mine. . .

In doing so, God offered Job—and through him all of us—a new understanding of the mysterious man-God relationship: it is not defined by that which distinguished question from answer but by that which separates one question from another.

What then is man? A question mark reflected *in* and opposed *to* and completed by another question mark. For there is quest in every question.

Man's quest for God and God's infinite quest for man. Both are in exile from one another—inside one another. Both are longing for an answer—perhaps the same answer.

That is why Job, right away, without hesitation, yields to God and submits to His will. He now understands that the essence of man lies in his ability to ask questions—and to receive them as well. That is why he does not argue his case but chooses immediate abdication; he understood that whereas he could question God's answer, he could not but accept God's questions.

The fact that God questions man was more important to Job than for God to answer. Is there a greater tribute the Creator could pay to His creature? "God spoke to Job in the manner a pupil addresses his teacher," says the Talmud. In other words: He addressed his *questions* to him. And for Job that was sufficient.

Is it for us as well?

The fundamental issue raised by the Book of Job is: did he come through his ordeal a winner or a loser? Was he a victim of injustice or his own victim? At the end of the story, we wonder: who carried the day?

What we do know with certainty is who lost. The three friends. God Him-self gives them a piece of. . . our mind. Job endured everything, says Kierkegaard, until his friends arrived; then he grew impatient. So do we. And so does God. "I am angry at you, said God to Eliphaz the Yemenite, at you and at your two friends: I am angry at you for not having spoken in the right manner as my servant Job did." God dislikes flattery—He does not need it. God—the source of truth—demands truth and nothing else. And so he dismisses the three false friends who had claimed to speak on His behalf. Human beings are defined by their attitude towards their fellow human beings. Had the three friends stood by Job in his distress, they would have come closer to God. But—wait a minute: the text speaks about three friends. What about the fourth, Elihu, who appears on the stage just before the denouement of the plot? He is the most vicious of them all: he repeats their arguments but uses insolence all his own. From the text it is clear that he is the youngest: he is ebullient, arrogant, offensive. Why has he arrived so late? He came when he felt that Job had already been weakened by others; he came only when he thought that there was no more danger. He spoke up when he thought that it was safe. Therefore God simply ignores him: He doesn't even refer to him. Elihu is the unworthiest character in the play. No wonder that, in some sources, he is identified as the reincarnation of Satan who used him to stage his own comeback.

On a totally different level: the real losers are Job's children. Alive, they were unhappy; they must have resented their father's constant—and possibly unwarranted—suspicion. Dead, they were maligned by their father's friends. They never had a chance: they died too young. The injustices inflicted upon them cannot be corrected.

Now—what about the chief protagonist, Job himself? For him, the outcome seems quite ambiguous. He won because his three or four adversaries lost. Still, did he in fact lose because God won? Here the logic is of a different nature: God's victory does not necessarily mean man's defeat—quite the opposite: it illustrates man's participation in that victory. And the other way around: "*Nitzchu ni banai*," means: my children's victory is mine, says God. When a person is sincere, when his—or her—outcry is genuine, and genuinely motivated, he or she cannot lose.

The fact is that, in his final concession speech, Job sounds humble and repentant: "I abhor myself," says he. I have sinned. I have erred. I am sorry. "I am but dust and ashes." I wanted to know what I will never know—things I am incapable of knowing. I wanted to understand things that lie beyond my comprehension. And now, it's all over. I will not do it again, I promise.

But. . . there is one sentence in this short but poignant passage that, upon rereading, strikes us as. . . significant. "*Eshalkha vehodieni*": I shall ask questions of You and You will answer me. It's exactly what God had told him earlier when, out of the whirlwind, He said: "Pull yourself together, man, *eshalkha vehodieni*," I have questions for you to answer. Why did Job use the same expression? To point to his secret resolve to continue the dialogue? To declare his determination to go on asking questions?

If he won't—we will. As far as I'm concerned, they remain unresolved. The happy-end is too abrupt. Too obvious. God says: let us forget our misunderstanding, and Job, a true gentleman, is willing to oblige. And, all of a sudden, Job is once again wealthy, respected and fulfilled. And "all his brothers and sisters and acquaintances from before came to break bread with him and console him and give him money, jewelry and gold as presents." How strange! Where were they when he needed them? When he needed them, they were not there. When he became rich again and influential, he suddenly discovered that he had so many relatives, cousins and uncles, neighbors and schoolmates. . .

Suddenly, he had seven sons and three daughters—and these daughters were all beauty queens: "the most beautiful in the land." Unlike the first set, these children had names, identities: they must have been famous in their own right.

But—one detail is missing here: did he remarry? No: he didn't have to. He was still married to the same wife. She had remained there throughout the entire year of his ordeal; she had heard every argument, every word, every insinuation. Yet while everybody took part in the debate, she kept quiet. Her silence is as impressive as their words—and perhaps more so. But now she reappears on stage. Together with her husband, she decides to embark upon a new beginning. Difficult? So what. Impossible? For a couple that has gone beyond its own despair, nothing is impossible. They rebuild their home, their lives, their hopes. Is that the lesson offered in their Book? That it is given to human beings to start all over again? To overcome anguish and bitterness? To affirm faith in life in spite of all that threatens and diminishes life? Is that Job's greatness: that he was able to once again assume his responsibilities as father and husband?

That his memory and his soul were covered with scars, however invisible, however intangible, is clear from the expression used to describe his death: "*Vayamat Iyov*," and Job passed away at the age of two hundred eighty years, *zaken*—an old man—*usva yamim*: old and saturated with years. This expression occurs also in the story of Isaac: both had enough. Having seen and endured too much—at the hands of too many adversaries—they were. . . fed up with life. Both were too elegant, too delicate to express that feeling: as long as they were alive, they celebrated its virtues. When death came, they allowed it to carry them without regret.

And so—Job remains my hero for many reasons: he suffered and rebelled against his pain, yet though he suffered, he did not make other people suffer. In our tradition, he symbolizes innocent suffering. Even though he was not Jewish, he symbolizes the universal implications in Jewish suffering.

Also: I like him because he never denied God—not even when he protested against Him. He stopped protesting as soon as God spoke to him out of the whirlwind. There is a time for protest and a time for restraint, a time for memory and a time for forgiveness, a time for rebellion and a time for penitence. One could argue that he should not have admitted to having committed sins that he knew nothing about. But he never said that he felt guilty; all he said was that he was responsible. Did he wish to make God feel guilty? If so, he died without knowing whether he had succeeded or not. All God said was that He too was responsible. The mystery of man's limitations was thus matched by that of God's limitless powers. What they have in common is the justification—or its absence—in the future of creation.

The drama of Job, the tragedy of Job as well as his troubling mystery can be found in one key sentence we have overlooked until now. It reads: "*Hen yikteleni lo ayakhel*." Usually it is translated as follows: "Though he will slay me, I shall continue to place my faith in Him"—or: "*I shall go on longing for Him.*" In other words: Job affirms his faith in spite of his suffering—in spite of his sense of loss and the presence of death around him. Which means: in spite of his doubts. He simply discards them.

However some sources indicate a different—if not contrary—approach. They spell the word "*lo*"—not *lamed vav*, which means Him, but *lamed aleph*, which means: NO. Let us now read the entire verse: "*Hen yikteleni*—though He could kill me and would—*LO ayakhel*," I shall not be longing for Him, I shall not offer my faith unto Him.

Thus the question whether Job did or did not lose his faith is condensed in this one brief verse. Is there an answer? Perhaps we could state—using talmudic precedents—that "*ele veele divre elokim hayim*:—both explanations may be true. But. . . aren't they contradicting one another? Precisely: the Talmud teaches us that there is nothing wrong with paradoxes. It is not given to man to solve contradictions but to assume them—to live them—and, in moments of grace, transcend them.

There exists a third explanation. . . you know. . . On the other hand. . . It is possible that Job kept his faith—and rebelled against it—at the same time. It is possible that, having reached the height of his despair and torment, he achieved something new: he showed us that faith is necessary to rebellion and, also, that rebellion is possible within faith. There exists a time when the two are intertwined so as to strengthen one another instead of negating one another.

Ultimately, Job learned that he lived in a world that was cold and cynical—in a world without true friends. It is in such a world that God seeks to join man in his solitude. The story of Job? A story to denounce hypocrisy.

Job thought that God had mistaken him for an "*Oyev*"—an enemy. True, the four letters are interchangeable. But I prefer to see the name in another light: in Gematria—numerically—*Iyov* is nineteen, the equivalent of "*Akhi*": my brother.

REFLECTING ON BIBLICAL CHILDREN
From Adam and Eve, Isaac and Jesus
To the Betrayal and Sacrifice of Our Children
André Stein

Even though many words were uttered against child sacrifice in the Hebrew Bible, child betrayal and even filicide, in fact, are rampant in the Book of Genesis. I propose that the exile of Adam and Eve, the drama of Cain and Abel, the Flood, the abandonment of Lot, the banishment of Ishmael, the binding of Isaac, Rebecca's trickery disinheriting Esau in favor of Jacob, her favorite, the treachery of Laban leading to the pathetic rivalry of Leah and Rachel, the abandonment of Joseph, are all instances of child sacrifice and betrayal. According to my definition of child sacrifice and betrayal, the Book of Genesis proves to be the first blueprint for what becomes one of the universal themes and sources of pain, anger and aggression in the Judeo-Christian and Islamic world.

That definition can be summed up as *any conscious/unconscious attempt against the life, truly best (intrinsic and independent of the well being of others) safety and security, dignity and social well being of the child.* With this definition in mind, I find it impossible **not** to discern in our biblical history the tendency, at least, toward indifference regarding the life and well being of children. In fact, we have scarce evidence in the Bible of the intrinsic value of a child's life.

Retracing our steps to the very beginning, what God had done to Adam and Eve, indeed, had no value for the life of the first couple. With the prohibition to sample the fruit of the pivotal tree in the Garden, we witness the birth of cruelty against children, the destruction of the concept of innocence. For whatever a child does during the first years of life is the result of natural ignorance, a penchant toward contrariness, adventure and little or no concern for the consequences of his or her actions. It is not his or her cognitive or emotional means to distinguish between good and evil beyond "that which I like and/or can get away with is good" and "that which I dislike and/or get punished for is bad." Thus, ultimately, regardless of the nature of the act or its consequences for others, a child is always innocent. To speak of an innocent child is redundant, in that the word "child" automatically encodes innocence. Failure to articulate and respect this reality leads to being committed to the cruel fiction of the guilt of children, their innate wickedness, their predilection for sin. Indeed, the concept of sin regarding children is the single most anti-child notion aimed at keeping children—young and not so young—downtrodden, shame-riddled and disempowered. Those who refuse to see the folly and evil of such nightmarish denigration of children inevitably become the enemies of children, the enemies of themselves, indeed, the enemies of life. Thus, in my reading of the biblical stories, sin replaces innate human fallibility.

The God of Adam and Eve—definitely childlike beings until their Father evicts them from their innocence—sets the tone for those parental figures and institutions that are poised to expect the impossible from children. Thus, when our youngsters, following the impulses of their tender years, falter and don't live up to adult expectations, their parents and their contemporaries attribute their children's actions to wickedness and corruptibility. This, indeed, is what happened to the first children of God, to their descendants in the patriarchal lineage of Genesis and, eventually, this is what leads in the most compelling manner to the *Akkedah*—the sacrifice of Isaac and eventually of its inevitable denouement, the crucifixion of Jesus. With the abandonment and betrayal of those two innocent sons by their earthly and heavenly fathers, everything is in place for the commonplace demise of an endless chain of sons. (To be sure, daughters were sacrificed as well. Their ordeal, however, took a different path. For a sacrifice to be credible, parents offered to the deity what they cherished most. Since, in biblical times, sons were of greater currency than daughters, the *de facto* sacrifices were reserved for the most beloved sons. Daughters were abandoned to secondary status, to invisibility and silence until they would emerge on some man's horizon as a trophy and a fertile womb.)

No sacrifice of a child is more blatantly just that than the crucifixion of the son of God. The prototypes having been in place for centuries, all that had to happen was to actualize a reality that had been a virtual fact all along. Once the idea of child sacrifice was tolerated, it was inevitable that it would occur at the perpetrator's whim. There is no evidence that the very thought of this "pagan" practice is abhorrent and that it would be severely punished until it was completely eradicated even as a possibility. And even if we disallow all the other instances of divine and human child sacrifices, the sacrifice of Isaac as *requested* by God of His favorite servant, Abraham, speaks eloquently about child sacrifice as a practice known to humans. Abraham and God come out of the *Akkedah* as eternal winners, to be venerated for this supreme act of faith and obeisance. And whenever, in the *rarissime* cases, Isaac emerges as a topic of concern in connection with his ordeal, it is never with compassion and fury against the perpetrators. More often than not, it is stressed that he was *spared*, without a hair of his being affected. Nowhere is there evidence of indignation or indictment of the culprits. The fact is that **Isaac had been spiritually,**

morally and psychologically sacrificed. He could never again take the love of his father for granted, nor could he trust Abraham ever again enough to be alone with him. We seldom hear the voice of empathy; what did the poor lad suffer during those moments when he was tied to the soon to be burning altar? What terror invaded his heart when he saw his father's knife poised to stab him to death? How does one keep one's vitality intact after such a betrayal? What happens to one's trust and optimism? This time the angel intervened; what about the next time? How could he even think that this was an isolated event, never to be repeated again? And if his father could be an instrument of destruction—his father who loved him as much as life itself, his father whose destiny was inseparably bound to Isaac's life—what about the rest of humanity? Myriad questions never on Abraham's horizon had to emerge in his son's mind and soul, questions that abscond with the child's innocence, his optimism.

After the *Akkedah*, we can no longer speak of ignorance. Isaac had been thrust into an arena of knowledge where everyone was a potential lion. Very much like a Jewish child during the Holocaust. Once you learned that a) your parents would abandon you, albeit for your own good, b) there is a law against your very existence, c) anyone can be the earthly emissary of the Angel of Death, even your own parents, you will have been evicted from your innate ignorance. Your childhood had been sacrificed before the actual destruction of your body. If, like Isaac, you survive the actual attack on your being, you can never return to your childhood as if you had just left it for a time-out. It is in this sense that I support those Midrashic interpretations of the *Akkedah*, according to which the sacrifice of Isaac had been completed.

Some commentators, however, raise a question about Isaac's binding; Why didn't he protest, resist, object? After all, he was thirty-seven years old! The crucifixion of Jesus is evidence that it would have made no difference had the son of Abraham protested. Jesus did protest. In the Garden of Gethsemane, he pleaded for his life—to no avail. Thus, the attitude that hides behind the question about Isaac's stance is indeed a scarcely veiled indictment of the victim, who was not guilty of any wickedness for which the death penalty could have been viewed as a logical and deserved outcome. Since he did not emerge as a subject of concern, we have no reason to think of him as anything but a child, regardless of his age. There was no indication that he represented any-thing but filial devotion. What seems quite possible is that Isaac was feared as the sole heir; should he be a second Abraham, with his youth and vigor in the balance, he might be the one to dethrone his father(s). And this is where the link between Isaac and Jesus is dramatically relevant.

Both sons were sacrificed because the intrinsic value of their respective lives did not emerge as the prime consideration for their father, mother and God, their Heavenly Father. No one stopped to ask: what if this life is snuffed out? Was this life brought into this world to be of service and nothing else? Is this life on earth worth so little that it pales in significance whether it is lived to its natural term? No one stopped to ask: what is the purpose of Isaac's or Jesus' life?

I am reminded of my little cousin Judit, who was conceived by my aunt to save our lives from certain death at the hands of the Nazis. When the "job" of saving our lives was completed, she passed away, at the age of six weeks. She had to endure six weeks of malnutrition at the breast of a milkless mother whose peace of mind and sense of culpability and doubt about what she had done ravaged her nights and days. Had she felt that it was perfectly justifiable to create a life for the sole purpose of preserving other endangered children, she would not have felt a visible torment within her conscience and she would not have felt a loss that remained frozen for over fifty years. In her mother's soul, she felt the loss of that tiny life that never had a chance to unfold. She felt instinctively that a terrible wrong had been perpetrated vis-à-vis Judit. I never saw or read any evidence that either Abraham or God—or, for that matter, Mary's parents or Mary herself—felt anything akin to my aunt's dilemma about bringing into the world a child who was to be, before all, a life saver. For my aunt, once she uncovered the darkest contents of her conscience, what became paramount was how to prevent the death of her newborn. She did not succeed. Was she able to derive solace from the knowledge that Judit's very existence *in utero* saved the lives of four small children? Judging from the profundity of her silence, it would be impossible to fathom that she could ever look into our eyes without seeing in them the tormented face of her sacrificed newborn. How is it that no such painful validation of the life of Isaac or Jesus ever came to our knowledge? And even if the hearts of Sarah and Abraham on the one hand, and Mary and Joseph—and, to be sure, God—had shattered under the burden of loss, how is it that the authors of the holy texts chose not to include a reference to their respective griefs? Is it possible that the reason for such void resides in the absence of any such feeling? Or perhaps that a child's traumas were of so little concern that the authors omitted any reference to them in a matter-of-fact manner, conforming to the values of the time?

In reading the stories of Isaac and Jesus, it is clear that there is no link between innocence and child sacrifice. We like to think that only the wicked deserve and do die violent deaths. But this, of course, is a cruel tale, a gruesome fiction to justify evil practices against children. Alice Miller and others have eloquently demonstrated that all theories proposing the innate wickedness of children are just perverted excuses for the hatred of children. And our fear of them makes it pressing that we get rid of them one way or another, lest they confront us with our own projected destructiveness. Our young ones become the recipients of our shame, worthlessness and guilt that had been coerced on us when we were children. In short, there is a circularity to this demon making, from which the way out is not through cruel practices toward our children, but self-acceptance and self-empathy. If we project these benevolent ways of treating ourselves as our children, we will have put an end to the torment and violence handed down to us by those who drafted our favorite myths about God, Adam and Eve and their offspring, including Isaac and Jesus, the children of the Holocaust, the child victims of all genocides, hunger, disease and all other versions of abandonment and betrayal.

Until then, we can expect no change in victimizing, betraying and sacrificing our children, for we will not be able to mete out to them a treatment we reserve for others—regardless all the surface rhetoric about child protection and about how we do everything for our children; after all, the future belongs to them. We must remember that God promised Abraham that his powers would be secured forever through the continuation of his beliefs by his son Isaac. And yet, sacrificing the son would abscond with all of the father's posterity. Abraham was willing to sacrifice his son, Isaac, his bridge to the future. Just so, God sacrificed His only son, Jesus, to buy back all the sins of others without regard for Jesus as a being in himself. In these two examples of child sacrifice we have the antipodes of the matter, illustrating that a) the child's life in itself does not matter; and b) the role the child may play in the future may or may not be a compelling enough factor to safeguard his life. What matters is the father's design at hand. I am reminded of those staunch and sanguine protectors of the unborn child who have no reservation about killing the living, or endorsing the death penalty and supporting vengeful or invasive wars. In short, the full spectrum of attitudes and behaviors has to be expected without reliance on any constancy of thought and values.

When all is said, we have to face the fact; we are both life-giving and life-taking, neither angels nor monsters—just following the path traced for us by our founding spiritual myths, with the God of the Bible as our most compelling role model. On the one hand He created Adam and Eve; on the other hand, He allowed the death of His son, Jesus. He created us corruptible, in bad need of redemption and to redeem our "sins" He chose a virtuous man who had all the reasons to remain in His good graces as evidence that it is within our means to be and to do good. Yet He took the life of Jesus, the good son, for the sake of those who had betrayed Him with their intolerable, wicked ways of living.

God subjected Abraham and his son to the worst ordeal. To what purpose? He toyed with Job, another paragon of virtue and righteousness; for what good? This is all about self-gratification on the one hand, and undermining His own accomplishment by tormenting His best offspring, on the other hand. What does He gain in this circular process of creation—destruction—creation—destruction...? What can we learn from such an example that could be of use in living our lives? That godliness is next to darkness? Far from leading to eternal peace and harmony, good will and service, attempting to emulate God leads to giving life and making it hard for that young life to thrive, to exist. We give birth to children and we rob them of their innocence, their childlikeness. We teach them to be generous, righteous and just, only to confuse them with the stories of the sacrificed biblical children and their mixed up, ambivalent, unaware parents.

How could the same God who handed down a commandment against killing endorse the cruel death of His children? How can God tolerate the death sentence for Jesus, the prototype of the innocent? He did so to serve a greater good—redemption. In reality, however, we kill only those of whom we are afraid. Did God let Jesus die because He was scared of the Nazarene whose teachings and exemplary life threatened to be more attractive to increasing numbers of people than "God fearing?"

Are we then surprised that ever since the infancy of our Western civilization, we have shown a particular fondness for draining the blood of the innocent? On the surface we torment the weak—children, women, homosexuals, the old, the sick, the poor, etc.—and those whose blood can be shed with impunity for they are dying for our sake. In reality, we need to kill them, repress and shame them, for doing so addresses our fear of the next generation evicting us from our parental privilege. We hate the weak and we are scared of them. The paradigm seems to have worked with flawless success ever since the creation of the Garden of Eden and its inhabitants.

In Uta Rank-Heinemann's words: "It is God's own son who must die, taking the place and atoning for the sinners, so that they may be redeemed from evil." But in reality, to snuff out Jesus' young life with the excuse that he is to suffer and be sacrificed for us is another version of perpetrating evil. "He had to die, and not only die but suffer horribly for me," says Elisabeth, a staunch fundamentalist Baptist, a psychotherapeutic client of mine. Where does she get the notion that anyone, including the son of God, has to suffer horribly before donating his life so that **she** can feel redeemed? And what does it do to her? Is she free of anguish about the day of judgment? No, not in the least. She can never refer to herself without insisting on being "bad," "sinful," "don't deserve to be alive."

This is a sad version of feeling redeemed and forgiven. In other words, as far as Elisabeth is concerned, Jesus died in vain, his Calvary has failed her and millions like her. For I propose it as a basic truth that no one can feel guilt-free and redeemed by the sacrifice of another human being, and even less by the sacrifice of a child. Feeling free of darkness in one's soul can only come about as a consequence of self-acceptance, self-empathy, taking responsibility and finding palatable choices. Only thus can we reach out to others and do Jesus' work—build a solid, honest, loving self, linking one's life to a like-minded partner (should one choose to live with one) and together giving life to children whose lives will be guided by two consciously good-bad parents. Only such people can set the horizon of the community ablaze with pure passion. To do so, we have to re-write our sacred founding stories, from Genesis to Gospel.

"What an arrogant project," Elisabeth exclaims in response to hearing of my project of re-writing the ancient stories that bind us to our painful past.

"You believe that millions of people will discard their faith in God the Father and embrace a story of Christ not crucified? This is preposterous!"

In fact, she needs to see Jesus killed, and remind herself of this sacrifice of a good man for her to feel that all is well in her world. On the other hand, she cannot understand why she is compelled to be so harsh, so critical and perfectionistic with her twelve-year-old daughter. According to Elisabeth, it all comes from love, of course. More realistically, however, the consequence of sacrifice, torture and cruelty can only lead to visiting upon our children the cursed knowledge that had been handed down to parents throughout the ages. It is not surprising them that all the prayers in the world do not do the job of helping Elisabeth to accept and like herself and her daughter. She has never learned how to be good to herself. Instead, she was taught to be God-like and God-fearing. She cannot achieve the first in spite of her best efforts; consequently, she has committed herself to self-hate and fantasies of surrendering her worthless life as a sacrifice for her daughter's well-being. To achieve the latter—embodied by her parents loving and accepting her only as long as she is God-fearing, she prays sincerely several times every day.

"Let us imagine that Jesus was facing his judge, Pontius Pilate, on Good Friday, awaiting his judgement for life or death, with a multitude of grateful disciples behind him, hoping that their master would be spared. Pilate posed the traditional question for that day: 'Whom shall I let go, Barrabbas the thief, or Jesus the Nazarene?' And the crowd would respond as one asserting and demanding voice—'The Nazarene!' And let us imagine that Pilate had done according to the people's wish, as it was customary on that day, and let Jesus go. What would have happened to Christianity, and you?" I asked Elisabeth.

"Christianity would have disappeared without the sacrifice of Christ. And I would be at a loss what to do with the burden of my sins, of which I have many."

In short, Jesus had to die so that he could free all the Elisabeths of the world throughout the ages. This appears to me as one of the most tragic wastes in our history since it is in our nature to commit dark deeds—"sins"—as well as bright shiny ones. Denying and attempting to purge our shadow side in prayer, as does Elisabeth, the enemy of her beloved daughter and her habitually philandering preacher father and his beloved wife pray to God together for forgiveness and salvation every day. In short, they live as it is to be expected—shuttling between good and bad—and everyone involved has to carry the burden of his or her secret shadow side, without the expectation that the sacrifice of a child, any child, would buy back their dark side. It is as if one side of their being had indeed been unequivocally cleansed and redeemed by Jesus' gesture, but their other side is bathed in darkness. Just as God and all His biblical family must contend with their dark sides, rather than act as if it did not exist, and consequently project it on to their children.

Independent of religious dogma and the tenets of theology according to which we must not think of God in human terms, I propose that it is impossible not to acknowledge that these stories and the *dramatis personae* in them have been viewed as role-models; their crises, conflicts and challenges have been confronted as if they were of our own family's history. As we contemplate God the Father and His biblical lineage, it is scarcely avoidable to look at His actions or listen to His speeches without being reminded of the fathers we know, our own fathers or the fathers we are. How can we witness His mistakes and cruelties, endure His expectations and relive the pain and confusion caused by similar mistakes, cruelties and expectations proffered by our very own human fathers? We cannot look at the biblical dramas and not recognize in them familiar scenarios in which we ourselves are or have been embroiled.

If we refuse to see in God the Father His shadow side, we cannot escape blaming humanity—God's children—for all that hurts and all that is evil, and praise God for all that is good—in Him and in us. For as soon as we adopt this anti-human stance, we permit and justify child sacrifice and betrayal. It would then make perfectly good sense to praise Him and only Him, to deprecate man as a natural sinner, to gleefully and enthusiastically offer our children to Him, to kill on His behalf to make the world suit His values and needs. To raise children to prefer martyrdom to a commitment to the life given to them as a bundle of potentialities. In this respect, the sacrifice of biblical children from Adam to Jesus is not only tolerable but also predictable and exulting.

To say the least, Adam, Isaac and Jesus should not have been betrayed. Had those founding myths been formulated in a pro-child vein, Western history and the history of childhood would have been fundamentally different. It is noteworthy that the Ten Commandments attend to all potential threats to society, protecting faith in God, parents, community, property, ethical values, but there is not a word about honoring and protecting the most vulnerable members of any community—children. The seven capital sins make no reference to the sin of hurting children. In the teaching of biblical masters and wise men, we see a lot more often the call for hurting children for their own good than to warn people—parents—against the monstrosity of hurting a child for his/her own good. In most of our fairy tales, horrible and perverted things are done to children and when they are rescued, it is often at the expense of their childhood—they are rescued into adult *dénouements*. Historically, we have mountains of documentation about how children have been robbed of their childhood, their potentials, their lives. Today, we sacrifice and betray our children by hurrying them out of their childhood and make them into miniature and inadequate adults at the expense of their reality as adequate children. None of the biblical stories in Genesis or, for that matter, the life of Jesus as related in the Gospels, show us a child in the midst of his childhood, doing what comes naturally to children. These biblical characters are born and next we see them involved in adult dramas. What have the writers done to the childhood of our biblical ancestors? What do we know about the childhood of our parents and grandparents? Why must children be invisible? Is there some rapport between this absconded childhood of humans and the silence about the "childhood" of God and His family? Including His own son?

What greater evidence do we need for the thriving of child sacrifice than the story of the child Mary, who was first ushered away from her childhood to grace the bed of old man Joseph and then to lend her womb to God's greater design of giving life to a son, half divine, half human? What concern was shown by her parents or God for her right to live out her childhood before she was called upon to function as a competent adult? What evidence do we have that Mary had the final say—or, for that matter, any say—about her body, her life? She was around thirteen at the time of the Visitation. Can we imagine today what would happen if such a child were told that a) she was to marry and old man and b) she was to have a child with a stranger of great power? Even in the Annunciation of the imminent immaculate conception as reported by Luke (1:31), we learn two important points about the divine fate meted out to Mary; 1) Do not be afraid...says God's messenger the angel—in other words, there is a good reason to believe that young Mary could or would be frightened by the interruption of her innocence by an exclusively adult matter—conception. 2) In what the angel announces to Mary, she becomes invisible: it is all about Jesus and his importance in the world. In that context what relevance does Mary's fate have? She is just an insignificant Jewish girl, already sold to an old man. So what concern should there be for her? If anything, she should bless the moment when she learns her chosen status of bearing God's son. What is a mundane childhood or an ordinary life in the context of being the mother of God's son? Isn't this a classical, textbook version of sacrifice of a child in the most modern way—except for the blood of the young virgin, no blood is spilled, so we can defocus really easily from what is about to happen to the child-woman because that fate is to eclipse a life that in itself seems to be inconsequential until it is given to the greater good of God the Father and His earthly patriarchal designs and institutions.

Furthermore, Mary was at the mercy of two powerful forces—both having to do with her eviction from her childhood and from her life as she had known it. The former is the decision to make her Jesus' mother, the latter with what effect this news had on her own contractually bound fiancé, Joseph. He had choices about what to do with her, including repudiating her, which could have led to her being stoned to death by her community. Mary, on the other hand, had no say about any of this even though it was her life that was at stake. In this context, the angel's reassurance not to be afraid had to be as incon-sequential and insufficient as Dr. Mengele, the Angel of Death at Auschwitz picking up Jewish children to calm their fears before being sent to the gas chamber. Just as in the case of Isaac bound on Mount Moriah, bewildered by what had to seem to him a certain death about to be meted out to him by his father's dagger, we must imagine Mary traumatized beyond words and reason at the prospect of lending her womb to God's son. There is no torment greater than not being able to make sense of what is likely to happen to oneself because others have total control over one's life. Death camp survivors can attest to that—there is a dehumanization process that sets in which absconds with one's self-worth because of the ultimate and immediate course of one's life is taken away from oneself. Mary, who is told, 'everything is in order, don't be afraid,' knows better; if Joseph so chooses, she is to face a horrible shame and untimely and painful death without even being able to protest.

As the story unfolds, we learn that Mary was handed down a non-negotiable order about what was to happen participation in her womb, without her active participation. What that would do to her life is not even hinted at. How she felt or what she thought about the whole thing didn't emerge as a matter of concern. In this context, the initial "Do not be afraid..." feels like another order. 'All these earthshaking things will happen to you with dire consequences *and* you are not to be afraid.' How many children can relate to this; they are told of frightening, at times life threatening, events to follow but they are *not* to feel fear or anything else that could be a nuisance for the parents or other caregivers. Kids informed of terminal illness, kids facing the impending horrors of war, persecution, sudden changes in fortune, orphandom, surgery, etc., know this predicament only too well. They are told: 'be brave, be a little soldier, a trooper, be strong, proud, be a "X" (fill in the family name), make me proud, don't embarrass me. Just do as you're told and all will be fine, yours is not to ask why, speak when you are spoken to...' In everyday life, children who have to face the divorce of their parents are often told: "Don't be afraid..." All these pseudo pep-talks and hidden or overt injunctions amount to anesthetizing the child to his or her natural fear or terror in the context of what feels like a threat to his/her well-being. Because children are less trouble when they are naturally numb about their own fate.

Indeed, Jesus was born to a child-woman. She was a sexual virgin and a psychologically and socially pure and virginally ignorant girl. His earthly father, Joseph, a descendant of David, was significantly older. While he didn't exercise his legal right to shun and abandon his fiancée for adultery, it is entirely possible that he had some repressed anger toward Mary *and* toward this "Son of God" in whose fatherhood he was called upon to participate. Was he safe from the rumors and evil tongues about the predicament in which he found himself, thanks to the advent of this child in whose conception he did not participate? After all, the community did not hear the voice of the angel nor shared Joseph's dream announcing Mary's privileged status of having been chosen as the recipient of God's child. Thus, pious as he might have been, magnanimous and righteous as he was likely to be as a direct descendant of the lineage of David, he was still likely subjected to an element of reasonable doubt fueled by community ridicule. Under the best of circumstances, his advanced age might have contributed to a distance between him and this chosen son for whose life the Holy Spirit borrowed Mary's womb. His values were likely to be different from Jesus' as they tend to be between an elderly father and his young son in ordinary circumstances. In fact, neither Joseph nor Mary understood what young Jesus had to say about his Heavenly Father (Luke 2:50). It is no accident that we hear no more about Joseph—he disappeared from his son's life. Is it just a commonplace abandonment, the kind millions of sons and daughters experience from fathers unable and/or unwilling to stay benevolently and actively in the life of their offspring, or did Joseph disappear because it was too hard to stay actively present in the life of this son who was also not his son? Who failed whom, who betrayed whom? Who felt threatened by whom? What kind of self-denial must one achieve to be free of the wound a man is likely to feel, knowing that he had not participated in the conception of his own son? That in fact, his own son is *not* his *own* son? What thoughts rush through his mind and his viscera each time he looks at his son, not finding himself reflected in the boy's being? What does he feel in his groin when he looks at his wife, knowing that she had sheltered another's seed? And if that other seed comes from God, what measure of insignificance might inch through his heart, having been displaced from his wife's womb by none other than the Almighty? Can we blame Joseph for disappearing? But is any of this a consolation to the child-mother or to her son who, in the process, loses his father and has to contend with his mother's pain and bitterness about her own fate?

Nevertheless, in spite of, or in addition to, our empathy for this relatively pathetic man, we must not forget that Jesus did not choose to participate in this primal drama of all primal dramas. He was still entitled to a flesh and blood father, just because he was born a flesh and blood child and that is how he lived. He had a right to a mother and father, like anyone else. As a boy, he needed guidance, affection, respect, and protection like any child, just for being a child.

Is it a surprise that of his childhood we know next to nothing and most of what we know has to be inferred from silences and absences. Such is the lot of an invisible child. We know so little of Jesus' childhood because the life of a child did not matter, nor does it matter today. What do we know about the lives of most children except for child prodigies or children who come to tragic ends? We learn about Jesus mostly once he had achieved some status as an adult teacher and, principally, upon his martyrdom; that is, once he had ceased being a child and became a *cause célèbre* as an adult and as the resurrected Son of God. There was nothing written about Jesus' childhood because his life had no intrinsic value, i.e., a value for its own sake, until he began to serve, live and die for others.

P.S. One of my fondest memories of Harry James Cargas seems appropriate here, On a recent visit to his home in St. Louis, Missouri, I asked

Harry if Jesus died for *his* sins? He was visibly taken aback and, in a rare moment of confusion, he asked for some time to think about my disturbing
question. The next morning, over breakfast, Harry gave me his answer: "I hope
not. My sins have been so small it would have been a tragic waste."

Elisabeth, so are your sins.

SINGLE OR DOUBLE COVENANT?
Contemporary Perspectives
John T. Pawlikowski, O.S.M.

Introduction

Chapter four of the conciliar statement *Nostra Aetate* inaugurated an entirely new era in theological discussions about the Church's relationship to the Jewish People. For nearly all of the Church's existence its theological perspective of Jewish-Christian relations was dominated by the so-called "displacement theology," developed during the Patristic era, in which the "unfaithful" Jews were replaced in the covenantal relationship with the Creator God by the "believing" Christians. In its brief statement on the Church's relationship with the Jewish People, Vatican II generated a theological revolution. By repudiating the so-called "deicide" charge against the Jewish community, underlining its ongoing covenantal relationship with God and stressing Christianity's profound debt to Judaism, the Council destroyed the very basis for the patristic "*adversus Judaeos*" tradition. *Nostra Aetate* also fostered the development of parallel statements within several Protestant denominations as well as ecumenical organizations.[1]

Nostra Aetate, as Dr. Eugene Fisher has noted,[2] was in many ways unique in the annals of conciliar statements. Most such statements rely heavily on previous church documents, the biblical tradition and the teachings of the Church Fathers. *Nostra Aetate* had only the New Testament to draw upon. And so it highlighted the imagery of St. Paul in Romans 9-11, where the church is depicted as grafted onto the tree of salvation whose trunk was Judaism. By implication, such imagery conveys the sense of continuing life for Judaism from a Christian theological perspective, for if the trunk has died the branches can hardly remain healthy.

Likewise, in putting to rest the historic deicide charge, the Council destroyed any credibility for the so-called "perpetual wandering" theology which basically argued that Jews were an accursed race perpetually doomed to roam the face of the earth in a degraded state for murdering the Messiah. This theology was responsible for much of the persecution of the Jews during the course of history and for Catholic opposition, including some opposition at the level of the Vatican, to the initial proposals for the restoration of a Jewish state in Palestine.

This *adversos Judaeos* theology was also the root of the twentieth century interpretations of Judaism which left little or no further role for the Jewish people in the ongoing process of human salvation. Gerhard Kittel, the original editor of the highly influential *Theological Dictionary of the New Testament*, exemplifies the continuing impact of that theology in this century. Kittel viewed post-biblical Judaism as largely a community of dispersion. "Authentic Judaism," he wrote, "abides by the symbol of the stranger wandering restless and homeless on the face of the earth."[3] And the prominent exegete Martin Noth, whose *History of Israel* became a standard reference for students and professors alike, described Israel as a strictly "religious community" which died a slow, agonizing death in the first century A.D. For Noth, Jewish history reached its culmination in the arrival of Jesus. His words are concise and to the point in this regard:

> Jesus himself...no longer formed part of the history of Israel. In him the history of Israel had come, rather, to its real end. What did belong to the history of Israel was the process of his rejection and condemnation by the Jerusalem religious community...Hereafter the history of Israel moved quickly to its end.[4]

A third example is Rudolf Bultmann, who exercised a decisive influence over Christian biblical interpretation for decades. Unlike Kittel, Bultmann's exegesis did not carry over into politics. But, theologically speaking, his understanding of Christology also left Jews and Judaism bereft of meaning after the coming of Jesus. In his *Theology of the New Testament*, he held to the view that a Jewish people cannot be said to exist with the emergence of Christianity. For Bultmann, Jewish law, ritual, and piety removed God to a distant realm while through the continued presence of Jesus in prayer and worship, each individual was brought ever closer to God. Bultmann's understanding of Judaism in Jesus' day was based on totally inadequate sources in terms of Second Temple Judaism and Jesus' relationship to its teachings.

The deep-seated tradition of anti-Judaic Christology begun in the Patristic era has continued to find expression even in very recent attempts at theological reformulation. Liberation theologians, for example, are not free of its shadow. Gustavo Gutierrez has written that since "the infidelities of the Jewish people made the Old Covenant invalid, the Promise was incarnated both in the proclamation of a New Covenant, which was awaited and sustained by 'the remnant,' as well as in the promises which prepared and accompanied its advent."[5] And Clark Williamson, in a detailed study of Jon Sobrino's *Christology at the Crossroads* in light of the basic anti-Judaic patterns for Christology set out by Tertullian, has concluded that "each aspect of this anti-

Judaic model is to be found in Sobrino's *Christology at the Crossroads*. Each theme can be documented in his text."[6]

If we are fully and finally to purge Christian belief of all remaining traces of antisemitism, we need to recognize that this *adversos Judaeos* tradition was unequivocally repudiated in chapter four of *Nostra Aetate* when the Council Fathers declared the continued validity of the Jewish covenant after the Christ Event. To the extent that we continue to rely on patristic sources as foundation for faith expression in contemporary Christianity, we shall have to employ writers such as Clement of Alexandria as a barometer for authentic appropriation of these sources without their underlying antisemitic bias.[7]

The challenge now facing Christianity in light of *Nostra Aetate* and parallel Protestant documents is how we can both honor classical theological claims about "newness" in Christ while remaining faithful at the same time to II Vatican's insistence that this "newness" does not involve the termination of the original covenant with the Jewish people as the Churches have often argues. Additionally, we shall have to decide whether the "old covenant-new covenant" terminology, so widespread in Christianity, helps or hinders our ability to face up to the post-conciliar theological challenge.

While individual Catholic and Protestant theologians (and recently a few Orthodox), as well as official Church documents, have begun to grapple with restating the theology of the Christian-Jewish relationship in a more positive way, no clear consensus has emerged as yet. The pre-conciliar approach, advocated by several scholars in the vanguard of improved Christian-Jewish understanding such as Charles Journet, initially became attractive to a wider group within the Church.[8] Rooted in Paul's "mystery" approach to Jewish-Christian relations, it was appropriated by Jean Danielou,[9] Hans Urs von Balthasar,[10] Augustin Cardinal Bea[11] and several others. While each of these scholars had a distinctive twist in his particular adaptation of this Pauline notion from the Letter to the Romans, they all remained uncompromising on the question of the centrality of Christ and the fulfillment that his coming brought to salvation history. Although all found ways to leave some theological space for Judaism after the Christ event, they made no sustained effort to reconcile the apparent tension resulting from these two assertions. Rather, they simply fell back on the Pauline contention that their compatibility remains a "mystery" in the divinely instituted plan of human salvation.

A decade or so after the Council, Catholic theologians began to move away from this "mystery" paradigm and search for bolder ways to restate the church-synagogue bond theologically. In general, two models have surfaced, though a few have advocated a third option. The two major models have generally been termed the *single* and *double* covenant theories. Each has several variants.

The Single Covenant Model

The single covenant model holds that Jews and Christians basically belong to one covenantal tradition that began at Sinai. In this perspective the Christ Event represented the decisive moment when the Gentiles were able to enter fully into the special relationship with God which Jews already enjoyed and in which they continued. Some holding this viewpoint maintain that the decisive features of the Christ Event have universal application, including to Jews. Others are more inclined to argue that the Christian appropriation and reinterpretation of the original covenantal tradition, in and through Jesus, applies primarily to non-Jews.

A single covenantal perspective has clearly dominated the many statements and speeches of Pope John Paul II on the theology of the Church's relationship to the Jewish people. He has now spoken more on this topic than any other pontiff in history. While a certain lack of clarity remains in the corpus of John Paul's writings on several issues related to the theology of Christian-Jewish relations, there is little doubt that the Pope firmly believes in the continued bonding between church and synagogue after the Christ Event. This bonding exists as a core element of Christian self-identity for John Paul II, who regards the Jewish-Christian relationship as *sui generis*. It is quite different, particularly, on the level of theology, from the relationships that the Church has with any other world religions.[12]

Several prominent Christian scholars have supported the single covenantal model, including the American theologian Monika Hellwig. While she has not pursued this question in earnest in recent years, her earlier writings portrayed Judaism and Christianity as pointing toward the same fundamental eschatological reality which still lies ahead. The two faith communities share a common messianic mission in terms of this reality, though each may work somewhat differently in carrying it out. For Hellwig, there is a "most important sense in which Jesus is not yet Messiah. The eschatological tension has not been resolved...Logically the Messianic Event should be seen as lengthy, complex, unfinished and mysterious."[13]

In Hellwig's paradigm, the one covenant forged at Sinai continues in force. This affirmation of continuing divine faithfulness to the Jewish people forces Hellwig into rethinking the fundamental significance of Jesus as the Christ. Her response is to see in the Christ Event not primarily the completion of messianic prophecies, but the possibility of all Gentiles encountering the God of Abraham, Sarah and Isaac. Jesus the Jew opened the gates for Gentiles to enter the covenantal election first granted to the Jewish people and to experience the intimacy with God that this election brought them. Hence Christians must look to God's continuing revelation in contemporary Jewish experience to grasp fully God's self-communication today. While some ambiguity remains in Hellwig's thought on this point, she also seems to imply that the revelation given humankind in and through the Christ Event serves as one barometer for Jewish faith expression as well. Her theology of Jewish-Christian linkage thus ultimately involves some rethinking of respective self-definition by both communities.

Hellwig is willing to grant that in the end it does not matter all that much whether we speak of one or two covenants in terms of the Jewish-Christian relationship. The crucial question is whether people in the Church describe Christianity as fulfilling everything valuable in Judaism so that the latter no longer retains any salvific role or whether, instead, Christians understand themselves as simultaneous participants with Jews in an ongoing covenantal relationship with God. She still prefers to stay with the vocabulary and imagery of a single covenant because it has a solid biblical basis and has the possibility of unfolding in newly constructive ways.[14]

An internationally known voice in theological discussions for the past several decades has been the Episcopal scholar Paul van Buren. His is without question the most comprehensive effort at constructing a new theological model for the Jewish-Christian relationship. *The Burden of Freedom* was his first, rather preliminary, statement in which he mainly emphasized the deficiencies in previous models.[15] This work was followed by his major trilogy which includes *Discerning the Way*,[16] *A Christian Theology of the People Israel*,[17] and *A Theology of the Jewish Christian Reality, Part III: Christ in Context.*[18]

Van Buren argues that Christianity has more or less eradicated all Jewish elements from its faith expression in favor of a pagan-Christian tradition. The Holocaust represents the pinnacle of this pagan-Christian tradition. The Church must now rejoin Judaism, no easy task in light of the "cover-up" which van Buren believes took place during the first century of Christian existence. When the Christian leadership realized that the promised signs of the messianic era were nowhere to be seen, the response was not to modify the Church's initial theological claims about the Christ event but rather to push the actual realization of these claims to the metahistorical, "higher" realm. This meta-historical realm of messianic fulfillment was penetrable through faith. It was not subject to historical verification of any kind. With the completion of this transfer, the path was cleared for the proclamation of the Easter mystery as an unqualified triumph on the part of Christ, a triumph in which the Jewish People had no continuing role.

In his more recent writings, van Buren has increasingly insisted on the need to recognize that Israel consists of two connected, but distinct, branches, both of which are essential to a full definition of the term. Christianity represents the community of Gentile believers drawn by the God of the Jewish People to worship Him and to make His love known among the peoples of the world. For van Buren it is not a question of the Church now suddenly abandoning its historic proclamation of Jesus Christ and the Son of God. But Jesus was not the Christ in one crucial sense. He was not the long-awaited

Jewish Messiah. And so post-Easter Judaism remains a religion of legitimate messianic hope rather than that of spiritual blindness.

The shared messianic vision of Judaism and Christianity leads van Buren to advocate the notion of the "co-formation" of the two faith communities. By this he means that both of the branches of Israel must grow and develop alongside each other, rather than in isolation. While each will continue to retain a measure of distinctiveness, both will experience a growing mutuality characterized by understanding and love. This growing together in love will increase each partner's freedom to be its distinctive self while maintaining an awareness of the necessity for mutual cooperation.

In his later volumes, van Buren also began to give some in-depth attention to the significance of Christ within his theology of Israel. Van Buren now interprets the new revelation in Jesus as basically the manifestation of the divine will that Gentiles too are welcome to walk in God's way. Through Jesus, the Gentiles were summoned for the first time as full participants in the ongoing covenantal plan of salvation. But the Gentiles' appropriation of this plan, van Buren admits, took them well beyond the circles of God's eternal covenant with the Jewish People. In no way, however, did it annul the original covenant. Nor can Christians by-pass the original covenantal people in their quest for bonding with the God of Abraham, Sarah and Isaac who was revealed to them through the ministry and person of the Jew Jesus.

Jesus did not expect a future in the ordinary sense of the word. From that perspective his message is ahistorical, much like the rabbis of his time. He anxiously awaited the coming of God's reign, which would replace the present era. He did reveal a deep, personal intimacy with God, but his relationship with God maintained a clear line of demarcation between himself and the Father. His sense of intimacy with the divine was very Jewish. Van Buren puts it this way:

> We can only speculate about what went on in Jesus' own soul, but we can know how the early witness presents him. It presents him as we could expect Jews to present a Jew wholly devoted to God. It presents him as one whose will was to do God's will. His cause was nothing but the cause of God. In this sense and in no other, he had no will of his own and no cause of his own to defend. In other words, he was strong-willed and stubborn in the cause of God. In short, he was a Jew.[19]

For van Buren any Christological proclamation today, particularly in view of the Holocaust, must make it abundantly clear that the divine authorization Jesus enjoyed to speak and act in the name of the Father did not exempt him from the realities of the human condition, and that the powers of death and darkness continued to hold sway after the Easter event. In short, a major modification of many classical Christological claims is demanded by a new understanding of Jesus' relationship to the Jewish community of his day, by the Jewish People's return to historical existence in the modern State of Israel and by the Holocaust. If we are to take one traditional Christological doctrine with utmost seriousness, it is the Incarnation. The Council of Chalcedon insisted that the Word **became** flesh, not merely that the Word had "put on" flesh. Jesus' participation in the human condition was total and real in every sense of the term.

Where van Buren ultimately winds up on the Christological question in his published writings is to proclaim Jesus *Israel's gift to the Gentile church*. His primary mission is to reconcile the Gentiles with God. This is still a hard saying, for most Christians who remain victims of the Church's erroneous first century belief that Jesus was expelled rather than given by Israel.

Van Buren also acknowledges that Jews may have some difficulty with his claim because Judaism has never recognized Jesus as its gift to the Church. But this latter situation is largely the result of the sufferings endured for centuries by the Jewish People in the name of Jesus. As the Church begins to move away from the "expulsion" theology of Israel, Jews will need to rethink their traditional posture towards Jesus as well. For if Israel remains bound to God, and if it is God who gives the Church the gift of the Jew Jesus, then Israel remains clearly implicated in this gift.

In giving their special allegiance in faith to Jesus, van Buren tells us, Christians follow, in the words of Paul to the Romans (15:8), a person who "became a servant to the Jewish people." Herein lies the basis of Israel's claim upon Christianity, a claim sealed through Jesus Christ. The Church can never escape this profound debt to Israel and profoundly corrupts itself when it tries:

> To acknowledge the claim of God's love, with which the Church is confronted in the witness to Christ, is therefore always to acknowledge the legitimate claim of Israel. No Jew need repeat that claim today, since it is repeated to the church again and again, whenever it rehearses the things concerning Jesus of Nazareth, by his reality as a Jew. It comes as his call to follow him in his service to his people.[20]

In some presentations to the Christian Study Group of Scholars, which is dedicated to the ongoing exploration of Christian understandings of Judaism, van Buren, a long-time member, has attempted to respond to criticisms that he has failed to explain adequately the uniquely Christian appropriation of the covenant with Israel in and through Christ. He has put forth the notion that the revelation in Christ involved making God "transparent" to humanity in a way that surpasses that present in the initial covenantal disclosure. Should van Buren pursue this track, it would place him closer to those sometimes categorized as "double covenant" proponents, for he would be arguing that the Christ Event involved not only the opportunity for Gentiles to enter the covenanted community, but the exposure as well to an enhanced understanding of God's link to humanity.

Another important representative of the single covenant position has been Norbert Lohfink. Much like van Buren, his view of the single covenantal tradition embracing Jews and Christians is more complex than first imagined. Unlike van Buren, he does not expand the term "Israel." Rather, he speaks of a twofold way to salvation within a single covenantal framework.[21] In concert with van Buren, he holds to the view that Christians and Jews appropriate this single covenant in different *ways*. The Christian *way* is strongly rooted in the New Testament's understanding that the eschatological fullness of the "new covenant" promised in the book of Jeremiah has already begun. But this sense of dawn of eschatological covenantal renewal is not absent from postbiblical Jewry. So one cannot posit a hard and fast distinction between Jews and Christians in this regard.

Lohfink interprets the "parallel" ways of Israel and the Church in a *dynamic* sense. They are not destined to remain separated permanently; otherwise God's salvific design for the creation would be thwarted. Hence his rejection of a double covenant approach, which he regards as a form of permanent separation between Jews and Christians that would undermine their jointly necessary witness against forces of power and sin in the world. He concludes that:

> One must speak of a "twofold way to salvation" in such a way that one does not deny to the other that it is God's instrument. But to condemn the two ways, facts that they are, to permanent parallelism for all time on the ground that there are simply countless ways to salvation would be to despair of the possibility of the actual salvation of this world, of that salvation of which the Bible speaks. This ends up, hard as it sounds, in unbelief before God's biblical word.[22]

Double Covenant Perspectives

The double covenant theory is frequently misrepresented. It is often understood in a way that renders the two covenants totally dichotomous. In point of fact, the double covenant model generally begins at the same point as its single covenant counterpart, namely, with a strong affirmation of the continuing bonds between Jews and Christians. But then it prefers to underline the distinctiveness of the two traditions and communities, particularly in terms of their experiences after the gradual separation in the first century C.E. Christians associated with this perspective insist on maintaining the view that through the ministry, teachings and person of Jesus, a vision of God emerged that was distinctively new in terms of its central features. Even though there may well have been important groundwork laid for this emergence in Second Temple or Middle Judaism, what came to be understood regarding the divine-human relationship as a result of Jesus has to be regarded as unprecedented.

A historical note must be introduced at this point. Increasingly, Christian and Jewish scholars are stressing the fluidity of the first century of the Common Era. A major transformation was occurring within Judaism. New groups were arising, one of which was the community of Christian Jews. This fact makes it impossible to speak of a single covenant in a linear way. Christianity and Judaism, as they emerged at the dawn of the second century, were postbiblical phenomena. While they remained in most cases deeply rooted in the biblical tradition, including the covenantal tradition, their period of intense separation which we now know from scholars such as Robert Wilken, Anthony Saldarini and Robin Scroggs lasted for most of the first century (even longer in some regions) left them quite distinctive faith communities. While the Church clearly began as a community of Christian Jews, as scholars such as James Charlesworth and Cardinal Carlo Martini have insisted,[23] this was no longer the case, except in a few areas, by the second century. This reality has been recognized by both Christians and Jews throughout the centuries. It accounts for one of my principal problems with the single covenant perspective, a problem that neither Hellwig, van Buren nor Lohfink have addressed in any significant way.[24]

One of this century's early pioneers in the effort to re-think Christianity's theological stance toward the Jewish People in light of the Christ Event was the Anglican, James Parkes. Over the years, Parkes developed his outline of the double covenant theory on the basis of what he regarded as the two different but complementary revelations given humankind through Sinai and Calvary respectively.[25]

One area in which Parkes' model has been frequently faulted is the scriptural. It does not seem clearly enough rooted in scriptural data. This certainly was not the case with another early proponent of the double covenant theory, the University of Chicago biblical scholar J. Coert Rylaarsdam. His approach was developed almost entirely from the scriptural tradition. He argued that any adequate theological viewpoint regarding the Jewish-Christian relationship must begin with an acknowledgement of the presence of two distinctive covenants *within* the Hebrew Scriptures.

The first of these covenants, the one with Israel, focused on God's union with the covenanted community in history. At its core stood a mutual pact of faithfulness and responsibility between God and the Jewish People. The covenant was future-oriented. Divine intervention in history on behalf of the chosen people was an ongoing, open-ended process. Since its basic elan did not mesh well with the initial proclamation of finality in the Christ Event within the apostolic church, it tended to be downplayed in the New Testament.

The second covenant revolved around the figure of David and bore a far more eschatological cast. In this covenantal strain, religious meaning was rooted in the holiness tradition associated with Mount Zion and the divine presence revealed through the Davidic dynasty. It looked to and celebrated a supra-temporal order of meaning. God was depicted as king of creation and of the nation, with the earlier biblical stress on Torah and history largely abandoned. The tension between these two covenantal traditions in late biblical Judaism led, Rylaarsdam believes, to the growth of several sectarian religious groups. One of these was the eschatologically oriented Christian church which arose out of the preaching of Jesus. This new faith community quickly found itself beset with some of the same tensions as Judaism. But, in early Christianity, the Davidic covenantal tradition rapidly assumed prominence.

Rylaarsdam thus posits the existence of twin biblical covenants; but they are not two chronologically successive covenants in the way Christians have traditionally explained them. Rather, these two covenantal traditions permeate both the Hebrew Scriptures and the New Testament. Recognition of these simultaneous rather than consecutive covenants forces upon the Church a radical reshaping of its understanding of the significance of the Christ Event and its consequent model of the Jewish-Christian relationship. For if both Judaism and Christianity continue to revolve around the same two covenants that are intimately linked, albeit in paradoxical fashion, then the church-synagogue relationship, whatever its specific tensions as any given moment, must be understood as one of mutual interdependence.[26]

Though there are valuable insights to be gained from the perspectives of both Parkes and Rylaarsdam, subsequent scholars have judged their models inadequate as the basis for building a new theological relationship between Jews and Christians. Somewhat more promising have been the viewpoints presented by Clemens Thoma and Franz Mussner. I include both of them within the "double covenant" category (not something they expressly do themselves) because of their insistence on a distinctive revelation in and through Jesus that clearly goes beyond that of the original covenant with Israel.

Clemens Thoma's approach to the Christian-Jewish relationship is deeply rooted in the Scriptures. He strongly emphasizes the profound connections between Jesus' teachings and the Jewish tradition both prior to and contemporaneous with him. The Hebrew Scriptures also occupy a central position in any expression of Christian faith for Thoma. He emphatically rejects any attempt to describe the basic theological tension between the Church and Israel as rooted in the acceptance/rejection of Jesus. There was no consistent, univocal notion of the messiah in Jewish thought at the time of Jesus. Many diverse understandings surfaced in a time of great creative renewal within Judaism. Some Jews had even reached the conclusion that the notion of messiah should be permanently discarded. Hence there exists no one Jewish expectation to which Jesus can be compared and no grounds for alleging Jewish rejection of Jesus' fulfillment of this expectation:

> It is not correct to say that the decisive or even the sole difference between Judaism and Christianity consists in the Christian affirmation of Jesus as the messiah and its denial by Jews. There are certain asymmetries and considerations on both sides that render unacceptable such absolute statements of the messianic question. For a better evaluation we must consider and compare the relative importance and place accorded the question in Judaism and Christianity... In the last resort, neither in Judaism nor in

Christianity is it a question of the messiah but of the Kingdom of God, of
"God who is all in all" (I Cor 15:28)[27]

For Thoma the uniqueness of Jesus is ultimately located in the
unqualified fashion in which he tied the kingdom of God to his own activities
and person. In so doing, he was following a trend already present in apocalyptic
interpretations of Judaism. But his sense of intimacy with the Father went
beyond what any branch of Judaism was prepared to acknowledge. Thoma puts
it this way:

> In his relationship to the God and Father, Jesus gathered together Old
> Testament Jewish traditions of piety in an original way and endowed them
> with new beauty. Yet, it would be a radical mistake to represent Jesus, on
> principle and in any way at all, as being in opposition to the God of Torah.
> However, he did experience this God in a uniquely close and intimate way.[28]

Franz Mussner's perspective bears many similarities to Thoma's. He
shares the same conviction about Jesus' deep, positive links to the Jewish
tradition. He likewise rejects any interpretation of the Christ Event over against
Judaism in terms of Jesus' fulfillment of biblical messianic prophecies. Rather,
the uniqueness of the Christ Event arises from the complete identity of the work
of Jesus, as well as his words and actions, with the work of God. As a result of
the revelatory vision in Christ, the New Testament is able to speak about God
with an anthropomorphic boldness not found to the same degree in the Hebrew
Scriptures.[29]

In answer to the question of what the disciples finally experienced
through their close association with Jesus, Mussner speaks of "a unity of action
extending to the point of congruence of Jesus with God, an unprecedented
existential imitation of God by Jesus."[30] But this initiation, Mussner insists, is
quite in keeping with Jewish thinking, a contention that many Jewish scholars
would no doubt challenge. The uniqueness of Jesus is to be found in the *depth*
of his imitation of God. So the most distinctive feature of Christianity for
Mussner when contrasted with Judaism is the notion of incarnation rather than
fulfillment of the messianic prophecies. But even this Christian particularity is
an outgrowth of a sensibility profoundly Jewish at its core.

Having laid out the basic principles of his approach to a theological
expression of the Jewish-Christian relationship, Mussner amplifies his model
with a discussion of what he calls "prophet Christology" and "Son
Christology." The "prophet" Christology is chronologically the older of the two
Christologies. It views Jesus as belonging to the line of prophets who
manifested the "pathos" of God and joined their words and actions to the divine
plan for human salvation. Christianity never completely abandoned this
"prophet Christology", not even in the gospel of John where the "Son
Christology" most clearly predominates. The two Christologies do not stand in
fundamental opposition. But the "Son Christology" adds a dimension of

superiority to Jesus as prophet that makes the differentiation between Christian and Jewish beliefs more pronounced.

Yet even this "Son Christology" in Mussner's analysis has some roots in the Jewish tradition. The claims in the past for an essentially non-Jewish basis for this "high" Christology are unfounded; "Son Christology" owes much of its language and imagery to the Wisdom Literature. Mussner has no illusions that calling attention to the connection between "Son Christology" and the Jewish tradition will remove all opposition to it on the part of Jews. But such an understanding might provide an opening for discussing the issue within the framework of the Christian-Jewish dialogue.

From the above survey of some recent scholarship on the theology of the Christian-Jewish relationship, it is apparent that the line of demarcation between the single and double covenant perspectives is far from rigid. Both perspectives acknowledge some measure of continued bonding because of the common rootage in the Jewish biblical and Second Temple traditions. Both likewise point to a degree of distinctiveness in Christianity's covenantal participation, even if this participation comes through the original covenant with Israel. Many scholars, myself included, remain dissatisfied with the present options of "single" and "double" covenantal language and we are not quite ready to move to the multi-covenantal approach advocated by Rosemary Ruether and (in a somewhat different way) Paul Kitter. Nor am I, for one, completely convinced by Norbert Lohfink's effort to bridge the gap by speaking of two paths of salvation within a single covenantal framework.

Given the present options, I remain convinced that a double covenant perspective more faithfully represents the reality of the Christian-Jewish relationship both historically and theologically. First of all, it helps to underline the distinctiveness of the revelation experienced in and through Christ. Jesus certainly represented the point of entry for the Gentiles into the covenantal tradition of Israel. But the Christ Event involved something more than that. A new understanding emerged over time of the profound linkage between humanity and divinity. Whether we express it in the "transparency of God" language with which Paul van Buren has recently experimented, in the more biblically based terminology of Clemens Thoma, in the "Son Christology" of Franz Mussner or of "Christology as the Manifestation of the Divine-Human Nexus" which I have outlined in my own writings,[31] the Christ Event involves more than "Judaism for the Gentiles." That is why I have objected, for example, to the title of what is otherwise a very fine book, Clark M. Williamson's *A Guest in the House of Israel: Post-Holocaust Church Theology*.[32] While the single covenant paradigm may somewhat better protect the sense of linkage between Jews and Christians, it fails to safeguard the unique contribution of the revelation in Christ. Christianity has something distinctive to offer to the covenantal partnership with Jews. Language such as the title of Williamson's book obscures that reality.

Several points need to be made about Christianity's distinctive revelation. First of all, it did not come instantly, but over a period of time. As Raymond Brown has correctly argued, the awareness of the enhanced divine-human nexus does not really appear until the latter part of the first century C.E. where it very likely had liturgical origins.[33] Prior to that, as Robin Scroggs has insisted, the Jerusalem/Palestinian community had little consciousness of a separate identity from Judaism.[34] So when we wish to speak about the theology of the Christian-Jewish relationship today, we cannot become excessively biblical in our approach. We must consider the historical developments that took place, both positively and negatively. This means, for one, that we must pursue the emergence of Christianity's distinctive revelation through the drawn-out process of Christian-Jewish separation into the second century and its gradual formulation in philosophical categories by the church fathers and the early church councils. Contemporary discussions about covenantal theology cannot totally discard this development; it is part of the authentic identity of Christianity. Neither, on the other hand, can we restrict discussions of covenantal theology from the Jewish side to the biblical period, a trend especially commonplace in some versions of the single covenant perspective. The Jewish community that emerged out of the renewal of the first century C.E. was not simply a reincarnation of Biblical Judaism. That is the ultimate import of the research of Neusner, Shmueli and Perelmuter.

But the process of developing a double covenantal theology will involve the purging of certain prevalent trends in articulating the distinctive Christian revelation. All forms of displacement theology must be jettisoned. Certainly that is demanded by chapter four of *Nostra Aetate*. So too with an excessive sense of "victory" or "triumphalism" as Johannes Metz and A. Roy Eckardt have emphasized. Finally, we shall have to pursue the issue of the distinctiveness of Judaism. Here the early reflections of James Parkes and J. Coert Rylaarsdam have some continuing value, even though we must take the question beyond their formulations. The sense of community, peoplehood, the dignity of creation, the importance of history—these are core theological values that have been seriously underplayed, or even obfuscated, in much of Christian covenantal theology.

While stressing the distinctiveness of the revelation of divine intimacy in and through Christ we must emphasize, as Mussner has and I do in my writings, that there do exist connections between this Christian sense of a new divine intimacy and developments in Second Temple Judaism. I have emphasized in particular the connections with perspectives found within Pharisaism as explained by the Jewish historian Ellis Rivkin.[35] It is not true to say, however, that Jesus' sense of divine intimacy was no different from the understanding shared by many of his Jewish contemporaries. But proof of this does not depend on a claim that Jesus had a special sense of God as "Abba," as

Schillebeeckx incorrectly argued, but on a panoply of sayings and actions on the part of Jesus.

My final reason for preferring the double covenant position over the single covenant model at present is that it better safeguards the distinctive experiences of the two communities since separation. Following the 1985 *Notes on the Correct Way to Present Jews and Judaism in Christian Preaching and Catechesis*, which underscores the importance of the post-biblical Jewish experience for Christian reflection, we must recognize that the history of antisemitism, the Holocaust and other events have impacted the communities in different ways. As a result, the vast majority of Christians and Jews now see the two faiths as quite separate, something we cannot totally ignore in our theological reflections.

In closing, I would add three comments. First of all, discussions of covenantal theology will have to be filtered through the experience of the Holocaust. Johannes Metz is absolutely correct on this point. In doing this, we must begin with the question of God and then move to Christology. No covenantal theology can by-pass the Holocaust. I have begun to address both the God and Christology questions in various recent publications.[36] Secondly, in the end Monika Hellwig may be correct in saying we should not over-emphasize the issue of single vs. double covenant. Perhaps we should be content with the formulation that Clark Williamson introduces in his volume mentioned previously when he speaks of Jews and Christians as "partners in waiting." Finally, whether one selects the single or the double covenant model as a framework for theological reflection on the Jewish-Christian relationship, it is clear that the language of "old covenant/new covenant" is seriously inadequate. First Covenant is probably the most acceptable terminology for the theological discussion. If it is used, then New Covenant may remain viable, although we must be aware of how a scholar such as Lohfink interprets its origins in the book of Jeremiah.

1. See Helgo Croner, ed., *More Stepping Stones to Jewish-Christian Relations: An Unabridged Collection of Christian Documents 1975-1983* (New York:/Mahwah: Paulist, 1985) and Allan Brockway, Paul van Buren, Rolf Rendtorff and Simon Schoon, eds., *The Theology of the Churches and the Jewish People: Statements by the World Council of Churches and its Member Churches* (Geneva: WCC Publications, 1988).

2. Eugene J. Fisher, "The Evolution of a Tradition: From 'Nostra Aetate' to the 'Notes'", International Catholic-Jewish Liaison Committee, *Fifteen Years of Catholic-Jewish Dialogue 1970-1985* (Rome: Libreria Editrice Vaticana and Libreria Editrice Lateranense, 1988), p. 239.

3. Gerhard Kittel, *Die Judenfrage* (Stuttgart: Kohlhammer, 1933), p. 73.

4. Martin Noth, *The Laws in the Pentateuch and Other Studies* (Edinburgh: Oliver and Boyd, 1966), p. 63.

5. Gustavo Gutierrez, *A Theology of Liberation* (Maryknoll, NY: Orbis, 1973), p. 161.

6. Clark M. Williamson, "Christ Against the Jews: A Review of Jon Sobrino's Christology," in *Christianity and Judaism: The Deepening Dialogue*, ed. Richard W. Rousseau, S.J. (Scranton: Ridge Row Press, 1983), p. 148.

7. See W. Barnes Tatum, "Clement of Alexandria's Philo-Judaism: A Resource for Contemporary Jewish-Christian Relations," in *Overcoming Fear: Between Jews and Christians*. Ed. James H. Charlesworth (Philadelphia and New York: The American Interfaith Institute and Crossroad, 1992), pp. 119-138.

8. Charles Journet, "The Mysterious Destinies of Israel," in *The Bridge*, Vol. II, ed. John Oesterreicher (New York: Pantheon, 1956), pp. 35-90.

9. Jean Daniélou, *Dialogue with Israel* (Baltimore: Helicon, 1966); *The Theology of Jewish Christianity* (Chicago: Henry Regnery, 1964); also see Jean Daniélou and Andre Chouraqui, *The Jews: Views and Counterviews* (New York: Newman, 1967).

10. Hans Urs von Balthasar, *Church and World* (New York: Herder and Herder, 1967).

11. Augustin Cardinal Bea, *The Church and the Jewish People* (London: Geoffrey Chapman, 1966).

12. See John Paul II, *On Jews and Judaism: 1979-1986*, eds. Eugene J. Fisher and Leon Klenicki (Washington: United States Catholic Conference, 1987); *Spiritual Pilgrimage: Texts on Jews and Judaism: 1979-1995*, eds. Eugene J. Fisher and Leon Klenicki (New York: Crossroad, 1995).

13. Monika Hellwig, "Christian Theology and the Covenant of Israel," *Journal of Ecumenical Studies* 7 (Winter 1970), p. 49.

14. Monika Hellwig, "From the Jesus of Story to the Christ of Dogma," in *Antisemitism and the Foundations of Christianity*, ed. Alan T. Davies (New York/Ramsey/Toronto: Paulist, 1979), pp. 118-136.

15. Paul van Buren, *The Burden of Freedom* (New York: Seabury, 1976).

16. Paul van Buren, *Discerning the Way* (New York: Seabury, 1980).

17. Paul van Buren, *A Christian Theology of the People Israel* (New York: Seabury, 1983).

18. Paul van Buren, *A Theology of the Jewish Christian Reality, Part III: Christ in Context* (San Francisco: Harper & Row, 1988). Also see, "The Context of Jesus Christ: Israel," *Religion & Intellectual Life* III:4 (Summer 1980), pp. 31-50.

19. Paul van Buren, "The Context of Jesus Christ: Israel," p. 47.

20. Paul van Buren, "The Context of Jesus Christ: Israel," p. 50.

21. Norbert Lohfink, *The Covenant Never Revoked: Biblical Reflections on Christian-Jewish Dialogue*. (New York/Mahwah: Paulist, 1991); Norbert Lohfink, *Das Jüdische Am Christentum: Die Verlorene Dimension*. (Freiburg/Basel/Wien: Herder, 1987).

22. Norbert Lohfink, *The Covenant Never Revoked*, p. 93.

23. See James H. Charlesworth, ed., *Jesus' Jewishness: Exploring the Place of Jesus in Early Judaism.* (New York and Philadelphia: Crossroad and the American Interfaith Institute, 1991) and Cardinal Carlo Maria Martini, "Christianity and Judaism: A Historical and Theological Overview," in James H. Charlesworth, ed., *Jews and Christians: Exploring the Past, Present and Future.* (New York: Crossroad, 1990).
24. See Wayne A. Meeks and Robert L. Wilken, *Jews and Christians in Antioch in the First Four Centuries.* (Missoula, MT: Scholars Press, 1978); Robert L. Wilken, *John Chrysostom and the Jews: Rhetoric and Reality in the Late 4th Century.* (Berkeley: University of California Press, 1983); Anthony J. Saldarini, "Jews and Christians in the First Two Centuries: The Changing Paradigm," *Shofar* 10 (1992); and Robin Scroggs, "The Judaizing of the New Testament," *The Chicago Theological Seminary Register,* 75:1 (Winter 1986). On developments within Judaism, see Jacob Neusner, *Death and Birth of Judaism: The Impact of Christianity, Secularism, and the Holocaust on Jewish Faith.* (New York: Basic Books, 1987); Ephraim Shmueli, *Seven Jewish Cultures: A Reinterpretation of Jewish History and Thought.* (Cambridge and New York: Cambridge University Press, 1990); and Hayim Goren Perelmuter, *Siblings: Rabbinic Judaism and Early Christianity at their Beginnings.* (New York: Paulist, 1989).
25. See James Parkes, *Judaism and Christianity.* (Chicago: University of Chicago Press, 1948) and *The Foundations of Judaism and Christianity.* (London: Vallentine-Mitchell, 1960). Also see John T. Pawlikowski, "The Church and Judaism: The Thought of James Parkes," *Journal of Ecumenical Studies* 6 (Fall 1969), pp. 573-579.
26. See J. Coert Rylaarsdam, "Jewish-Christian Relationship: The Two Covenants and the Dilemmas of Christology," *Journal of Ecumenical Studies* 9 (Spring 1972), pp. 239-260.
27. Clemens Thoma, *A Christian Theology of Judaism.* (New York/Ramsey: Paulist, 1980), pp. 134-135.
28. Clemens Thoma, *A Christian Theology of Judaism,* p, 115.
29. Franz Mussner, *Tractate on the Jews: The Significance of Judaism for Christian Faith.* (Philadelphia: Fortress, 1984); "From Jesus the 'Prophet' to Jesus 'The Son,'" in Abdoldjavad Falaturi, Jacob J. Petuchowski and Walter Strolz, eds., *Three Ways to the One God: The Faith Experience in Judaism, Christianity and Islam.* (New York: Crossroad, 1987), pp. 76-85.
30. Franz Mussner, *Tractate on the Jews,* p. 226.
31. See John T. Pawlikowski, O.S.M., *Christ in the Light of the Christian-Jewish Dialogue.* (New York/Ramsey: Paulist, 1982); *Jesus and the Theology of Israel.* (Wilmington: Michael Glazier, 1989); "Judentum und Christentum," TRE, XVII:3/4, pp. 386-403.
32. Clark M. Williamson, *A Guest in the House of Israel: Post-Holocaust Church Theology.* (Louisville: Westminster/John Knox, 1993).
33. Raymond E. Brown, "Does the New Testament Call Jesus God?," *Theological Studies* 26:4 (December 1965), p. 546.
34. Robin Scroggs, "The Judaizing of the New Testament," p. 8.
35. Ellis Rivkin, *A Hidden Revolution: The Pharisees' Search for the Kingdom Within.* (Nashville: Abingdon, 1978).
36. See John T. Pawlikowski, "Christian Theological Concerns After the Holocaust," in Eugene J. Fisher, ed., *Visions of the Other: Jewish and Christian Theologians Assess the Dialogue.* (New York/Mahwah: Paulist, 1994), pp. 28-51; "The *Shoah*: Continuing Theological Challenge for Christianity," in Steven L. Jacobs, ed. *Contemporary Christian Religious Responses to the Shoah.* (Lanham/New York/London: University Press of America, 1993), pp. 139-165; "Christology in Light of the Jewish-Christian Dialogue," *Proceedings of the Forty-Ninth Annual Convention,* Catholic Theological Society of America, 49:1994, pp. 120-134.

CHRISTIAN-JEWISH RELATIONS
An Historical Overview and Prognosis
Eugene J. Fisher

It is an honor to have been invited to contribute an essay to this *festschrift* for my dear friend and colleague, Harry James Cargas. It has been over three decades since the Second Vatican Council's declaration, *Nostra Aetate*, urged us all to replace the ignorance and misunderstanding of the past with a drive to reconciliation between Jews and Christians in the present for the sake of a better future of joint witness to the spiritual heritage we hold in common though diversely understand. Over all that period, Professor Cargas has embodied the spirit of the Christian side of this historic moment of reconciliation between our two communities. He has put into words, often emotional and challenging, the sense of repentance with which the Christian today must encounter the too often tragic past we share with the Jewish people. He has put together book after book analyzing that past, especially the great tragedy of the Holocaust, but always with an eye to establishing a firm foundation for a better future. He is truly a pioneer whose work joins that of other pioneers to make real the exciting promise of Catholic-Jewish dialogue. It is our task to ensure that the success of the dialogue in our generation will be handed down to succeeding generations for them, in turn, to build upon. It may not fall on us in our time to complete the historic turning to each other of the Church and the Jewish people, but we can make a solid beginning to consolidate what we have done together after centuries of isolation.

To gain perspective on the significance of the work of Harry James Cargas and of other individual and joint actions taken by Jews and Christians in this historic period, I offer first what I have called the "six stages" of Christian-Jewish relations over the past two millennia. Obviously, it is a summary, the barest outline of what needs to be considered to appreciate our present unprecedented opportunity and challenge to change the course of that ancient history and to better it for the next millennium. I offer it, of course, primarily from the Christian perspective, in terms of fundamental options made in times of crisis, of decisions made by real people each of which profoundly affected the lives and faith of succeeding generations of Jews and Christians alike. It is my argument that the present generation, representing the sixth "stage," is one such moment. Indeed, we are in a very real sense the first generation of Jews and Christians to have open to us the possibility of making such a change in many centuries. Then I will assess some of the recent documents of my own and Harry's Roman Catholic tradition in terms of their contributions to the common Christian-Jewish endeavor.

The Six Stages of Jewish-Christian Relations Over the Centuries

A. The first stage of Jewish-Christian relations was the briefest. It encompassed the period from Jesus' ministry to the destruction of the Jerusalem Temple by the Romans in the year 70 of the Common Era. In this period, the earliest Christians were practicing Jews who observed Jewish law and worshiped with Jewish rituals. They faced the task of how to embody in their own rituals what they had and were experiencing of the Risen Christ in their lives. They did this, quite naturally, in and through the rituals and sacred texts of their people, seeking understanding through re-reading the Jewish Scriptures in the light of the Christ event and defining this new meaning for themselves and for all future generations of Christians by adapting their own Jewish rituals to the sacred significance of what was for them now the seminal event in the history of divine-human relations. It is not accidental that the Christian Eucharist adapts aspects of typical synagogue services of the time, combined with the ritual of the Passover Seder and the underlying theology of the Temple sacrifices. Embedding Christian faith and worship in Jewish ritual and biblical self-understanding would have significant implications for future decisions of later Church leaders, as we shall see. For it made of Christianity always and forever a spiritual entity with a sacred bond to the faith, history and life of God's People, Israel.

A major reflection of the Church's earliest appreciation of its sacred bond with Judaism can be found in St. Paul's letter to the Romans, chapters 9-11, upon which the Second Vatican Council relied for its re-evaluation of Christian understandings of Judaism. Thus, while Paul's successful argument throughout his epistles for the inclusion of gentiles into the Christian community without the prerequisite of first converting to Judaism led to a gradual "gentilization" of the Church, the same apostle's positive views of the "irrevocable" covenant between God and the Jewish people has enabled a more positive theology of Judaism to develop in the Church today.

B. The second stage has been aptly called **"the parting of the ways."** This was in fact a complex phenomenon that took place gradually, reaching maturity and definiteness around the middle of the fourth century when certain basic decisions, such as moving the weekly worship from the Sabbath to Sunday (to celebrate the Day of the Resurrection) were consolidated. Another major decision in the same period concerned the liturgical calendar overall, which was originally Jewish but gradually adapted, keeping the structure of Passover

(Pesach, Easter) and Pentecost (Shavuoth) but replacing the liturgical High Holy Days of Judaism with the Solemn Easter Triduum as the core celebration of the religion's essential understanding of itself. The early part of this period saw the setting down of the four Gospels and the later, non-Pauline epistles, such as the epistle to the Hebrews with its radical vision of the sacrificial death of Jesus replacing and transcending the Temple sacrifices.

During this stage, many of the New Testament and patristic polemical themes against Judaism were developed, such as the negative portrait of the Pharisees in Matthew and Justin Martyr's apologetical "Dialogue with Thrift." These often reflected the competition and consequent confrontations between the emerging church and developing rabbinic tradition, although the Mishnah (the earliest and core volume of the Talmud), written at the end of the second century, contains remarkably little anti-Christian polemic. Contrary to much popular opinion, the famous "curse" clause of the rabbinical "18 Benedictions" against the *minim* (heretics) does not seem to have reflected an attempt to exclude Christians from synagogue prayer. The polemical tradition of the early Church culminated in the fulminations of St. John Chrysostom of Antioch in the 4th Century, who reflected his frustration at the continuing habit of Christians, seemingly gentile as well as Jewish, in attending Synagogue services. Thus, the reflection in John's Gospel of an expulsion of Christians from the Synagogue seems to have been an event of local significance for John's community but did not represent general Jewish practice.

One great decision of this stage for Christians was how far to part with Judaism. We saw above some of the liturgical innovations and continuities. In the second century, Marcion of Pontus proposed a radical break with Judaism, to the point of arguing that the Hebrew Scriptures should be suppressed from the Christian canon because, in effect, they preached a different God than the New Testament. Christianity, for Marcion, had superseded Judaism in God's plan of salvation and anything too "Jewish," even major portions of the New Testament itself, should be set aside. While Marcion's radical vision was rejected by the Church as one of the first major heresies in Christian tradition, many of his polemical categories (such as "Old" versus "New" and "God of Wrath" versus "God of Love") remained in Christian catechetical teachings for centuries.

C. The third stage begins at the end of the 4th Century and beginning of the 5th with the establishment of Christianity first as a licit religion (which Judaism already was) and then as the official religion of the Roman Empire. The rejection of Marcion now became important for the next great decision faced by the Church: What to do with the large portion of the Jewish community that did not see their salvific "fulfillment" in the Risen Christ or the Christian interpretation of what was now known as the "Old Testament." During the following centuries the Church was to use both force and persuasion to suppress every other religious tradition in the old Roman Empire except one—Judaism. Framing the theology that facilitated this remarkable development was, chiefly, St. Augustine of Hippo. Augustine argued that since the Church's proclamation of the Gospel required its continuity with the

Hebrew Scriptures, the people who wrote and therefore witnessed to the sacredness of the Bible were to be preserved. Since they resisted the fulfillment of their own prophecies, however, their dispersion witnessed as well to the triumph of the Cross, so it made sense to keep them from being visibly prosperous or having authority over Christians. Gregory I, who was elected to the papacy in 590, embedded Augustine's theory in canonical legal principles that held throughout the Middle Ages. Further, he prohibited any attempts at forced conversion of Jews, since this might lead to insincerity and a "worse state" for their souls than remaining faithful (if ignorant) Jews. Thus Judaism alone among all the religions of the ancient world was allowed to survive in Christendom over the centuries and even, in some places and times, to thrive.

D. The fourth stage began in 1096 with the massive violence perpetrated against the helpless Jewish communities of the Rhineland by marauding Crusaders, despite strong protestations by the Pope and local bishops. During this period, the teaching of contempt against Jews and Judaism escalated dramatically, perhaps, it has been theorized, as a means of rationalizing the murders of so many Jews by the Crusaders. In any event, it is this period which introduced many of the practices of oppression and even persecution of Jews that some equate with the whole of Christian history. In the 12th Century, the first exile of Jews was enforced by England and the first burning of the Talmud in France. The blood libel and well poisoning charges that were to re-occur over centuries had their beginnings in the 13th and 14th centuries, as did the Passion Plays which did so much to "demonize" the Jews in the popular mentality. This period, in many ways the nadir of Jewish experience in Christian lands until the 20th Century, culminated in the expulsion of Jews who would not convert from Spain in 1492 and the subsequent development of the Spanish Inquisition (to catch less than sincere converts!). By 1492 the Jews had been expelled from virtually all of Western Europe with exceptions such as the Italian peninsula where medieval canon law and papal tradition still prevailed to protect them and which welcomed many of the refugees of the Spanish Expulsion. It is necessary also to report that the great Christian Reformers of the period, by and large, did not really seek to reform the ancient and medieval teaching of contempt toward Jews but merely carried it forward into their own preaching and teaching. Here again, as in all of the categories of this list, proper nuancing is required. While Luther's rhetorical flare distilled and, it can be argued, worsened the process by which the Jews were "demonized" in Christian culture, Calvin's great respect for the Hebrew Scriptures as a divine model for human social organization led at least some of his followers to ameliorate the condition of the Jews in their midst. Thus some Jews were able to find refuge, for example, in The Netherlands. Despite such exceptions as Holland and the Papal States, however, by the end of this period, on the eve of the Enlightenment, the Jewish communities of Western Europe were decimated and severely oppressed. The center of European Jewry shifted to Central and Eastern Europe. In countries such as Poland, Hungary and Lithuania, Jewish communities expanded in size and Jewish learning flourished.

E. The fifth stage lasts from the Enlightenment to the eve of World War II. Though freed from the ghettos and contributing significantly to European culture and society, Jews were still considered at best as tolerated "outsiders" by much of European society. Simultaneously, this period saw the development of pseudo-scientific racism, in great part as a means of rationalizing colonization and the slave trade to the New World. These "racialist" theories sought to justify what was being done to native peoples on the grounds that they were lower forms of humanity. Native and African Americans could thus be treated in ways that fully recognized human beings could not. The racialists sought to hide their fear and contempt of the human communities they brutalized behind a veneer of "enlightened" and "scientific" language. They also extended their theory to the most visible "alien" group within Europe in order to hide the fear and guilt that Western Europeans felt toward a minority community which, as we have seen, had been subjected to increasing oppression since the 12th Century.

One can sense here an Enlightenment at war with itself, with "the Jews" serving at once as the symbol of "medieval superstition" by some thinkers and as the symbol of "anti-Christian secularism" for others. The great Enlightenment thinker Voltaire, for example, opined that Jews, no matter what they did or what was done for them, could not be assimilated into "enlightened" European society, even if they abandoned their ancient "superstitions" (such as adherence to the Bible). They were too different—another race, really, from that of Europe. In such thinking, Voltaire seemingly paved the way for the flowering of "modern" racial antisemitism in the 19th and early 20th centuries in which pseudo-scientific "evidence" was marshaled by racialists such as Gobineau, Chamberlain and Wagner from such "sciences" as phrenology to prove the inferiority of the sub-human races.

Nazism carried these absurd theories to their utmost extreme. Western Europe, in which the moral restraints of Church teaching had been discredited and abandoned among many by an Enlightenment carried to its own extreme of replacing a sense of divine order with a human-centric view of Creation, proved to be all too vulnerable to the Nazi caricature of science. Theories which should have been laughed out of court in universities found a place in academia as well as in politics. Further intellectualized by Nazi theoreticians, racism and the "science" of antisemitism proved, in potent combination with lingering medieval Christian portraits of Jews in league with the devil, to be sufficient for many Germans and other Europeans to dehumanize their neighbors, to see them at once as less than fully human and yet, ironically, as a potent enemy, a threat which needed to be "exterminated." These (and several other factors which need to be evaluated in order to account for the very different attitudes toward Jews between and often within individual European countries) coalesced to provide a veneer of rationalization for the cold and systematic murder of two-thirds of Europe's Jews. The Holocaust thus represents a crisis not only for church teaching but also for western civilization as a whole.

F. The sixth stage begins with the liberation of the death camps by the Allied armies, and with the shock of realizing what had happened there. A high point was reached when a Jewish state was reestablished in the land of Israel, manifesting the Jewish people's renewed ability to hope. This spirit of hope for the future continued as the churches began to embark upon profound examinations of conscience and renewal, resulting in the Second Vatican Council's *Nostra Aetate* and similar soul-searching statements by other churches.

I shall now turn to an examination of the American Catholic responses to Zionism and Israel, on the one hand, and official Catholic theological developments on the other. Again, this is not to imply that developments in other churches are any less significant than in my own, simply that I know my own best.

Zion—Zionism—and Catholic-Jewish Relations in the United States

Rabbi James Rudin, in his excellent exposition of the ambivalent reactions of Catholics to early Zionist claims (*Israel for Christians*, 1985), uses as his paradigm the dual response of Pope Pius X to Theodore Herzl's 1904 plea for official Catholic support for the Zionist cause. Pius' immediate, spontaneous response to Herzl during the audience itself was not a political, but a theological one, perhaps reflecting the ancient theological "teaching of contempt" which saw in the destruction of Jerusalem in 70 C.E. and the dispersion of the Jewish people throughout the world, a divine rejection of the Jews for their supposed "rejection" of Jesus:

> We are unfavorable to this movement. We cannot prevent the Jews
> from going to Jerusalem, but we could never sanction it... the Jews
> have not recognized our Lord. Therefore, we cannot recognize the
> Jewish people. (*Diaries*, Dial Press, 1956, 429).

Herzl had cast his plea in religious terminology, a terminology he had used and would use to greater effect with Protestants, particularly the British, for many of whom millennial categories were comfortable ones (as they still are, for example, with many American fundamentalist and evangelical Christians).

Catholics, however, tend to be more reticent about such eschatological, "End Time" theologies and predictions perhaps because our cultural/historical "memory" is so long. Our memory of such "end of the world" claims and the damage these claims have done over the centuries in disrupting society is quite immediate to those steeped, as was Pius X, in Church history and tradition. Thus Herzl, perhaps miscalculating his audience and viewing all Christians as basically the same in theological outlook, received a papal "No" to his theological request. But was it a "No" to Zionism as such? Or rather was it a response to certain of the broader theological claims some Zionists have liked to project to Christian audiences?

Evidence for the latter interpretation is seen in the much less celebrated, but far more important *considered* response of the Holy See delivered to Herzl's entourage some two weeks later by no less a figure than the Vatican Secretary of State, Cardinal Merry del Val:

> If the Jews believe they might greatly ease their lot by being admitted to the land of their ancestors, then we would regard that as a *humanitarian* question. We shall never forget that without Judaism, we would have been nothing.

This positive, moral-political response, of course, also has a theological content—traditional respect for Jews and Judaism as bearers of God's Word to the world and acknowledgement of the Church's permanent debt to the Jewish people's faithfulness to that witness without which, Catholics believe, neither Jesus nor the Church would have been possible. It was on these latter, positive theological categories of Catholic tradition that the Second Vatican Council relied in developing the scheme for its Declaration on the Jews, *Nostra Aetate*, No. 4.

Dr. Ronald Brown of Harvard, in his 1986 thesis for the University of Geneva, has filled in with admirable depth our understanding of Catholic press reactions to the creation of a Jewish State in the Holy Land, *Eretz Israel*. Again, one finds numerous expressions reflecting elements of the ancient teaching of contempt, and more contemporary fears that the Jews would, having gained political power over the Holy Places, act in a manner similar to that of the Crusaders during their brief moment of power in that gloriously tragic land. The actual history of the State of Israel since its founding has alleviated that fear considerably, though it must be said that the grandiloquent boastings of outspoken, if numerically small, right-wing Israeli groups to deny Christians the right to live in certain areas of Israel are capable of triggering ancient Christian fears raised in the early 4th century by the Emperor Julian of Rome (whom we call, not affectionately, the apostate), with his threat to rebuild the Temple of Jerusalem and to disallow all Christian claims in the area. These are not, needless to say, the views of any Israeli government, including the present one. But the reader will recall that the Christians of Israel, while loyal to the State, are a "minority within a minority," and so may be forgiven a bit of the paranoia that understandably attends minority status in societies experiencing change and an uncertain future. Ironically, as we American Christians, who form the dominant majority in our own democracy, listen with sympathy to the concerns of our fellow Christians in democratic Israel, we may also come to a better understanding of what it feels like to be a minority in a society and culture dominated by another religious and cultural tradition. This, too, properly understood, may enhance dialogue between Jews and Christians in the long run.

American Catholic attitudes toward Zionism have been over the years distinctly different from those of many American Protestants (cf., Martin Marty, *Modern American Religion*, (Univ. of Chicago Press, 1996 Chapters 4 and 12 on Protestant responses to Zionism; and Brown on the U. S. Catholic Press 1947-1950). There have been very few "Catholic Zionists" in the sense not uncommon among Protestants in American history. By and large, being immersed in our own problems of immigration and survival against anti-Catholic discrimination in this country, we left such matters to the Holy See in the 19th century and the first half of this century. So the history of U. S. Christian interest in the Holy Land (from missionaries to biblical archaeologists) has been until recently largely a Protestant one. American Catholic involvement in such activities was largely left to the Franciscans or to the French.

Yet the shared immigrant experience with Jews has brought some of us Catholics into the debate on U. S. foreign policy. The history of the labor movement, for example, is to a great extent a history of Catholic-Jewish collaboration. American labor's strong support for Israel over the years is evidence of the close ties wrought by the labor struggle in this country, a dynamic intensified by the fact that, from its founding until the late 1970s, Israeli politics was dominated by the Labor party there. Look, then, at the voting records of Catholics in Congress both before and after 1948, to the present, and you will see a consistency of support for Israel-related causes perhaps unparalleled by any other group of American non-Jews. The reader may also note in passing the quick denunciation by the NCCB, twice reiterated, of the obscene U. N. resolution equating Zionism and Racism, until its repeal.

Despite these natural communal ties, it is true that some Catholic public rhetoric in the 1940s and 1950s, for example articles and editorials in *Civilita Cattolica* in Rome and the *Brooklyn Tablet* here in the U. S., at times reflected what amounted to a fear of a Zionism triumphant. Concerns were expressed, for example, that "the Jews" would act toward the religious minorities of Israel as did those who previously held power. The Crusaders were arguably the worst offenders against the religious liberty of other groups during their relatively brief stay, so perhaps we Catholics were engaging in a bit of psychological "projection" in expressing these concerns, but they were real nonetheless. If one thing is certain, it is that virtually every debate concerning the Middle East, to be fully understood, must begin with its origins in centuries-old disputes.

Yet despite expressed concerns, sometimes laced with remnants of the teaching of contempt against Jews and Judaism, when it came to key votes in the U. S. Congress, over the years Catholics most often sided with the Jews, which since 1942 is to say with the Zionists, "By their deeds shall you know them."

The Catholic "anti-Zionist" rhetoric of the 1940s was not a rejection of the idea of a Jewish State as such. The fact of a Jewish State was never much of a problem (Cardinal Merry del Val's statement typified a consistent "humanitarian" pro-Zionist or neutral-Zionist policy through the years). Rather, the interests of the Holy See centered on the disposition of the Holy City—Jerusalem—and, since 1967, on the needs and aspirations of the Palestinians in the occupied territories. The "local church" it should be recalled, is composed primarily of Palestinian Christians whose witness in the Holy Land is seen as vital to the Church as a whole by the Holy See.

In 1965, the Second Vatican Council, despite opposition from some right-wing Catholics (e.g., the late Archbishop Lefevre), and many Arab states, issued *Nostra Aetate*, ending forever any speculation that Jews were doomed to eternal exile as punishment for supposed collective guilt for the death of Jesus.

The year 1967 also saw a major change, with the Israeli take-over of all of Jerusalem. This ended the Vatican's active support for the idea—which was part of the 1947 U. N. Partition plan and a possible reason for the strong, if tacit support of the Vatican for that plan—of placing Jerusalem under international control. In 1947, it might be noted, U. N. control, for all practical purposes, would have meant Christian and especially Catholic influence since, as mentioned, the Latin American countries held enough votes to swing almost any resolution proposed to the U. N. General Assembly.

Post-1967 papal policy began to introduce phrases such as, "Whoever has sovereignty over Jerusalem, these principles should apply"—religious liberty, access to the Holy Places, and respect for the rights of the two peoples (Jews and Arabs) and three major religious communities (Judaism, Islam and Christianity) that make up the Holy City's population. These principles have traditionally been acknowledged by the government of Israel and, indeed, are reaffirmed in the 1993 "Fundamental Agreement" between the Holy See and the State of Israel. The commitment by the State of Israel in its signing of the historic 1993 Accord with the Holy See to preserve the Status Quo, was an important component, in the eyes of the Holy See, of the exchange of ambassadors with Israel. Having now a recognized, legal stake in the Jerusalem equation, the Holy See feels able to place on the table informally some creative approaches to the question of Jerusalem (cf., *Origins*, Oct. 3, 1996).

It is not, then, that the Holy See ever refused to "recognize" the State of Israel. As its statements over the years; e.g., *Redemptoris Anno* (1984) and that by the Pope in Miami (1987) clearly show, it did acknowledge the reality and legal validity of the Jewish State. The Holy See even mandated for all Catholic religion classrooms a positive attitude toward "the religious attachment" of the people Israel to the Land of Israel, and to the State as a recognized entity under international law (cf., Vatican *Notes*, 1985, Part VI). Certainly by 1986 these were no longer issues but official Church affirmations. There is still a sense of caution today, however, about grandiose, theological claims of eschatology such as those of some American Christian "fundamentalists" (see Thomas Stransky, *America*, 1996), but one can find equal caution about such claims within Zionism itself. The use of the phrase, "The beginning of the redemption," for example, as applied to the State of Israel, finds strong resistance in some quarters of contemporary Judaism.

The problem here is that symbols can and do overwhelm reality. The Holy See's cautious diplomacy continues to be viewed with some skepticism in the Jewish community. The reality is that U. S. Catholics, bishops included, over-whelmingly endorse the essential aspirations of Zionism, and the validity and importance of the State of Israel. It should also be understood that we have a great reverence for the Palestinian Christian community in the region, since it provides a vital living witness to the life and deeds of Jesus, and therefore to the redemptive significance of the Christ event. So our feelings of protectiveness toward our co-religionists in the Middle East are motivated not only by humanitarianism but by a sensitivity that flows out of our inner spiritual lives as well. Some actions understandably taken by successive Israeli governments to ensure the security of all of the people of Israel, such as the closures, have had unintended but devastating side effects for the Palestinian Christian minority, religiously as well as economically. It is often easier, for example, for foreign Christian pilgrims to gain access to holy sites in Jerusalem and Bethlehem than it is for Palestinian Christians whose ancestral homes fall on the wrong side of a particular checkpoint. So I would argue for very sensitive treatment of these issues on the part of the Israeli administration, perhaps even special training for key administrators who make decisions "on the ground" which can profoundly affect the religious lives of the Christian minority.

This, of course, is a principle many Israeli and American Jews would espouse. It is a matter of careful listening and sensitive implementation of shared values in very practical situations.

As a Catholic, I have argued and will continue to argue within my own community for a greater Catholic sensitivity to the symbol and sign of *reality* for Israel and for Jews. The Catholic thinks here in terms of *sacraments*, of the State of Israel as the incarnation in the present of the universal hopes of the people of Israel, despite the current turmoil and all too human fallibility of all involved. While we Jews and Catholics rightly celebrate together the present state of diplomatic relations between the Holy See and the State of Israel, we acknowledge, as does the preamble of the "Fundamental Accord" itself, that this is but one aspect of the deeper, and we believe divinely-inspired, relationship between our two peoples of Faith in the One God, Father of us all. It is this faith, and the covenant bond that it forges between us, that impels us, along with our third "sibling," Islam, to turn our hearts and minds toward the ancient streets of Jerusalem, seeking there some way, in justice and in hope, to make it truly a "City of Peace," not only for ourselves but for all humanity. Stranger things have happened, such as the unlikely miracle of the Jewish State coming to be in the first place.

From *Nostra Aetate* to the Catechism

For Catholics, the history of reform in Jewish-Christian relations begins with Pope John XXIII's call for a universal or "ecumenical" Council of the world's bishops. This Second Vatican Council tackled enormous challenges theologically, liturgically and in the structure of the Church itself. Windows long thought forever closed were prudently and cautiously opened to let in fresh breezes and, we sincerely believe, God's Spirit, a Spirit which has literally transformed the ancient Church of Rome.

One of the first issues which John XXIII mandated the Council Fathers to take up was the issue of the Church's understanding of Judaism and attitude toward the Jewish People. So sensitive were the deliberations on this topic that it would not be until close to the very end of the Council, on October 28, 1965, that its Declaration, *Nostra Aetate* ("In Our Time") would be overwhelmingly passed.

Nostra Aetate is a remarkably short document given the profound changes it brought about. In only 15 Latin sentences, it addressed and gutted the very heart of the ancient "teaching of contempt" towards Jews and Judaism into which so many Christians had drifted in the course of centuries. It replaced the old negative stance of the Church toward its "elder brother in the faith," as Pope John Paul II has aptly called the Jewish People, with an attitude of "mutual esteem" and positive respect for the ongoing salvific validity of Judaism as a divinely revealed religion. It condemned as wholly false the ancient charge of "deicide" against the Jews, the idea that Jews were collectively to blame for Jesus' death, and so were to be seen as "cursed" by God. Relying on fresh understandings of key passages in the Epistles of Paul, such as Romans 9-11, and the Gospels themselves, it presented for Catholic reflection a positive appreciation of the continuing role of Judaism and the Jewish People in God's plan of salvation for all humanity.

The Council's small step of turning toward rather than away from God's People, Israel, has in the past three decades resulted in the greatest burgeoning of dialogue between our two peoples in the entire history of our relationship. In country after country bishops' conferences issued major statements seeking to implement the Council's vision in Catholic teaching and preaching. History will record that the first "Guidelines for Catholic-Jewish Relations" ever issued in the history of the Church, anywhere in the world, were issued by the American Bishops early in 1967. These were followed over the years by bishops' conferences, first in Western Europe during the 1970s, then in Latin America in the 1980s, and, with their emergence from Communist domination, in Eastern Europe, beginning with Poland, in the 1990s. These episcopal statements were greatly facilitated, indeed, mandated by documents issued in 1975 and 1985 by the Holy See's Commission for Religious Relations with the Jews to give guidance for the implementation of *Nostra Aetate* by local churches around the world. Seminaries and Catholic school religion classes will never be the same again, thanks be to God.

What was in the late 1960s and early 1970s the work of experts and great pioneers in the field has increasingly entered the mainstream of Catholic life, certainly here in the United States, but increasingly also around the world. Given the ancientness of the Catholic Church and its traditional caution in approaching change where truly important things such as liturgy and doctrine are at stake, the speed of the change within the Church approaches the miraculous. Allow me to give a few examples of what has been taking place.

When I first began my present position almost twenty years ago, I had to define for Catholic audiences what the term "Holocaust" meant for Jews, but could presume an awareness of "Christ-killer" or "Deicide" charges. Today, happily, it is the opposite. Catholics are very much aware of the Holocaust and what it means for Jews and Christians, while terms such as "Deicide" and "Christ-killer" have virtually dropped out of the Catholic vocabulary.

Other measures of progress are not hard to find. In the late 1950s, before the Council, a series of textbook self-studies of Catholic, Protestant and Jewish religious education materials was initiated by the American Jewish Committee.

Catholic texts and teachers' manuals were studied by Sr. Rose Thering, OP, as her doctoral dissertation for Saint Louis University. The results were depressing (and in fact were supplied to the drafters of *Nostra Aetate*) in the largely negative portrait of Jews and Judaism that emerged. When, using the same methodology, I updated the study in the mid-1970s on teaching materials produced after the Council, I noticed substantial progress in developing a more positive image of the Jewish "other." Most of the blatant anti-Judaic themes of the "teaching of contempt" had been eliminated and replaced with positives. In the early 1990s Dr. Philip Cunningham, also controlling for analytical methodology, reported continuing progress in improving Catholic under- standing of and appreciation for Jews and Judaism.

One of the major factors accounting for this continuing progress—and of course much more needs to be done across-the-board—has been the remarkable pontificate of Pope John Paul II. It can be said without exaggeration that no Pope in the history of the Church has spoken more often with Jewish communities nor spoken more positively about Jews and Judaism than has John Paul II. A volume containing his addresses on the subject was published by the Catholic Bishops' Conference and the Anti-Defamation League of B'nai B'rith in 1987. A much thicker update of this volume was published in 1995.

Pope John Paul II has done what no Bishop of Rome, at least since St. Peter, ever did. In 1986, he visited the Great Synagogue of Rome and prayed there with its Chief Rabbi and congregation. One cannot imagine a stronger affirmation of the validity of Jewish prayer. In December of 1993, the Holy See and the State of Israel, in a very real sense representing the aspirations of the Catholic Church and the Jewish People, announced a "Fundamental Accord" that paved the way for the exchange of full ambassadors in the succeeding months. This should remove from the mind of even the most cynical the last doubts about the sincerity of the Church's repentance for past misdeeds against Jews. Having affirmed Jewish validity religiously in the Second Vatican Council and subsequent teachings, the Church now affirms without ambiguity the validity of Jewish polity as well.

In April of 1994, Pope John Paul II, again sitting alongside the Chief Rabbi of Rome, presided over a profoundly emotional concert for the victims of the Holocaust to commemorate Yom HaShoah. *Kaddish* was prayed. The concert was shown on European television and made available also to PBS in this country. The Pope's experiences during the Nazi occupation of his native Poland, and the murder by the Nazis of so many of the Jewish classmates and friends of his youth, have given him an intensely personal awareness of the magnitude of the tragedy for Jews, as one can see in the very moving chapter on Judaism in his best-selling book, *Crossing the Threshold of Hope*, and also in the remembrances of "Lolek" Wotyla's boyhood friend from Wadowice, Poland, Jerzy Kluger.

Finally, as evidence of the effectiveness of the Church's *heshbon hanefesh* (reconsideration of the soul, which we Catholics call an examination of con- science), one might mention the new *Catechism of the Catholic Church*. Does this text, destined as it is to have a lasting impact on Catholic teaching on the grassroots level for decades, perhaps generations, reflect the more positive attitudes toward Jews and Judaism announced in the official documents mentioned above? I believe that in many ways it does.

Under the rubric of interpreting Article 4 of the Creed of the Catholic Church ("suffered under Pontius Pilate, and died"), the *Catechism* devotes a major section (all of paragraphs 571-598) to breaking down religious and social prejudices against Jews and Judaism. As Father Edward Flannery states in his study of the *Catechism*'s understanding of Judaism: "The *Catechism*'s treatment...is the fruit of the dialogue that has gone on between Christians and Jews for the last decades. One can sense in it a conscious effort to repudiate those anti-Judaic beliefs which have led to the alienation of Christians and Jews. The age-old canard that the Jews killed Christ is forcefully rejected, and the true Christian teaching is reasserted." Father Flannery then quotes the *Catechism*'s own conclusion to its discussion of Jesus' death:

> The Church has never forgotten that all sinners were the authors and ministers of the sufferings of Christ, and does not hesitate to impute to Christians the gravest responsibility with which they too often burdened the Jews. (para. 598)

In conclusion, I would like to list briefly what I consider to be the key principles of the *Catechism*'s approach.

1. The Church's understanding of God's People, the Jews, is stated in the present tense, not the past tense. "Israel is the priestly people of God, 'called by the name of the LORD,' (Dt. 28:10) and the first to hear the word of God, the people of 'elder brethren' in the faith of Abraham" (63).

2. Whatever the historical involvement of individuals, *Jews as such are not collectively responsible for Jesus' death* (597). The *Catechism*'s insistence on this principle and its numerous implications for classroom presentation of the New Testament is driven home by it extensive treatment under article 4 of the Creed, "suffered under Pontius Pilate, was crucified..." (571-630). It is under this overarching rubric, rejecting the very essence of the old teaching of contempt, that the *Catechism* organizes its major discussion of Jesus' relationship to the faith of his people ("Israel, Law & Temple"—574-586), to which we shall return, below.

3. "God's Covenant with the Jewish People is irrevocable" (839, 840, 2173). The New Covenant has neither abrogated nor superseded "the First Covenant" (522). The *Catechism* is quite explicit: "The Old Covenant has never been revoked" (121). This is a reference to Pope John Paul II's framing of the issue in his extraordinary address to the Jewish community of Mainz, Germany, where he boldly likened the contemporary dialogue between the Church and the Jewish People to the relationship between the Sacred Scriptures.

4. The Hebrew Scriptures are to be presented "as the true Word of God" with their own permanent integrity and dignity. As the *Catechism* states, "the Church has always vigorously opposed the idea of rejecting the Old Testament under the pretext that the New Testament has rendered it void

(Marcionism)" (123). Thus, there should be an emphasis on "the unity of the divine plan" (140). As the 1974 Vatican *Guidelines for Implementing Nostra Aetate* fleshed out this principle: The Hebrew Bible and the Jewish tradition founded on it must not be set against the New Testament in such a way that the former seems to constitute a religion of only retributive justice, fear, and legalism, with no appeal to love of God and neighbor (Dt 6:5; Lev 19:18; Hos 11; Matt. 22).

5. While Christians validly see in the Hebrew Scriptures "prefigurations of what God accomplished in the fullness of time in the person of his incarnate Son" (128), typology and fulfillment are not the only valid approaches to interpreting the Hebrew Bible. "Such typological reading discloses the inexhaustible content of the Old Testament, but it must not make us forget that the Old Testament retains its own intrinsic value as revelation reaffirmed by Our Lord himself" (129). This paragraph of the *Catechism* reflects section I of the Holy See's 1985 *Notes on the Correct Way to Present Jews and Judaism in Catholic Preaching and Catechesis*, which deals at length with "the relations between the Testaments." The *Notes* urge catechists to "profit discerningly from the traditions of Jewish reading" of the Bible from ancient to modern times.

6. The *Catechism* in two paragraphs (839-840) distills what it considers essential to an understanding of *"the relationship of the Church with the Jewish People."* The first echoes the Second Vatican Council's *Nostra Aetate*, the Pope's 1986 address at the Rome Synagogue and the prayer "for the Jewish people" from the reformed Good Friday liturgy of the *Roman Missal*: *"When she delves into her own mystery, the Church, the People of God in the New Covenant, discovers her link with the Jewish People, 'the first to hear the Word of God.' The Jewish faith, unlike other non-Christian religions, is already a response to God's revelation in the Old Covenant,"* citing then Romans 9:4-5 and 11:29, as did the Council. One will note here the distinctive intimacy of what the Council called the Church's ongoing "spiritual bond" with Jews and Judaism and why the Pope called the Jews our "elder brothers" in the faith in the present tense and not as a past event exhausted in New Testament times (See also 63).

7. Catechists need to look beyond past and present in speaking of "fulfillment" and imbue their teaching with eschatological urgency. "When one considers the future, God's People of the Old Covenant and the new People of God tend towards similar goals: expectation of the coming (or the return) of the Messiah." Acknowledging frankly the very real differences in Messianic beliefs between Jews and Christians (and, one might add, *among* both Jews and Christians), this framing allows the fulfillment theology of the *Catechism* to be freeing and challenging rather than exclusivist or supersessionist. As the section of the 1985 *Notes* of the Holy See, on which the *Catechism* here relies, states: "Attentive to the same God who has spoken, hanging on the same word, we Jews and Christians have to witness to one same memory and one common hope in God who is the master of History. We must accept our responsibility to prepare the world for the coming of the Messiah by working together for social justice...and international reconciliation."

8. Reiterating the words of Pope John Paul II to representatives of Bishops' Conferences in Rome (March 6, 1992) and the emphasis in the 1985 Vatican *Notes* which followed from the Pope's words, the *Catechism* declares that **"a better knowledge of the Jewish people's faith and religious life as professed and lived even now can help our better understanding of certain aspects of Christian liturgy"** (1096). This section goes on to spell out the Jewish roots of Christian liturgical practices such as the proclamation of Sacred Scripture, response of praise and intercession for the living and dead, the structure and lectionary cycle of the Liturgy of the Word and of the Hours, central prayers such as the Our Father, the great feasts of the Church and the liturgical cycle itself, especially the Passover, which "both celebrate." Again, the eschatological caveat ("already here/not yet here") calls Jews and Christians into a dialogue of mutual reconciliation, expectation and working together to prepare the world for God's Reign, a task Jews call *tikkun olam* (repairing the world).

"SEPARATE BUT EQUAL"
The Model for Christian/Jewish Relations?
Franklin H. Littell

The familiar phrase comes, of course, from Plessy v. Ferguson (1896), when the case against segregated facilities was denied by the Supreme Court of the United States. *Apartheid* was legitimate, provided the citizen's claim to equal treatment was honored. In 1954, in Brown v. Board of Education of Topeka, the issue of segregation or separation itself was confronted. "Separate" had not been accompanied by "equal," and the principle of fairness controlled the decision against tax-supported segregated schools.

"Separate but equal" failed as a working model for the school experience of American youth. Can it function as a working model for adult American religion(s)? The rapid embrace of "toleration" as a primary religious virtue, accompanied by the assumption of most Americans—according to a recent special issue of *The New York Times Sunday Magazine* (6 December 1997)—that at most religions are "all right, as long as you have one," suggests the victory of a pattern of blending (*Gleichschaltung*?) rather than separation in mutual respect.

Harry James Cargas has been one of the pioneers in pushing the issue of how best the Jewish minority and the several larger Christian minorities are to be related to each other in a pluralistic society. Is integration—perhaps the "melting pot" of Israel Zangwill, OR radical separation—like the "pillarization" (*verzeulen*) of Dutch society before World War II, the best model? or is there a Third Way?

The question is not how "Jews" and "Christians" are to relate to each other. At the level of individual contact that is no real problem in America today: personal friendships which cross communal lines are very common. Where occasional regressive attacks on individuals—so-called "hate crimes"—occur, criminal penalties are appropriate and usually applied.

In our devotion to long-range goals of changing the mindsets and converting the souls of the bigoted and unregenerate, we professional educators frequently tend to forget that the jail and the penitentiary are also powerful educational forces during times of social tension. But we are thinking about structures, not about how individual cases should be managed.

Neither do we ask how "the synagogue" and "the churches" are to relate to each other. At the level of inter-religious cooperation, the National Conference of Christians and Jews (founded in 1928) led the way on the national level, with campus programs at Iowa, Cornell and Michigan opening the doors to inter-religious dialogue and understanding. In recent decades the NCCJ has been succeeded by a host of national, regional and local academic and communal programs and institutions. The chaplaincy in the armed forces set a high standard during World War II, making "Cooperation Without Compromise" a noble practice as well as a high ideal. In civil life, too, there are now ample channels for rabbis, priests and ministers and their lay people to work together for the common good as fellow-citizens.

There are major differences in the way Jews and Christians relate to organized religion. "Going to church" is a significant clue to identify "Christians." But to use connection to *shul* as a way of defining "the Jews" ignores the fact that the primary meeting of religious significance is around the dinner table, in the family. Applying the Christian standard to Jewish religious "membership" also ignores the fact that in America, as in Israel, fully 50% of Jews have a different self-definition. This half or more is often called "secular Jews," although this expression seems more polemical than scientific.

Also, and this is perhaps more crucial, being understood and being officially defined solely by religion—has proven dangerous for Jews. In the Germany and Hungary of Hitler's empire, for instance, Jews who thought of themselves as "citizens *mosaischer Glaube*" ("of the Mosaic faith") were politically naive as well as philosophically impoverished. Mordecai M. Kaplan's classic—*Judaism as a Civilization* (1934)—was a contemporary call to a more sturdy and comprehensive self-definition which, however, reached many too late.

This discussion refers primarily neither to the experience of individuals nor to the inter-agency relations of communal leaders.   We are using a definition of the problem that makes it possible to speak of "the Jewish *people*" and "Jewish civilization" in their totality, and to discuss the collective form and impact of the Christian communities.

We are greatly indebted to Martin Buber for bringing us the philosophy of "dialogue" (*I and Thou*, 1923, 1937), now so important also in organized interaction between Jews and Christians. Yet Buber, like most of his generation, remained set in the context of European "Christendom:" in one of his great essays he contrasted Judaic collectivism with Christian "individualism" (*Two Types of Faith*, 1951). He never experienced, obviously, the individualism of many American Jews and the militant "*we*-consciousness" of many Americans of the Free Churches. His perception of the interaction was based on his experience in Europe, where the *shtetl* and the *ghetto* were the underside, and—in their structures of power—the darkened mirror image of "Christendom." In that setting "dialogue" remained the prerogative of the university elite; in America "the dialogue" too has been "democratized," slowly but profoundly influencing the self-definitions of both communal entities.

American Jews, like American Christians, often fail to note the radical difference between the role and place of religion in Europe and its function in America. In the first settlements in North America, Christianity functioned as a spiritual peninsula of European "Christendom." From time to time, some American church leaders still strike the pose of the leaders of established churches—but even their own adherents do not believe them.

The Jews remember the painful underside of "Christendom." Carrying over from their experiences of bigotry, repression, persecution and genocide in European "Christendom," many American Jews mistakenly refer to America as a "Christian" nation and commonly use the terms "Christian" and "gentile" inter-changeably. But, as already stated, the Christians in America are gathered in a number of large minorities. The largest dozen of these minorities total over four-fifths of the total Christian percentage, but it is a mistake for any to suppose that the Roman Catholic Church in the USA, the Southern Baptist Convention, the Church of Jesus Christ of Latter Day Saints (commonly called "Mormons") and the United Methodist Church will inevitably act with any more harmony on a given issue than will the agencies of Reconstructionist, Orthodox, Conservative and Reform Jews.

"Christians" are gentiles who are defined by their relationship to the faith and disciplines of Christianity. As we have seen by the wholesale apostasy of the baptized where the Marxist and Nazi ideological establishments prevailed for a time, baptized gentiles can revert to their pre-Christian condition and place in history. They can apostatize. Although a very few Christian isolates may be identified in the last two thousand years, by and large the Christian is formed and defined by his or her membership in a community of faith. As a great British theologian (Peter Taylor Forsyth) put it, against those who scorn formation in community: "a spirit without a body is a ghost." Buber's work notwithstanding, to discuss Christian behavior apart from the record of the Christian churches is a basic error (even though in some periods of history, including the German Third Reich, the idea is attractive).

We have, therefore, to discuss the much more complicated and ambiguous issue: the interaction of the Christian and Jewish communities in a land where our liberties are Constitutional (if we can keep them), and where the cultural patterns and social mores have yet to catch up with the legal realities.

The Burden of History

Not until the Civil War, nearly a hundred years after the break with the British sovereign, did it begin to become clear what kind of a society "the American dream" required to sustain it. Three great acts of Congress shaped the future. Emancipation and the Homestead Act determined that the plantation system should yield place to free labor and the family farm. The Morrill Land Act extended the principle of free public higher education to college level.

What was the pattern of religion to be? In the New World, whose discovery was considered providential in human history, a radically new relationship was to develop between church and state. This was not clear at first. Would the United States carry on, like Latin America, the millenium and a half of cooperation between church and state that had been one of Western Christianity's chief characteristics? For more than two centuries the answer in the English-speaking colonies was—like the answer in the Spanish, Portuguese and French-speaking colonies—given in the affirmative.

With the exception of Pennsylvania and little Rhode Island, the independent colonies—indeed, from 1776 to 1791 the independent states— patterned their religious life on the model of European "Christendom." Even in Pennsylvania, Roman Catholics could not vote or hold public office until after the Revolution. Although the Virginia Bill of Religious Freedom (1784-86) and the First Amendment to the Federal Constitution (1789-91) set a high standard of separation for the nation, not until 1843 was the last major state church (Massachusetts) disestablished. In one New England state (New Hampshire) Jews were constitutionally disfranchised until 1912.

Nevertheless, all through the 19th century the religious pattern was shifting in the United States from the solidity of Protestant state churches and cultural domination to acceptance of the realities of religious pluralism. The massive Roman Catholic immigrations of the 1840s through 1860s, and the flight of Jews from tsarist Russia following the series of pogroms 1873-1905, confronted the older Protestantism with the brute necessity of finding a new model of self-understanding. This change had been required in principle by the Constitutional mandate of Religious Liberty. With the demographic change, decisive reformation and reconstruction could no longer be avoided, requiring fundamental alterations in ancient doctrinal, liturgical and disciplinary practices.

In truth neither Christians nor Jews have found easy the radical change from establishment to Religious Liberty.

"Christian America" is a myth still appealing enough to evoke atavistic political responses. When Pat Robertson or Pat Buchanan and their allies promote the myth and build a political campaign based upon it, they are evoking memories and patterns of behavior that go back more than a millenium and a half in the history of Christianity. From the time when the Emperor Constantine gave Christianity the backing of the full force of the Empire (325 C.E.), imperial administrative practices and the Theology of Triumphalism ruled European "Christendom." The time of separation in America has been comparatively brief, and some of the basic lessons are yet to be learned. (The time of toleration—**not** Religious Liberty—was shorter yet in Germany during the Weimar Republic. After twelve years of religious uncertainty during the German Third Reich, the largest Protestant church—the *Altpreussische Union*—reverted to the official treaty of 1931 with the state, and the Roman Catholic Church after 1945 continued the Concordat negotiated between Hitler and Pacelli.)

The behavior of the Russian Orthodox Church and the Roman Catholic Church in Poland today, after long decades of wintering through bitter Soviet ideological persecution, only adds another load of evidence as to how difficult it is for Christians in Western civilization to abandon the ways of coercion and persecution. In the edicts of the rulers, in the privileged status of the established churches' professionals, and thus in the mindset of the peoples, the persecution of "Jews" and the persecution of "heretics" were piously linked from the time of Constantine's decrees and Justinian's Code.

Official Christianity was dominated by a blend of imperial administrative practices and theological triumphalism, both of which were little changed by the 16th century Reformation. The attitude to the Jews was little bettered by the 18th century Enlightenment. Voltaire, as well as most of the *Encyclopedistes,* was a flaming antisemite. The teaching of contempt for the Jews was little changed in the churches. There were small Judaeophile groups in the 16th century Radical Reformation, in 17th century Radical Puritanism and in 18th century Radical Pietism, but the picture changed little in the Christian establishments.

Even in the Social Gospel, which opened such broad vistas of Christian social concern at the opening of the 20th century in America, was unable to relieve the anxieties of American Jews. Among prominent churchmen, only Reinhold Niebuhr strongly took positions that supported Jewish survival. While journals such as *The Christian Century* and the Canadian *United Church Observer* accused "the Jews" of an unpleasant resistance to assimilation, Niebuhr from 1928 opposed missionary efforts that targeted "the Jews." He was the first Christian leader to advocate the founding of a Jewish state (in *The Nation,* February of 1943). He remained a loyal, if not uncritical, friend of Israel until his death in 1971. Niebuhr was, however, post-Holocaust Christian—like Harry James Cargas in his generation, who has also made the pilgrimage with those Christians concerned for the lessons of the Church Struggle and the Holocaust, and calls himself a "post-Auschwitz Christian."

The Holocaust (Shoah) and the German Church Struggle (*Kirchenkampf*) visit upon Christianity the most serious credibility crisis in its two millennia of history. No matter the excuses—and all have been tried!—the brute fact remains that 6,000,000 Jews were deliberately murdered in the heart of "Christendom" according to a program carried out by baptized heathen counted as Roman Catholics, Eastern Orthodox and Protestants. Few church leaders spoke up for those who had no voice, to intervene for the powerless. During the Holocaust the people lost one-third of world Jewry. European Jewry lost 60%, including the important centers of learning and culture of both religious and secular movements.

The Jewish people and leadership emerged with **three burning concerns** that have subsequently affected their relationship with the governments and peoples of Western civilization: 1) Christian missions aimed at converting Jews; 2) inter-marriage between Jews and gentiles; and 3) support for the security and well-being of the Jewish state, Israel, which came forth like the Phoenix from the ashes.

All three areas of confrontation remain highly volatile, in America as well as in Europe. In America, however, where the communities are both "separate" and "equal," the solutions must be found in forms quite different from those that have followed traditional lines in Europe. By what means and in what style are Christian churches to maintain their unity and formation when they are burdened with neither political persecution as "heretics" nor state sponsorship for services rendered? This is the same pair of questions that confronts Jewry in America.

How are we to talk about these things? "Dialogue" is difficult in Europe: there is a shortage of Jews in Germany, where the concern for finding a new way is most lively among the churches and in the widespread Societies of Christian-Jewish Cooperation. In Britain and France and elsewhere, the heavy shadows of "Christendom" and Auschwitz darken counsel but provide no driving thrust for change. "Dialogue" is virtually impossible in Israel, for there is a shortage of Christians coupled with a genuine paucity of Biblical theological energy among the tattered remnants of ancient and once great churches.

Only in America can the inter-religious dialogue flourish today. Only in America are the free exercise of religion *and* the prohibition of sectarian preference or privilege rooted in the law of the land. Only in America are the Jewish, Protestant and Roman Catholic communities enjoying a tremendous flowering of spiritual and cultural, economic and political energy. Since 1907 American Catholics have been the chief support of the Vatican. Since 1938 more than two-thirds of all the missionaries in the world have come from the American Free Churches. Since 1945 the Jewish communities have enjoyed the greatest renaissance of intellectual, spiritual, cultural, economic and political influence since at least the Golden Age before 1492 in the Iberian peninsula.

Themes for the Inter-Religious Dialogue

Israel now flourishes as the City of Refuge for the Jews of the world, and as a high-tech paragon. But there are half again as many Jews in the United States as in Israel, and they are not threatened with annihilation by neighboring despots and dictators. Therefore they have the opportunity, and the responsibility as well, to work out with their neighbors the implications of this new thing: religious membership that—like other free associations—is uncoerced, voluntary, and uncorrupted by any civil force. And in the American situation, the solutions are debated while the neighbors listen in.

Let me summarize the steps that the Christian churches must take if Christians and Jews are to move through "cease fire" to armistice to reconciliation to trust—and toward *Shalom* (peace, harmony).

First, the Christian churches must remove words and phrases in their catechetical texts, their Sunday School lessons, their official Study Units and their liturgies that refer to "the Jews" with contempt. The negatives at last are being noticed and deleted, although a recent 800-page dissertation in our Department of Religion at Temple University showed that the Catholic liturgies still contain a heavy load of theological antisemitism. Nevertheless, the slow and thorough purging from catechetical materials of what never should have been there in the first place is continuing, country by country, under the Bishops' Conferences.

Expressing regret for bad teaching in the past, with removal of the offending words, is only prophylactic. Unhappily we do not yet have in America a single denominational press that has moved over to the affirmative, nor even study units on the lessons of the Church Struggle with Nazism—let alone on the lessons of the Holocaust.

Second, the Christians must insert words into the teachings and liturgies that express the indelible indebtedness of Christians to their Jewish heritage and praise God for the continuing survival of the Jewish people. So far the most thorough and courageous official position in this respect has been issued by the Synod of the Protestant Church of the Rhineland (January, 1980).

Third, they must close down missionary efforts that target "the Jews." Again, we are not talking about individual cases, where a Christian teacher or pastor is free to counsel a Jew who is contemplating conversion just as he would meet a Dane or Japanese or Zulu where he is. The same principle applies to gentile conversion to Judaism. Dr. Alexander Schindler, the retired head of Reform Judaism, has been fearless (and helpful) in reciprocal response: he has understood that in America a good rabbi—like a good minister or priest—strives to make the option attractive and is prepared to welcome and train converts.

To return to the discourse about patterns and structures, the Jewish people does not have the same place in the providence of God as other tribes, clans and nations. My late friend Will Herberg was once challenged with the question by a speculative critic, "If the Jewish people is 'elected,' why not the Teutonic *Herrenvolk*?" He gave the answer of Jerusalem, not of Athens: "Because one is true and the other is false." Franz Rosenzweig, in *The Star of Redemption* (1921), elaborated a model to express the complementary work of Jews and Christians: the Jews are to form and fashion a covenant people who witness to the Way of Life (*Torah*), while the Christians are to carry the good news of that Way to all the tribes of the earth.

Fourth, the Christians must cease nursing their double standard, expressed in hypercritical and constant criticism of the democratic State of Israel. Israel is the only democratic society in the Middle East. It is surrounded by dictatorships and despots; it has four times been the object of rattlesnake attacks by combinations of aggressive military forces; it has declarations of war out against it by surrounding countries, only two of which in the last fifty years have agreed even to an armistice. As citizens in a democracy, Israelis are entitled to make their own mistakes; as the post-Holocaust City of Refuge for Jews around the world, Israel is entitled to the good will of Christians who take their history and their Bible seriously.

Unfortunately, the theological and cultural levels of antisemitism in the Christian churches are still so thick, even among those who would be ashamed of being identified with modern political and ideological antisemitism, that the opportunities are seldom missed publicly to criticize Israel for faults that would not even be noticed in other governments' conduct of their affairs. The writer is sorry to say, having been a Methodist clergyman for more than sixty years, that the World Methodist Council is one of the worst offenders. We are in choice company, however, in dependably anti-Israel postures of the National Council of Churches. And, as a recent statement of the World Council of Churches on the status of Jerusalem makes clear, the malaise of antisemitism still stains the public countenances of otherwise admirable ecumenical leaders.

What might we ask of the Jewish communal leaders and agencies?

First, we might urge that concern for "the free exercise of religion" be stronger, and that there be more understanding of the path of Christianity in America from establishment to pluralism. Too often the reactions to bad experiences with established and coercive religion in Europe have been transferred without adjustment, and some Jewish spokesmen find high profile as opponents of every public manifestation of the traditional religion of the land. In a coercive "Christendom," the power structures themselves were the enemy of liberty of conscience; under Religious Liberty, the dangers lie elsewhere—in knee-jerk reaction to any public manifestations of religion.

What about evangelism on the streets? Who is hurt when two courteous, well-dressed young people come along to pass out their tracts and try to debate the last things? Such activity would not be permitted to "heretics" in "Christian" Europe, of course; but in America, why not take their pamphlet and give them one of your own. In the long haul, "the empty public square" (Richard J. Neuhaus' potent phrase) is as dangerous for Jews as it is for Christians.

Second, now that Judaism enjoys virtually universal acceptance as a valid religious option, more active intervention in behalf of the life and liberty of the modern "heretics"—so-called "sects and cults"—would seem in order. We should not forget that the repressive edicts for more than a millenium and a half in "Christendom" were directed against "Jews *and* heretics." It is a grievous mistake, as well as politically and theologically wrong, to have in prominent position in one of the Jewish defense agencies a man who has profiteered enormously in recent years from his activities as a cult-basher. It was a serious practical error, as well as legally and religiously wrong, for a member of the House of

Representatives who is a Jew to be one of the most articulate defenders of the murder of the misguided "Branch Davidians" near Waco, Texas. Most Christians, and not only the spiritual descendents of Hiram and Joseph Smith, Jr.—"Mormons," the Church of Jesus Christ of Latter Day Saints—still remember when their fathers and mothers were defamed and lynched as members of a "sect" or "cult." Now all but the most obtuse would agree that "Mormons" are as worthy of their citizenship as any of the rest.

Jews have as much reason to support a disciplined and truly American police and public safety network as have gentiles (including the Christians). In recent years we have had appalling cases of justice thwarted because of criminal actions by officials in police and public safety. We have been visited repeatedly by the shadows of Rodney King's assailants, by the apparitional uniformed killers at Waco and Ruby Ridge, and by the very real presence of policeman Mark Fuhrman in Beverly Hills. We are paying a heavy price to learn a simple fact: you cannot convict a criminal "beyond reasonable doubt" if you have to rely on evidence from a corrupt police force. The other side of the coin is this: you cannot secure your own safety by undermining the Constitutional rights and liberties of ethnic or religious sects with whom you share neither color nor creed.

Citizens and communities are entitled to protection in all of their liberties, and especially—we believe—exercise of their Religious Liberty, unless charged and prosecuted in due process of published law. Jews and Christians should be united in demanding uprightness and truth-telling from those entrusted with the stewardship of power and physical force, and they should work together to restore uprightness whenever and wherever and by whomever the rule of law has been breached. This now reaches to the highest level, for in the infamous **Smith** Case (494 U.S. 872 [1990]) the Supreme Court reversed two centuries of religious progress, radically amending the First Amendment to the detriment of Religious Liberty.

Third, and here again inter-religious cooperation is called for, the Jewish communities could speak more loudly to what Catholic teachers call "the option for the poor." As good Pope John XXIII pointed out in his great encyclicals, we "must take account of all those social conditions which favour the full development of human personality" (*Mater et Magistra*, 15 May 1961), for every human person "has the right to life, to bodily integrity and to the means which are necessary and suitable for a proper development of life... to respect for his person, to his good reputation, the right to freedom in searching for truth and in expressing and communicating his opinions...And he has the right to be informed truthfully about public events." (*Pacem in Terris*, 10 April 1963).

This is a season in American history to remember the words by which nations and generations are judged, raised up if righteous or broken on the wheel of history if found wanting. The Gospel of Greed is blowing loudly from the trumpets, while in the dark alleys of the cities a voice of crying is heard. A recent study reports that one out of every three young black men has jail experience. This is true because never in American history have we had political "leadership" so single-mindedly determined to use "the penitentiary solution" to morally and religiously outrageous social and economic injustices. Let both Jews and Christians harken to the message of the prophet: "Woe unto them who lie on beds of ivory, who lay house to house and field to field, who grind the faces of the poor!" (Isaiah) *Woe to the wicked City!*

Fourth, every rabbi and synagogue should reach out to the seeking gentile. Across the years this writer has learned to value and love the spiritual and Biblical culture of the synagogue and family services. Until the laws of "Christendom" penalized conversion, Judaism kept its doors open to seekers and friends. May we anticipate that, emerging from the long tunnel of restraint and persecution, the Jewish people will again offer its religion and culture as a winsome option?

Stating the same truth in the negative: sectarian hostility displayed toward the gentiles is no more lovely than antisemitism, and it reflects a parallel spiritual distortion—even if it does not present an equal danger in civil life.

In the End

We have come to a decisive moment in American legal, cultural and religious history. A return to the mythic "Christian America" of some peoples' Golden Age is impossible, even if it were desirable. Shall we in theory and at law thicken and raise higher the walls between the Roman Catholic, Protestant and Jewish communities? As the Dutch and Swiss decided after the communal and cantonal armed conflicts of the 19th century, a harsh separation is indeed better than even harsher shooting wars. But in both areas, today, static establishments have lost the vast majority of their citizens to hedonism, materialism and substitute *Ersatzreligionen*. Or are we propositionally committed to the opposite solution—a blending that obliterates all lines of separation, so that our great-grandchildren in time to come will sport the beautiful light chocolate color of many Caribbean islanders, talk Esperanto, and worship in the high spiritual and ethical fellowship of an eclectic religion?

The creative tension can be broken in either direction. As we look for further enlightenment in the life of covenant and spirit, we may remember that—in both Jewish and Christian teaching—to those in tune the ways of the Almighty are "wonderful" and "surprising." Both a dogmatic alienation between our peoples and a propositional flattening out somehow strike discordant notes. We need to welcome the possibility of a Third Way, whose outlines we cannot yet discern, but whose Spirit is familiar to us in the dialogue. Especially at Yom Kippur we are taught to welcome the cleaning of the slate, followed by a sudden light that lifts the heart and brings joy to life.

In this continuum of history—past, present, and future—we are enlightened by dialogue with those who have died in the faith and by those present. And in that dialogue, instead of insolent confrontation we practice the things of our peace, our *Shalom*. Let our peace, our *Shalom*, be translated as the Hebrew *harmony*, not as the Aristotelian immovable dead stop.

Our path into the future is illuminated by a vision of things not yet seen and heard. In what heaven do we have hope? Our beliefs about the last things—when we are reminded—set the pitch and the beat for our present music. Let us listen to the sound of the other's hope for the things unseen, for the time to come, for our *Shalom*. As for me, I hope that the angelic choirs—on the pitch and hearing each other with joy—shall sing in harmony, and in unison only during antiphonals.

HOLOCAUST STUDIES IN A CATHOLIC SETTING
Richard Libowitz

One of the significant results of Vatican II was the opening of the Roman Catholic Church to greater contacts with other religious faiths and denominations. Within the United States, this new openness was demonstrated through significant increases in ecumenical and interfaith activities at a number of levels, including the archdiocesan, the individual parish and within many institutions of higher education. These activities were being generated at the same time and may have been abetted by the growing pride in ethnic identification and heritage which arose in the late 1960s and which stimulated a demand for ethnic studies, including Jewish Studies, at many colleges and universities, public and private alike. As a Jewish undergraduate at the University of Notre Dame during those years, I experienced this trend in the form of curiosity about Jews and Judaism on the part of my classmates, whose many questions, fortunately, were sufficiently basic to be answered from an educational matrix of five years of Hebrew School. A generation later, I find myself still responding to Catholic undergraduates' questions about Jews and Judaism, but the questioners are now my students rather than my classmates. I have been engaged in teaching various topics of Judaica at Saint Joseph's University, a Jesuit institution, for nearly fifteen years. During ten of those years, I taught similar courses at Rosemont College, an undergraduate institution operating under the auspices of the Sacred Heart of the Child Jesus religious order. Although the impetus for ethnic studies long ago faded from its peak of the late 1960s-early 1970s, students continue to enroll in these courses, often in greater numbers than is convenient from a selfish pedagogic standpoint. The following analysis is based purely on my own experiences within college classrooms in a Catholic setting. If the results are anecdotal rather than empirical, they underscore a lesson learned from Elie Wiesel; the telling of the story is of primary importance.

I

They walk into the room as students do for any first class of the Winter semester and look for a psychologically positive and comfortable place to sit. The room is one of the largest on the floor but the humidity grows and the air begins to feel close as more than thirty-five men and women enter, select seats, shrug off their coats and wait for me. I watch them as they go in, from the vantagepoint of an office shared by several Theology instructors. As a rule, I arrive early to my classes but, on this opening night of the semester, I deliberately linger at my desk across the hall for a few extra minutes. I want the students to be uncomfortable.

Once I enter the classroom, our first meeting begins in the perfunctory manner, although my introduction to the course may seem relatively lengthy. Following the normative announcements regarding books, writing requirements, office hours and the like, I surprise the students by beginning to interrogate them. "Why are you here?" I ask. "Hasn't anyone warned you that this is meant to be the most difficult course in the university? Do you know that if this is not the most difficult course you take, I will consider myself to have failed?"

The students look at me with curiosity. The majority is white, the progeny of middle and lower middle-class families. While there is an occasional Jewish, Muslim, Buddhist or Hindu student, almost all are Roman Catholic, a significant percentage of whom have matriculated from parochial schools in the Phila-delphia area. Most have never met a rabbi before. (Although I use my academic title in the classroom, I am listed as "Rabbi Libowitz" in the University Course Catalogue and many of the students seem to prefer addressing me by the religious title.) They are also unaccustomed to professors speaking in so discouraging a manner about their own courses and their wonder is apparent; what is he talking about? Is he trying to scare us?

Of course, that is precisely what I want to do, to winnow the chaff from the grain. "This will be the most difficult course you take, not because of the amount or length of the assignments but because of their nature. You will read, hear about and see things that never should have occurred," I warn them. "You will be asked to question the basic nature of humankind and examine the acts of your own Church. You will be required to think of God in a critical manner that is foreign to most of you. Should you persist and complete this course, I can promise that you will have been confronted by many questions, but I cannot guarantee a single answer."

I then tell a story I first heard from Elie Wiesel; "in a *shtetl*, a little village in Poland, there was a man who had a question with no answer. And in another *shtetl*, far away, another man had a question, also without answer. Neither man knew about the other, which was a shame, because the second question was the answer to the first. When you understand that story, you will begin to understand the questions we must ask about the Holocaust."

II

It has been my good fortune to teach at two Catholic schools of higher education since the mid-1980s. At each institution, in different ways, I was able to introduce the study of the Holocaust into the religious studies curriculum. Rosemont College, a women's institution, first engaged me as an adjunct instructor almost fifteen years ago. I was assigned two courses on Judaism, a text course alternating with an historical survey during autumn semesters; from the first, I devoted a unit to the Holocaust within the latter class. Shortly thereafter, I began teaching similar survey courses at Saint Joseph's University, a co-educational Jesuit institution. In the late 1980s, with the enthusiastic support of Joseph Gower, then Chairman of Saint Joseph's Theology Department, I received permission to offer a course on "Jewish and Christian Responses to the Holocaust." The class was offered initially within the University College, our evening division, as a Third Level Theology course and cross-listed as a graduate course in Education. Within a few years, I was asked to alternate the course between the (day) College of Arts and Letters and the University College. By the mid-1990s, student demand led to parallel courses in the day and evening divisions.

III

Although its title indicates an emphasis upon post-Shoah religious writings, the students' near total unfamiliarity with the events of the Holocaust and its victims necessitates that a lengthy portion of the syllabus be devoted to introductory and background materials. In earlier works, I have discussed the development of Holocaust courses within many colleges and universities and identified three categories or phases in the evolution of course offerings.[1] Phase One courses remain the most common variety. These are survey courses, usually historical in nature, which present broad rather than in depth studies of the Holocaust. Phase Two offerings provide a narrowed focus of attention, with concentration upon particular places, events or personages, and present those topics in greater detail than would be possible within the Phase One format. Phase Three courses, which are the most recent additions to the curricula, tend to be less about the Holocaust than to use it as a starting point for broader studies, such as investigations of medical ethics or political responses to genocide.

The Saint Joseph's course was intended to focus upon theological writings and could be considered sufficiently specialized for inclusion within the Phase Two variety, but the need to supply both historical and religious background materials resulted in a course that straddles Phases One and Two. The class makes use of historical, sociological, theological and philosophic texts, articles from a variety of fields and sources, films and guest speakers. The manner of class presentation varies with the given topic or sub-topic and may include lecture, seminar style discussion or student presentations (individual and group). In addition to mid-term and final examinations, each student is responsible for a research project which culminates in an 8-12 page paper or its equivalent (some students have made films or other creative projects to satisfy this requirement). A second writing assignment involves the preparation of a detailed review of a survivor memoir (the authors ranging from Primo Levi to Nehama Tec) selected from an approved list. Students also maintain journals of their reactions to the course (personal responses to the readings, films, conversations in and out of class, etc.) as well as to "outside" Holocaust materials—including newspaper and magazine articles, telecasts, films and theater productions—about which they become far more aware and sensitive during the semester. The journals, while kept confidential, are collected and read twice during the semester; they are not assigned a grade, *per se*, but remain a fundamental requirement of the course. Over the years, in addition to fine tuning the various assignments and requirements, I have revised the syllabus and changed at least one book every year; classes have read numerous texts reviewing the history of the Holocaust, memoirs, scholarly collections, theological studies and creative works, including art, novels, poetry and drama. This practice has served a dual purpose, taking advantage of newer publications while preventing the course from growing stale from repetition.

To prevent reduction of the materials to abstract numbers, place names and dates, students' sensitivities are challenged by audio-visual resources. Like the books, these selections have changed through the years and range from U.S. Army Signal Corps films of concentration camps to Hollywood productions to documentary works; titles include Lanzmann's "Shoah" (selected portions) and Jon Blair's "Schindler," German language films, such as "Triumph of the Will" and "The Tin Drum," and interviews of survivors and rescuers, such as "Courage to Care" and "Weapons of the Spirit."

Each presentation of the course begins with a series of background lectures, intended to provide students with a basic knowledge of the fundamentals of Judaism. These lecture topics include Jewish religious beliefs and practices, texts, the calendar and life cycle. A rapid, if necessarily sketchy, race through the outlines of European Jewish history locates Jewish communities throughout the continent, traces the essential pattern of eastern settlement following a series of expulsions from the west, takes notice of the uneven and often uneasy relationship between Jews and Christians—on both individual and institutional bases—and establishes the conditions of Jewish life at the dawn of the "modern" age.

The pace begins to slow with entrance into the late eighteenth century with its twin phenomena of European Enlightenment and Jewish Emancipation. Jewish responses to the new possibilities of freedom and acceptance are reviewed, including a change in demographics (a return to western Europe as well as increased emigration to the United States), the beginnings of the Reform movement in Jewish religion and the development of both Neo-Orthodoxy and Conservatism in response to Reform. The final decades of the nineteenth century carried with them another popular movement, racial antisemitism, which the class examines in both its American social form and the European political version with its epicenter in Vienna, the city where Adolf Hitler claimed to have learned his antisemitism.

Entering the twentieth century, the discussion highlights the situation in Germany immediately before, during and after the first World War. The Treaty of Versailles is reviewed in detail, followed by a look at the Weimar Republic that attempted to govern Germany under the restrictions of that treaty. The creative nature of life in Weimar is compared to that of the United States in the "Roaring Twenties," with the latter's restrictions on immigration, Prohibition, bans against the teaching of Darwin's theory of Evolution and the revival of the Ku Klux Klan. The erosion of living conditions due to the economic strictures of the Treaty of Versailles resulted in hyperinflation which, along with the massive unemployment of the Depression, paved the way for the entry of Adolf Hitler into the government in 1933. The class examines the life and rise of Hitler and the Nazi Party, with an eye to the development of the party ideology, its growth in popularity and strength.

IV

Scholars differ in their belief when the Holocaust may be said to have begun. Some date it from the Wannsee Conference (1942), others from the invasion of Poland (1939); still others push back the date to Kristallnacht (1938), while the most radical place the start at Hitler's entry into the government in January, 1933.

Tracing this path to genocide, the class reviews the development of anti-Jewish legislation, increasing efforts to leave Germany and focuses on the events of 1938, including the *Anschluss*, the Evian Conference on Refugees and Kristallnacht. Isolated and abandoned by the world, European Jewry entered 1939 and the beginning of the war and mass murder.

It has long been my belief that we make a serious error when we entrust the Holocaust solely to the historians or attempt to teach about the subject in terms of data transfer and memorization. By presenting students with a course laden with dates, names and numbers, we imply that the Holocaust may be quantified and thereby reduced to a set of tables and statistics. In so doing, students come to understand their task as the memorization of the dates, learning of the numbers, and the gaining of facility with the jargon. Left to these devices, students will never have to confront the Shoah as a whole, an act of monstrous evil, a reality that Arthur A. Cohen referred to as "the tremendum." Their tone will be one of detachment and lack any sense of awe and foreboding.

Having said this, I do not include myself among those individuals at the other extreme, who say the Holocaust is so utterly different from the normative events of human experience that it can never be understood but must be regarded with mystical awe. They are guilty of an emotional deconstruction of the events which serves, whether intentionally or otherwise, to justify the helpless attitude with which the Nazis' victims faced their plight. After all, if the dilemma they faced was not only unprecedented but also absolutely unique in human history how could anyone have been expected to combat it? One might even argue that the victims' deaths are, in this way, "justified" because of their defenselessness against an inhuman onslaught. My concern is that in placing the Holocaust ultimately beyond description we encapsulate it—and ourselves—from a full confrontation with its reality. Just as it would have been impossible for the victims to do anything, so it becomes impossible for the investigators to learn much. So why bother?

This attitude is far different from that expressed by Cohen, Wiesel and others, that we may never find answers to all of our questions or that (at least in a mystical sense) many of our questions will be answered either "No" or with silence, but such responses do not negate and, I would argue, further demand the investigational process. The study of the Holocaust is as much about questions as answers; therefore, students must be encouraged:

1) To ask questions
2) To ask the right questions
3) To accept additional questions as answers.

One of the areas subject to criticism within a traditional Roman Catholic education has been the limited tolerance of questioning and variation in religious matters. It has been my experience that many of my students were raised in a catechetical tradition which controls the range and nature of theological questions and limits the answers within a set of sanctioned responses. Dissent in matters of faith is discouraged, while faithful defense and maintenance of the mysteries of the Church is lauded. Part of my task is to encourage students to question matters and areas they are not accustomed to or comfortable challenging, without seeming to be anti-Christian in general or anti-Catholic in particular.

As the class enters the Kingdom of Night itself, reading becomes secondary in significance to visualization of the story. For this, I rely upon a series of films, beginning with Alain Resnais' "Night and Fog." Resnais' universalizing agenda, leading to the omission of the word "Jew" from both the French narration and the English sub-titles, is disturbing and can be misleading but the starkness of his camera (and the brevity of the work) begins to provide students with a sense of place.

The United States Army Signal Corps, under the direction of Hollywood director George Stevens, filmed Allied discoveries in a series of camps and hospitals. Available commercially as "Nazi Concentration Camps," it is an unrelenting 60 minutes of graphic witness to atrocities. Although the quality of the film stock is poor by today's standards, students stare in silence, turn their heads away then turn back again, to view torture equipment and the scars marking the survivors, buildings filled with rotting bodies, exhumations and mass burials, the sight of Generals Eisenhower, Bradley and Patton looking on sternly, as townspeople are forced to view the remains of events about which they had claimed complete ignorance.

For many students, the ultimate scenes involve the liberation and clean-up of Bergen-Belsen, by its British Army liberators. The officer in charge, after declaring conditions to be "beyond description," announced with typical understatement that each soldier was doing his bit and things were now getting organized. Because typhus was racing through the camp, the British finally used bulldozers to push many of the corpses into their mass graves. It is not unusual to have a student leave the room at this point. Many faces are streaked by tears. For me, one of the most memorable scenes involves the interrogation of the chief doctor at the Hadamar "sanitarium," site of at least 20,000 "mercy killings." The expression on the face of the American officer conducting the questioning is one of total contempt as he orders the guards to remove the prisoner.

When the scenes of horror are done, the class reads of attempts to rebuild a shattered world. During the first months after the war, many thousands of Jews wandered the face of Europe looking like the ghosts they seemed to have become, some unwilling to return to empty homes, others unwanted in the places where they had once lived "normal" lives. Eventually many found themselves in Displaced Persons camps, either because they had nowhere else to go or because the British had captured them as they sought refuge in Palestine ("*Aliya Bet*"). Zionism, in 1945-47, was a nationalist movement divided by many philosophies—including Political, Spiritual, Religious and Revisionist. In the immediate post-war years, while political negotiations with Great Britain and the United Nations continued, efforts were made to bring the survivors to Mandate Palestine. Emissaries and agents were sent to the DP camps to teach, serve as doctors and nurses, and prepare people for new lives in the traditional Jewish homeland. Students react with shock and anger at stories of survivors—including members of my own extended family—being kept under guard by British troops in former concentration camps until 1948, when the independence of Israel caused the gates to be thrown open.

Physical rescue and resettlement having begun, the syllabus turns, at last, to theology, beginning an examination of Jewish and Christian writers, who have sought *sophia* for the unknowable. Any discussion of the Jewish effort to comprehend—if not to rationalize—the murder of two-thirds of European Jewry must begin with Richard Rubenstein. Reading from *After Auschwitz*, students wrestle with Rubenstein's insistence upon the death of the traditional God-idea (omniscient, omnipotent, omnipresent, loving) and his conclusion that the universe is a vast, cold, lonely and uncaring place. From Rubenstein, the class turns to Emil Fackenheim, listens for the "commanding Voice" of Auschwitz and contemplates the "614th" commandment, "Thou shalt not permit Hitler a posthumous victory." Other voices are heard as well; Irving Greenberg and Eleazar Berkovits, among others.

When the class begins to read Christian theologians, they discern a new set of questions, which deal less with the victims than with their killers and the bystanders who permitted it. Paul van Buren, Franklin H. Littell, Darryl Fasching, Clark Williamson and Harry James Cargas are among the authors, representing a wide range of liberal and conservative denominations, who want to know how this could have happened in the heart of what was once known as "Christendom," at the hands of men and women who were baptized Christians.

Without question, this is the most sensitive portion of the curriculum and can require the most careful management of class discussions. Despite the strenuous efforts of a myriad of scholars, educators, religious leaders and others over the past twenty years, there are many people who continue to view the Holocaust as, in its essence, a Jewish issue and a Jewish problem. One of the ongoing educational tasks we face is to convince people that the Holocaust was an event of *universal* significance, despite its focus having been upon *particular* groups. Fifty years after the gas chambers were destroyed, the Shoah remains a watershed event for Jews and Christians alike, raising questions critical for both groups' self-understanding. However, the challenges and questions differ for each group. Elie Wiesel has said, "For Jews, the questions are about the victims. For Christians, the questions are about the killers." As a non-Christian, lacking the *bona fides* of membership within the religious group being placed under a theological and moral microscope, I think it important to withhold my personal opinions from the conversations (a caution that is noticeably absent in my critiques of Jewish authors).

From a personal and educational perspective, it is desirable that the critics of Christianity and its failures during the Holocaust be themselves members of the faith in question, representatives of both liberal and conservative denominations and able to declare "we," rather than "you." This desideratum becomes even more important when attention is on the Roman Catholic Church. The public silence of Pope Pius XII remains a flashpoint issue, yet it is one of the most frequently selected topics for students' research papers. To avoid any possible accusations of anti-Catholic bias and to prevent the students from withdrawing into an "us versus them" shell, every effort is made to utilize materials prepared by Catholic authors, including John Morley, the American Jesuit who was the first scholar permitted access to the Vatican archives of the period, and that Catholic author who refers to himself as a "post-Auschwitz Christian," Harry James Cargas.

One result of this effort is to allow students to draw their own conclusions from the historical records. If the questions are raised and the accusative fingers pointed by class members, the flow of the subsequent discussions can be controlled without any appearance of a negative agenda on the part of the professor.

Whenever possible, the course concludes with a special guest speaker, a Survivor. Year after year, students list this session—the opportunity to listen to and question one who was there—the highpoint of the semester.

Approximately four hundred Saint Joseph's University students have studied these aspects of the Shoah with me over the last decade, a period during which the classroom populace has undergone a transition from second to third generation since the Holocaust. I no longer ask students to inquire of their parents, uncles or aunts about the second World War and what they knew or experienced; more than half a century removed from the events, it is their grandparents' generation to whom students must turn for personal information. Within this same decade, the development of Holocaust resources has become an industry; the annual production of scholarly and popular materials causes one to be hard pressed to keep track of new publications, films, CDs and WEB sites, let alone be thoroughly familiar with them. In spite of this new wealth of resources, and the inclusion of Holocaust study within the mandated curricula of a growing number of states, I have found only a marginal increase in *a priori* knowledge among the students in my courses. Many have read Elie Wiesel's memoir, *Night*, often as a high school assignment. Curiously, fewer have read the *Diary* of Anne Frank than was the case ten years ago. A growing number of students from the east coast have visited the United States Holocaust Memorial Museum in Washington, and that experience has proven most significant. Perhaps it must be said, when all the book learning is placed in one scale, a first-hand experience remains the most effective teaching/learning technique. The long-range effects of this intense exposure are measured in behaviors and attitudes passed to the next generation and elude the statisticians. Hate is a learned behavior; so, too, is respect.

THE ROLE OF THE UNIVERSITY
IN RETHINKING ISSUES OF SOCIAL JUSTICE
Marcia Sachs Littell

My first meeting with Harry James Cargas was in 1980. He was one of the featured speakers at a Yom HaShoah Program at the University of North Carolina in Charlotte. It was one of those rare encounters one is privileged to have in a lifetime. Within minutes we had an immediate bonding and sharing of interests and concerns. It was as if we had known each other always and had been conversing everyday. I was moved by his courage as a "Post-Auschwitz Christian" and the brave way in which he has been attempting to get his own church to face the necessary issues regarding the Holocaust. At the same time, he never wavered from his faith and commitment to his religion. Most of all, I was impressed by such a well balanced human being—a first-rate scholar, brave thinker and magnificent writer with a wonderful sense of humor who was also a basketball coach and sports enthusiast.

One of the pressing issues dominating the life of Harry James Cargas has been the question of Social Justice and the Quest for World Peace. Our conversations often move to the relevance of morality and ethics within the campus ministry and the role and responsibility of higher education in such matters.

Even though we have been spared the threat of another World War with the disappearance of the U.S.S.R., the years of our friendship have been scarred by on-going conflicts around the world—in Uganda, Kuwait, Rwanda, Bosnia and Herzegovina and, as this article is submitted, we have been on the verge of yet another war with Saddam Hussein in Iraq.

We come to realize more than we like that the lessons of history are yet to be learned. Much of our fate, as well as the future of our children and grandchildren, rests in the hands of the Generals and the men of the universities who created the modern engines of war. We are vulnerable. We are all, some would say, gamblers seated around a roulette table.

Is this then the point to which the churches and the modern university have brought us? Are we truly in a game of chance? Are there lessons from our past which give some signals, at least a little light to guide our feet? Our thoughts naturally turn to World War II and the encounter with another dictator and his screaming, bloodthirsty followers.

What have we learned? Fifty-three years have passed since the death camps of Nazi Germany were liberated. Since that time, those most deeply involved in the study of the Holocaust—in which study of the conduct and misconduct of the churches and their leaders is an important aspect—have become increasingly aware that not only the pathological event must be studied but also the implications for the present and future must be drawn. We not only tell the brute facts of the Holocaust: we also claim to point out its lessons.

As people of religion and also as people of the campus we are confronted by the Holocaust in painful ways. The more we examine the Holocaust the more we see how the church leadership failed the people. And we see how the products of the modern university, the alumni of the great universities of the Weimar Republic, the graduates of an institution once referred to as *universitas fidelium*, served an evil cause and even conceived evil programs. The professors operated the great engines that turned out thousands of competent technicians whose morals, ethics and commitment to human life were not a notable part of the record. These were modern men—of the university, of science, of high technology. They were governed by the premise that whatever *could* be done—*would* be done.

Professionals did more than cooperate with the Reich. Architects, engineers and chemists did the research required to build the Death Camps and make them efficient. University professors of philosophy, history and biology did the necessary theorizing to make Nazism appear legitimate. They revised biological theory to justify human breeding camps, enslavement and mass murder. Attorneys found legal precedents to justify monstrous crimes. Professionals like Josef Mengele, a man with two doctorates (a Ph.D. and an MD) who performed diabolical experiments on helpless human guinea pigs, symbolize the learned form human evil can take in modern society.

Mengele and professionals like him were not the products of Nazi-run universities, but of institutions widely regarded as among the best in the world. It was the pre-Nazi universities of the 1920s that failed to infuse ethics and humanity into their graduates but, instead, produced masses of technically competent barbarians.

The question for those concerned with peace and justice, with the dignity and integrity of the human person, is this: What have we learned from this watershed event in Western Civilization? Are our modern universities in 1998 doing a better job in preparing doctors, lawyers, business executives, scientists, theologians and teachers with a more sensitized understanding of the value of the human person, with a deeper commitment to life? Do our skilled scientists and nuclear physicists have a commitment to maintain the highest level of morals and ethics, a commitment to social justice that equals their devotion to technical proficiency?

In seeking some of these answers relating to the modern university, I turned to a former best seller, a book written by the Dean of the Faculty of Arts and Sciences of Harvard University: *The University: An Owner's Manual.* Dean Henry Rosovsky reviews the mores and mission of America's colleges and universities. He directs a special message to each of its "owners." Among these "owners" he includes students and their families, alumni, faculty, donors and trustees.

In discussing the role of the university and academic governance, Dean Rosovsky takes the view that only limited subjects are of concern to university administrators and professors; namely, "what do we teach, whom do we admit, how do we select professors, how do we govern ourselves and determine tenure procedures...." These Dean Rosovsky considers the fundamental issues. He declares that these are "for universities, the true, difficult, and timeless questions. They never go away." He is clearly able—in his manual—to segregate his moral and ethical accents from his responsibilities as a citizen.

Rosovsky says he does not believe that education can solve the problems of social justice or rectify "social ills." He relegates issues of general "social justice" to the category of "external relations" (community relations), which he does not think to be a major concern to the university "owners." The impingement of social issues on the university, he states, lie within the jurisdiction of the college presidents. Too many of us, he states, tend to confuse good education with good character. "The relation between character and education is weak." Finally, he concludes, "the university can produce new knowledge, teach professional skills, and the liberal arts. We cannot alone eradicate racism, poverty, the use of drugs." He does however spend a bit of printed space on faculty relations with students (including sexual harassment), strongly advising faculty and administrators how to stay out of trouble. We cannot, he says, "be a paradise island in a sea of discontent." Thus, according to the Dean of Arts and Sciences at Harvard University, "we train students in the state of the art while attempting with all energy to change the frontiers of that state." His perspective, as winsome as it is in some respects, is introspective, insular and clannish. In sum, the Dean of Harvard College takes the same position as the German intellectuals before Hitler came to power, namely that the university itself and its professors are *above politics.*

The modern university is **not** above politics and never has been. The modern university has a very definite role in relation to matters of social responsibility. It created the structures of western civilization and advanced industrial society. It also created the Holocaust and the war machines that now propel both sides in the Persian Gulf. Until the rise of the modern university the dominant elements were—in something called "Christendom"—invested in the clergy. Not so today; the stealth bomber, chemical weapons and nuclear fission are products of the modern university.

In attempting to understand Nazism, to explain Hitler's rise to power, to measure the responsibility of a literate people for the devastation wrought by the German Third Reich, we continue to ask, "How was it possible?"

It would be easy for us to understand if Germany had been a nation of ignorant, superstitious, illiterate savages. But with a nation where learning and culture were so greatly acclaimed, it seems beyond comprehension how people could have stood by and watched their country slide into a killing program of such magnitude.

Many people want to think Nazism was an outbreak of irrationality. To the contrary; the tragedy is that the programs of the Third Reich expressed rational purposes, however perverse. The killing centers were, like their inventors, products of what had been for generations one of the best systems in the world for training and honing the life of the mind. Himmler was always proud of the high percentage of Ph.D.s in his officer corps. He warned his men against yielding to the human touch, praising the *eiskalt* quality of a cold-blooded and "objective" performance of their task. Out of the 14 department heads whom Reinhard Heydrich gathered at the Wannsee Conference (January, 1942) to plan an efficient operation of the "Final Solution," eleven had doctorates. It is fair to say that without the cooperation of the educated professional elites, the Nazi regime could not have gained power, ruled the Continent for a time, and threatened the entire western world.

Thinking themselves to be "above politics," the German professors created an environment within the universities that promoted conformity, passivity and a contempt for democratic political action. At the same time, they opened the minds and hearts of their students to the nationalism and romanticism that flowed into Nazism.

Some historians have sought to explain Nazism by the economic depression, by a psychological predisposition to submission to authority on the part of the German nation, or by the power vacuum created by the Kaiser's abdication. While all of these factors are relevant, one must keep in mind two major negatives pointed out by Professor Franklin Littell in his book *The Crucifixion of the Jews* (1975). Littell demonstrates the failure of the church leadership to take a strong stand against Nazi idolatry, a capitulation that permitted the killing machine to function.

To this "credibility crisis of Christianity" was added a second: the moral failure of the modern university, with the resulting "credibility crisis" for higher learning and its chief representatives. The credibility crisis of Christianity is of course a problem for Christians. The credibility crisis of the modern university is something that calls for the attention of Christians, Jews and all others of conscience.

Dr. Alice Gallin, within her doctoral study at Catholic University, also illuminates the latter theme, the "credibility crisis of the modern university." She has added to the mounting evidence indicting the German professors as facilitators of the emergence of the Third Reich.

We have stressed the German crisis, but all of Europe was affected. As early as 1926, writing in France, Julien Benda pointed out in *The Treason of the Intellectuals* that the professors were betraying their calling. Benda thought the intellectuals should maintain truth against transitory fads and keep to the high standards of civilized society. Instead, he warned, the intellectuals of the 20th century had lost their moorings and were in tow to political and economic forces. He detailed in his book how the educated elite abandoned cultural leadership in the West, allowing an atmosphere of ethical and intellectual relativism to justify their retreat into their own professional concerns.

During the height of American concern over the role of the university in public policy in the late 1960's, Benda's book was reissued here in popular form (1969) in New York. Examination of Weimar Germany was being used to explore Post-World War II America. The topic still torments us.

The historical study of pre-Nazi universities in Germany has continued to be a major theme for those re-thinking our value systems. Immediately following World War II, in 1946 under the imprint of the Yiddish Scientific Institute (YIVO), Max Weinrich pointed out in *Hitler's Professors: The Part of Scholarship in Germany's Crimes Against The Jewish People*, how the intellectuals had made themselves technicians rather than persons of wisdom. They accommodated to the spirit of the times and the demands of the Nazi movement. Professor Weinrich dealt in specifics, including the evil actions of certain named professors, among them Nobel Laureates.

Almost twenty years after Weinrich, George Mosse also conducted a study of the intellectual problems and failures that allowed such cooperation between university leadership and genocide: *The Crisis of German Ideology: The Intellectual Origins of the Third Reich.*

We earlier mentioned Alice Gallin's published study, *Midwives to Nazism: University Professors in Weimar Germany, 1925-1933.* She investigates the role of the professors in preparing the way for the Nazi Third Reich, likening their function to that of a midwife. The midwife, with her special skills and training, facilitates the birth of a child and assists the parents at the crucial moment when the new being is ushered into the world. The midwife, of course, never is held responsible for the conception nor for how the child turns out later in life.

Alan Beyerchen showed how this same procedure worked with scientists: *Scientists Under Hitler* (New Haven, Yale University Press, 1977). Beyerchen showed that the vast majority of scientists were neither pro-Nazi nor anti-Nazi: they simply wanted to be allowed to practice their trade undisturbed, "above politics." The few who opposed the regime resigned—for example Einstein, Franck, Haber and Stern. Their resignations served the Nazi purpose of removing all opponents.

G. W. Blackburn showed that while the Nazis were not particularly interested in academic course content, they were involved in a massive re-education effort to control the minds of the youth of the New Germany. Teachers caved in to simplified heroic legends and all-or-nothing comparisons. Marxism and Christianity were both presented as enemies—ideological and spiritual—and the past was manipulated to support Nazi racial theories. (*Education in the Third Reich*, Albany, S.U.N.Y. Press, 1984). Blackburn built on an earlier work by Werner Richter (*Re-Educating Germany*, University of Chicago Press, 1945). Richter detailed the collapse of the education system. He showed that the Nazis were easily able to manipulate teachers because the teachers in the common schools were trained solely as technicians, with the emphasis on methods rather than cultural content. They were pleased to have their position enhanced, to the disadvantage of the university elites whom they envied. In *The German Phoenix* (1960), Franklin Littell showed how the post war re-education of all of the German professions was invariably a matter of restoring the balance of ethical and cultural content over against mere technical competence.

Robert Lifton's *The Nazi Doctors: Medical Killings and the Psychology of Genocide* (New York, Basic Books, 1986) depicts the psychological power of the accoutrements of science and medicine in creating a submission to sterility and uniformity, thus providing authoritative support for genocide. New research done in Germany by Benno Mueller-Hill presents the same process at work in pre-Nazi and Nazi Psychiatry.

These studies of the ways in which various professions failed to stop the Nazi regime and then served it loyally all spotlight the conditions in the modern university and the collapse of professional ethics. The professors turned their backs on the social contract theory and other Western understandings of the relationship between a people and its government. The academics joined the masses in approving a notion of *Volkstum* (race, nationality, peoplehood) that preceded and transcended the state, an idea rooted not in geographic or political boundaries, not in constitutions but in blood, soil and *Volk*.

Most German professors believed that academia and politics could be divorced. Yet they represented a powerful political factor, whether they recognized it or not. Their retention of nationalistic and monarchical views and their failure to support the republic opened the way to the Nazi alternative.

A clear example of this is evident in the report of an interview with Albert Speer in his home in Heidelberg, after he had served 20 years in Spandau prison. In reflecting upon his actions during the Third Reich, Speer makes it amazingly clear how as an educated man he was able to compartmentalize his mind.

At Nuremberg, he took "full responsibility" for crimes against the Jews. Yet it remains evident that the German university that trained him failed to provide its student with the ability to think critically and to ask the proper questions in the political sphere. We will not even hint at any effort to form a fully integrated human being—committed to the soul as well as the mind.

The university as such, disloyal to republican principles but not vigorously formative of persons of ethical and professional discipline, could not produce resistance to Nazism. There was one bright incident in the record of the universities during the Hitler period, but it came from students. Hans and Sophie Scholl took their stand against Nazism from lessons learned from their parents. Their parents had imbued in them a strong sense of right and wrong, along with the courage and strength to take action. Unfortunately these were not qualities to be learned from their professors. The one exception was their friend, professor and fellow martyr, Dr. Huber—a rare bird in the professorial ranks.

German professors clung to outmoded patterns of thought and action, perpetuating myths of *Volk* that undermined liberty and pluralism. Like Albert Speer, they never fully understood the role they played in bringing the Third Reich into being. Unlike Speer, most of them never admitted their complicity, even in retrospect.

Among the professionals and intellectuals who did not go into exile, a few theologians were able to mount the most effective and active opposition to Nazi doctrine and practice. Protestants in particular were more likely to be able to maintain control over symbols, ideology, professional identification and community organization. This is seen in *The German Church Struggle and the Holocaust* (Wayne State University Press, 1974) and in Robert Ericksen's *Theologians Under Hitler* (1986). Yet among the theologians the opposition was limited to a few individuals and a comparatively small number of parishes. Eberhard Bethge's biography of Dietrich Bonhoeffer, and the 1990 release by Burton Nelson and Geffrey Kelly—*A Testament To Freedom*—discuss Bonhoeffer's writings and ethical position and the failure of ranking Christian theologians to oppose the Nazis on ethical grounds. Bonhoeffer himself was a martyr. Wolfgang Gerlach indicates in his analysis (*The Cross and the Swastika*) that by 1933 it was clear that organized Christian resistance would follow Karl Barth, who stressed dogmatic rather than ethical opposition to Nazism. Thus, by ignoring Bonhoeffer's ethical position, the question of the treatment of the Jews and others consigned to concentration and death camps was relegated to secondary importance even by concerned Christians.

The lessons of the Nazi period have taught us that the university must serve as a model. The university **is not** above politics and is unable to escape modern society and its problems. It must serve as a model of higher ethics and of higher morality. The university cannot preach social justice unless it practices that virtue within its own ranks. A campus may provide a forum for public policy. But the most effective method of teaching within the modern university is through its actions.

The modern university has a clear and definite responsibility to confront the Holocaust—the bitter fruit of its perversion and the corruption of its elite— and to provide a worthy model of human relations. Regardless of what the school catalogs say about the institution's devotion to values, republican principles and democratic politics, regardless of what the professors and administrators say about "objective" scholarship, most of the universities today in America are doing what the modern university has always done: producing technicians for the market place.

Is that enough? Does the record validate that limited achievement? Can we, so soon after Auschwitz, relegate study of the Holocaust to "Jewish Studies" and bury the fundamental lessons of that event?

I would like to leave you with a challenge to change, a challenge well expressed in some words of Reinhold Niebuhr: "Nothing that is worth doing can be achieved in a lifetime; therefore we must be saved by hope. Nothing which is true or beautiful or good makes complete sense in any immediate context of history; therefore we must be saved by faith. Nothing we do, however virtuous, can be accomplished alone. Therefore we are saved by love."

ON THE CITY WHICH NOURISHED US
Reminiscences and Reflections
Hubert Locke

This small tribute to a dear friend departs from the customary festschrift essay in which colleagues, who usually share the same discipline with the honoree, prepare and present an article that reflects their scholarly expertise in the honoree's field. Harry James Cargas and I do not work in the same discipline, although we share a long-time common interest in studies regarding the destruction of European Jewry during the era of the German Third Reich. Over the course of our friendship, we discovered we also share an added bond; although we did not know each other at the time, we spent our formative years in the same city and both took our first graduate degree at the state university, forty miles away, which we attended a year apart.

As a testimonial to Harry James, I wish to offer some reflections on the urban community that nourished us both, in an era in which strong ethnic and racial neighborhoods in American cities served both to give one a sense of one's own identity as well as the incentive to establish close bonds and relationships—personal and intellectual—which transcended one's ethnic or racial roots. It is our common, although unconnected, experience in Detroit—at one time the Motor Capital of the world and during the years of our youth the Arsenal of Democracy—that I strongly suspect has brought both Harry James and I in our adult years to our preoccupation with the destruction of the Jewish communities and most of their inhabitants in Europe, and especially with the records of our respective religious faiths as they confronted that great horror.

Harry James and I are both Detroiters but, for the sake of accuracy, Harry James grew up in Hamtramck, a small municipality which is completely surrounded by Detroit and which, at one time, was reputed to have one of the largest Polish populaces of any city in the United States. Hamtramck was a cornucopia of Polish culture, with its Catholic churches where Polish was spoken for Saturday confessions and Sunday sermons at the Masses, where Polish bakeries and butcher shops abounded on virtually every commercial block, with a Polish language newspaper and Polish social clubs and countless other manifestations of Polish life and culture in abundance. Curiously, Black people lived throughout Hamtramck, in much smaller numbers but side by side with their Polish neighbors.

I grew up less than four miles away, in what was then one of four areas of the city in which Black Detroiters lived. In legal terms and by city tradition, my neighborhood was a ghetto; prior to the 1948 decision of the U. S. Supreme Court, it was one of the four areas of Detroit in which Black citizens could but homes. But the terms "ghetto" risks conveying the wrong imagery or impression, since today it is used—or misused—as if it were a synonym for slum. My West Side Detroit neighborhood was one of well-kept homes and clean streets; it was as culturally rich a Black community as was Harry James' Polish Hamtramck. We, too, had our churches and social clubs and barber and beauty shops—the functional equivalents of the general store in villages and small towns—where gossip was exchanged, newcomers to the community scrutinized, and politics and community issues discussed and debated. Our neighborhood, together with the other three Black areas, were served by two—and, at one time, three—Black newspapers; there were Black labor, political, and cultural organizations in abundance.

Geographically midway between my neighborhood and Harry James' Hamtramck was Detroit's Jewish community with its commercial thoroughfare on the street that, in 1967, would be the flash point for the city's tragic riot. But like Hamtramck with its Black populace, the Jewish community was largely but not exclusively Jewish; a large Catholic parish, an Episcopal church and several other sizeable Protestants congregations were well within its precincts. Their existence reflected an element of diversity even in the city's tightly-knit Jewish community.

There is, I believe, an important clue in these strong—if, in some cases, involuntarily created—racial and ethnic communities which somehow managed to adjust to and accommodate "outsiders" in their midst. Detroit was far from a racial utopia in the period in which Harry James and I grew up there. It was, in fact, frequently depicted as the most "Southern" city in the North, a charac-teristic derived in no small measure from the vast numbers of White, as well as Black, Southerners who migrated to the city during the periods of industrial expansion and particularly during the war years. It was also a label that described the city's racial climate and practices.

But unless one resided in one of the wealthy suburbs to the east or the far north of the city—and in the 1930s and '40s not only were these areas off-limits to Black residents but also to most Poles and Jews as well—it was virtually impossible not to encounter and thereby be obliged to come to terms with others who were outside the orbit of one's racial or ethnic kin.

The public schools in Detroit—perhaps unwittingly—reinforced both the development of strong ethnic and racial identities as well as the tendency to reach beyond the limitations these barriers, if taken too seriously, might impose. At the elementary level, the schools conformed to the segregated hous-ing patterns, enhanced by some racial gerrymandering of the school district's own making. In my neighborhood, therefore, the elementary was an extension and reflection of the community itself (with the curious exception of some White youngsters who lived in a church-operated orphanage opposite the school and who kept very much to themselves). Day in and day out, Black youngsters went to school and played in a neighborhood which gave us a sense of place and security within its borders.

At the high school level, at least on the West Side of the city, the rigid restrictions of racial separation broke down. My high school was almost evenly divided between Black and White students, with a large number of the latter being Jewish. When we entered college, either the city university in Detroit's midtown or, for the "brains" among us, the University of Michigan forty miles away (where Harry James went), experiences of racial or ethnic exclusivity broke down entirely, unless one deliberately chose to maintain them. But they disintegrated for young people who had a fairly healthy sense of their own individual heritage and thus, without obliging us to abandon our "roots," gave us access to a far wider range of opportunities and experiences than we might otherwise have enjoyed.

In much of the foregoing, there is nothing unique to Detroit. The experiences of a White lad of Greek-Polish extraction and of his Black counterpart whose parents hailed from the South and the Midwest were echoed in the lives of other African-American and Caucasian youths as well, in the decades prior to and during World War II in the industrial cities of the American North. These cities performed the functions that cities have managed, with varying degrees of success, throughout history: accepting, accommodating and adjusting migrants in their midst to a more urbane, cosmopolitan existence.

American cities proved to be particularly adept at this process and managed to do so not with virtually homogeneous populaces—as was the case in most European cities until recent times—but with large numbers of ethnically and racially diverse groups. The history of most American cities in the Midwest, in fact, can be written as the stories of ethnic and racial enclaves which absorbed and transformed migrants from the Old World and the American South to the urban North. In the inter-war years, those enclaves served to strengthen and reinforce strong ethnic and racial identities on the part of their inhabitants, often as much as a consequence of external hostility as internal cohesion. In the post-war period, access and exposure to other urban institutions and processes—the university, expanding opportunities in the workplace—began slowly to break through the insularity of the city's enclaves, just as they were also beginning to be replaced by the ersatz cities of suburbia.

Even in their most isolated periods, the enclaves of Detroit did not comprise a single ethnic or racial group. Black residents lived among the Poles of Hamtramck, Protestants and Catholics lived in the Jewish neighborhoods along 12th Street and Linwood, even Whites—likely those too poor to move elsewhere—could be found in the city's Black neighborhoods. It was a residential pattern found in other cities also; the sociologist Gerald Suttles, in his study of Chicago, notes that very few of what he terms "defended neighborhoods" (those in which residents attempted to seal themselves off "through the efforts of delinquent gangs, by restrictive covenants, by sharp boundaries, or by a forbidding reputation") were totally successful in doing so. "Very few of the defended neighborhoods in Chicago seem now to have been exclusively or almost exclusively occupied by a single ethnic group."[1]

These neighborhoods, Suttles argues, create "a new mosaic in the city which crosscuts rather than reflects only those distinctions already present in such items as race, ethnicity, income and social background. In this sense, the defended neighborhood is a social reality in its own right because it provides an additional basis for social differentiation and social cohesion."[2] This "cross cutting" process was much in evidence in the Detroit of Harry James' and my youth. By no means did it effect a large percentage of the Black populace, either in Detroit or elsewhere, but by breaking down and apportioning large ethnic and racial blocs on a more manageable scale in which one group might be dominant but not predominate, some neighborhoods of northern cities—augmented by the city's public institutions—forced, however reluctantly, insular racial and ethnic pockets to come to terms with the cultural, religious, and social realities of other groups and with the fact that they were not the sole proprietors of the city or its precincts.

Not every northern city and its residents, of course, underwent this metamorphosis. The Bridgeport neighborhood where Richard Daley, longtime mayor of Chicago, was born and died, has long remained a balkanized outpost of White ethnics in that city. South Boston fought, literally at times, efforts to racially integrate its schools, long after most of the South had succumbed to this inevitability. Nor was this cross-cutting process normative, by any stretch of the imagination. Large swaths of the urban Black populace remained quite unaffected by its dynamics. But where it did occur and for those of us who were its beneficiaries, the effects were life-transforming.

It was easier for young urban dwellers such as Harry James and I to adjust to this cosmopolitizing process than for our parents and many of our peers, We had the advantages not only of youth but also the liberalizing instincts of college life, and of what was perhaps the unique benefits of an era in which the nation was going through a cycle of self-confidence and optimism. America with her allies had just been victorious over the worst nation-state experience in unbridled racism in modern history. Our parents had partaken in the economic boom that the war against the Axis powers made possible. We were able to go off to college full of ourselves and the possibilities for helping to bring about a better society and world.

While we did not realize it at the time, this tendency of the city toward the cosmopolitan and the humane was already beginning to break down as the growth of suburbs exploded on the urban landscape in the post-World War II era. White residents began to abandon the industrial cities in droves and Black residents became their principal inhabitants. The resultant polarization of city and suburb along Black-White lines, rather than the admittedly sometimes tense but essentially effective set of interactions which the structure and processes of our old neighborhoods forced us to undergo, has produced an urban malaise in contemporary America that is the despair of nearly everyone except the politicians who decry it the most and who benefit immensely in the process. For those of us who remember the industrial American city in happier times, it is an especially sad development.

If Detroit was not an exception to the norm of the industrial city in mid-America in the inter-war period, it was unique in several respects.

Perhaps the most important was the fact that Detroit was a labor town in a period in which organized labor was one of the most powerful influences in American society. Detroit was heavily influenced by the presence of the United Automobile Workers union, which had its national headquarters on the near-East Side of the city. The unremitting harshness of life in the automobile factories was ameliorated, in part, by the wage gains, job security, and the benefits—health care, disability pay, paid vacations, sick leave and pensions—which the UAW secured for its members. Between the automotive companies and the union, it became possible for unskilled workers to buy homes and cars, to send their children to college or, at least, not require their immediate employment after high school to help supplement the family income, and thereby to take the critical steps necessary to enter the American middle class.

Although it was much longer in occurring, the UAW and the rise of several Black labor organizations came to have a decided impact on the racial politics of Detroit. By the early 1960s, an era of political liberalism became the order of the day. It came too late to avert the calamity that befell Detroit in the summer of 1967 but it reflected a deliberate, if belated, attempt to reverse Detroit's reputation as the most southern of northern cities in America.

Detroit also had a strong and very powerful Jewish community—large enough to have a secure sense of its place in the life of the city and, following the tradition of Jewish communities across the nation, thoroughly committed to issues of social justice. Its core was composed of German Jews who became, as they did in cities across America, the elite of a community which, after the turn of the present century, was heavily dominated by Jews from Eastern Europe. The German Jews in Detroit espoused strong assimilationist views; they sought to be "an integral, undistinguishable—if distinguished—part of the greater secular society."[3] The second and third generation of eastern European Jews followed this same trend so that the prominence of Jews in Detroit's business, civic and political life was a notable feature of the city.

Detroit has been termed, in a recent publication, a "city of contradictions" and nowhere is this more the case than in its racial ethos. This is yet another of its unique features. If it was a city in which its Jewish citizens rose to positions of prominence and influence, it could be said also that "few cities have matched Detroit for venomous antisemitism."[4] If it provided exceptional opportunities for unskilled Black workers and their families to move, in large numbers, into the ranks of the middle-class, this occurred in a city in which issues of race were always of tinderbox quality—a city which experienced two devastating riots within a twenty-five year span. In retrospect, however, it may be these very contradictions that served to produce the remarkable set of Black-Jewish relations that I remember as characterizing Detroit and the Catholic\non-Catholic interactions that I suspect were formative in Harry James' career and thought.

In the annals of antisemitism, Detroit holds a special place. It is irrevocably linked with the names of Henry Ford and his newspaper, the *Dearborn Independent,* and with James Coughlin, the fiery priest whose radio broadcasts in the 1930s spewed invectives against the Jews on a weekly basis. (Both men operated from suburban enclaves—Dearborn for Ford, Royal Oak for Coughlin—but that is beside the point.) According to recently uncovered correspondence between the Archbishop of Detroit, Edward (later Cardinal) Mooney, and the Vatican, Mooney was only mildly interested in curbing Coughlin and the Vatican even less so. Coughlin left a tragic stain on the Catholic Church in general and the Detroit Archdiocese in particular. How much that stain affected Mooney's successor, Archbishop John Dearden, is not known but, during the latter's episcopate a climate of inter-religious dialogue, accord and respect on the part of Catholics became increasingly discernible in the city. By the 1960s, collaborative efforts between Catholics, Jews and Protestants, such as those spearheaded by the Detroit Roundtable—one of the strongest branches of the National Conference of Christians and Jews—and by such groups as the Citizens Committee for Equal Opportunity, of which Archbishop Dearden was Vice-Chair, were commonplace.

The contradictions were equally visible on the racial front. The opportunities for economic advancement for Black residents were offset by the rigid patterns of discrimination, not only in housing but also in places of public accommodation and many sectors of employment above the unskilled level, and by the notorious reputation of the city's police department. As late as the 1950s, Detroit's hospitals routinely segregated patients by race, many restaurants and hotels refused service to Black patrons, and police maltreatment of Black Detroiters was routine.

These contradictions had several consequences. They produced, in both the Jewish and Black communities in Detroit, a fiercely committed, well-organized backlash against the city's antisemitism and racism. The Detroit chapters of the Anti-Defamation League and the American Jewish Committee were among the strongest in the country and the Detroit chapter of the National Association for the Advancement of Colored People was, for decades, the largest in the nation. At a very early period, these two sets of organizations began to engage in collaborations that, when combined with the influence of the UAW and the Democratic Party, gradually brought new, liberal leadership to the fore in the city and the state. This occurred, in fact, during the heyday of social and political liberalism in America and it could not help but have an impact on the interests and commitments of two young lads preparing for college and their subsequent careers.

To a greater extent than either of us realized at the time, those experiences also undoubtedly pointed both Harry James and I toward our life-long study of the Shoah—the annihilation of European Jewry. We are both products of an era of liberalism in American history in which one learned to have a healthy intolerance of intolerance. We are also products of a city in which we saw and experienced intolerance as a frequent occurrence. We had the good fortune of education at some of the Midwest's finest universities where our passion for justice and disdain for intolerance became disciplined by our studies, sharpened by our involvement in the numerous causes for social justice of the time, and deepened by our commitments to the precepts of our faiths. It was inevitable that when we came to a knowledge of the supreme intolerance of the modern era, we would be compelled to undertake a continuing consideration of its significance and implications for our time and the future.

Much of our consideration has focused on the large and, in many respects, tortured saga of the Christian community—both Roman Catholic and Protestant—in its response to the Shoah. Many parts of that saga remain unknown; enough is known, however, for both of us to share a decided ambivalence about the religious impulse and its prospects for contributing to a less intolerant future. I draw strength from Harry James' tireless effort as a prophetic voice within his Church on the Shoah and its implications for what he terms a post-Auschwitz Christianity. Both of us, I believe, labor in hope that "Never Again" will be as much a cry of the Christian Church as it is of the Jewish People.

1. Gerald Suttles, *The Social Construction of Communities*, (Chicago: University of Chicago Press, 1972), p. 27.
2. Ibid., p. 28.
3. Sidney, Bolkesky, *Harmony and Dissonance: Voices of Jewish Identity in Detroit, 1914-1967*, Detroit: Wayne State University Press, 1991, p. 22.
4. Ibid., p. 182.
5. Gerald Suttles, *The Social Construction of Communities*, (Chicago: University of Chicago Press, 1972), p. 27.

TEACHING LIFE
Reflections on Some Voices I Have Heard
John K. Roth

Then the Lord spoke to you out of the midst of the fire; you heard the sound
of words, but saw no form; there was only a voice. (Deuteronomy 4:12)

In 1993, Harry James Cargas published an important book called *Voices
from the Holocaust*. It has much to say because the book consists of twelve
important interviews that Cargas obtained from Simon Wiesenthal, Emil
Fackenheim, Elie Wiesel and other insightful witnesses and interpreters of the
Holocaust. The significance of Harry Cargas' many contributions to Holocaust
studies is immense. None of those contributions, however, is more notable than
his distinctive ability to engage people in thoughtful conversation, which he
then reproduces so that their voices can be heard by many others. As Cargas
keeps the focus on what others have to say, it is too easy to overlook how his
own voice is essential to create the context in which those men and women
reflect and speak. As my way of expressing gratitude and esteem to a close
friend, I want this essay to correct that oversight.

When I think of Harry James Cargas, I think of voices I have heard.
When I think of his voice, the others I have in mind are not always the voices
that I speak about the most. They are instead the ones that shape the context in
which I speak. Cargas' voice looms large among them—not because his voice
is always at the center of my attention but for the very important reason that his
ways of teaching life help to create the crucial background for the work of
teaching and writing that I gladly share with him. To put the point another way,
the voice of Harry Cargas helps me to find my own. Such an influence is as
precious as it is subtle, as forceful as it may be indirect, as challenging as it
supportive. On this occasion, then, I want to pay tribute to his voice by placing
it among other voices I have heard, ones that inform all that I have to say even
if it is only from time to time that I speak of them directly in my own teaching
and writing.

"When you write, you lay out a line of words."[1] That's how a gifted
American author named Annie Dillard begins a sensitive reflection called *The
Writing Life*. Her small book focuses on the challenges of writing well and on

the discipline that craft requires. But her meditation about writing covers even more, because *The Writing Life* is a book about teaching life.

As the voice of Harry Cargas reveals, teaching life involves multiple dimensions. At the very least, for example, it suggests communicating about life, exploring what has happened to persons, mapping the fate of societies and the destiny of traditions. In addition, teaching life implies informing, training, edifying—it moves beyond description about what has been and moves toward prescription about what ought to be. And third, of course, teaching life requires teachers who can do all these things with skill and care.

Teaching life involves lines of words—laying them out, seeing what they mean, testing their significance, wondering where they may lead. As Annie Dillard likens such lines of words to "a miner's pick, a woodcarver's gouge, a surgeon's probe,"[2] she might have Harry Cargas' voice in mind, for she is talking about lines of inquiry and questioning that show what is valuable and what is not, that differentiate beauty from ugliness, that find out what's wrong and, if possible, how to correct and even heal what is weak or diseased. Writing that way, teaching life that way—such work is as vital as it is long and hard. So, one of Dillard's lines insists, "write as if you were dying. At the same time," she adds, "assume you write for an audience consisting solely of terminal patients. That is, after all, the case. What would you begin writing," she asks, "if you knew you would die soon? What could you say to a dying person that would not enrage by its triviality?"[3]

I have never met Annie Dillard, but in *The Writing Life* there is a voice that I have heard. It belongs to a chorus of voices that have spoken deeply to me, because Dillard's words about writing sound to me like words about teaching life in its multiple dimensions. If you experience something similar in your life, you will understand that voices of this kind are often among those that work behind the scenes. Some of them one may speak about directly; others live in the silences of one's life. In either case, they are present, and they govern much that teaching life has to say.

So when I title this essay "Teaching Life: Reflections on Some Voices I Have Heard," the voices I have in mind are not always ones I have heard firsthand. They are mediated through the silence of writing and reading, and yet I want to stress that they do speak and that they communicate best, however paradoxically, when they are *heard.* That realization came home to me one day as I read Eudora Welty's autobiography, *One Writer's Beginnings.* At one point this Pulitzer Prize-winning storyteller, who has sketched so many rich portraits of life in her native Mississippi, reflects in the following way:

> Ever since I was first read to, then started reading to myself, there has never been a line read that I didn't hear. As my eyes followed the sentence, a voice was saying it silently to me. It isn't my mother's voice, or the voice of any person I can identify, certainly not my own. It is human, but inward, and it is inwardly that I listen to it. It is to me the voice of the story of the poem itself.

The cadence, whatever it is that asks you to believe, the feeling that resides in the printed word, reaches me through the reader-voice. I have supposed, but never found out, that this is the case with all readers—to read as listeners—and with all writers, to write as listeners. It may be part of the desire to write. The sound of what falls on the page begins the process of testing it for truth. . . . Whether I am right to trust so far I don't know. By now I don't know whether I could do either one, reading or writing, without the other.

My own words, when I am at work on a story, I hear too as they go, in the same voice that I hear when I read in books. When I write and the sound of it comes back to my ears, then I act to make my changes. I have always trusted this voice.[4]

The reader-voice of which Eudora Welty speaks has more than one thing to say. If each of us has a "reader-voice" that we hear as it speaks, then what it says—as well as where, when, and how it speaks most forcefully—may differ not only for each of us but also for ourselves as times and circumstances change. But in teaching life, the particularities of our different "reader-voices," I suspect, share quite a bit in common. In any case, I have encountered many meaningful voices on a path of teaching and scholarship that has forked in two directions.[5] One fork explores American culture and specifically what the concept of "the American Dream" reveals and hides. The other leads into the darkness formed by genocide and particularly the Holocaust. Thus, much of my life as a professor of philosophy has been governed by dreams and questions. Many of the dreams are visions of American life that continue to be influential in making the United States, and indeed the world, what it is today and will be tomorrow. Many of the questions are posed by Auschwitz—how and why has it scarred the earth?

To probe those lines of words, consider that a book called *Labyrinths* contains of brilliant examples of the philosophical *ficciones* composed by the Argentine master, Jorge Luis Borges, a writer who also intrigues Harry Cargas. One of them, "The Library of Babel," suggests that the universe is a Library. Although no two of its volumes are the same, the Library contains every possible book.

People dwell within this Library's "indefinite and perhaps infinite number of hexagonal galleries."[6] Among these librarians, as they are called, are some who say: If the Library contains all possible books, then "on some shelf in some hexagon . . . there must exist a book which is the formula and perfect compendium *of all the rest.*"[7] Presumably this book would clarify and justify everything. One tradition says that such a book not only exists but has even been read at least once. Although by this time nobody can identify either the reader or the book, there have been, Borges tells us, "official searchers, *inquisitors*" who have hoped to find "a clarification of humanity's basic mysteries." Apparently failure's accumulation, however, has worn them down. Presently, we are told, "no one expects to discover anything."[8]

If such futility exists, it may have something to do with what George Orwell thought would happen in *1984*. He compressed it into one grim image. Winston Smith, that novel's protagonist, lacks belief in God but does profess faith in "the spirit of Man." Soon, however, Winston will be broken. O'Brien, his interrogator, aims to ensure that Winston will learn to love Big Brother. Winston once thought O'Brien was his friend, but that hope shattered when the "friend" turned out to be one of the most cunning members of the Thought Police. A specialist in the subtleties of betrayal and human domination, O'Brien has even less use for God than Winston does. As for Winston's faith that "the spirit of Man" will prevail, O'Brien gives a blunt rebuttal: "If you want a picture of the future," he taunts, "imagine a boot stamping on a human face—forever."[9]

The journalist-scholar Gitta Sereny learned about boots stamping on human faces some time prior to 1984. Early in April 1971 she met for the first time a man named Franz Stangl. Formerly the commandant of Nazi death camps at Sobibor and Treblinka, Stangl was beginning a life sentence in a West German prison after being convicted of war crimes. Sereny got permission to interview him, hoping the result would be, as she put it, "some new truth which would contribute to the understanding of things that had never yet been understood."[10] Specifically, she wondered, could Franz Stangl have left the path that took him to Treblinka? And if he could have left that path, would his doing so have made any difference?

Sereny recorded her findings in a book called *Into That Darkness: An Examination of Conscience*. It remains among the most instructive studies of the Holocaust, which was Nazi Germany's planned total destruction of the Jewish people, the actual murder of nearly six million of them, and the annihilation of millions of non-Jewish victims who were also caught in that catastrophe. Summing up her findings, Sereny drew the following conclusions: Individuals remain responsible for their action and its consequences, but persons are and must be responsible for each other, too. What we do as individuals, Sereny contended, "is deeply vulnerable and profoundly dependent on a climate of life" that reflects "the fatal interdependence of all human actions."[11]

That phrase—"the fatal interdependence of all human actions"—bears remembering. I often hear its voice, I even hear it echoing in Harry Cargas', and, when that happens, something else resounds as well. It comes from a contemporary of Franz Stangl's. But on a summer Sunday in 1943, when Stangl was probably ordering more victims to their death at Treblinka, Reinhold Niebuhr was conducting a service of worship in a tiny village church at Heath, Massachusetts. During that service Niebuhr, who remains, arguably, the best Christian theologian in twentieth-century America, offered a famous prayer that he had written hastily that day on the back of an envelope. "God give us grace," he petitioned, "to accept with serenity the things that cannot be changed, courage to change the things that should be changed, and the wisdom to distinguish the one from the other."[12]

How does one find such grace, courage, and wisdom? I have heard part, if only a part, of a sound response to that question in the voice of a slim book that was given to me some years ago by a student. Jennipher Goodman was from Pitzer College, and she inscribed her gift with words that said: This book has made "a small but significant difference in my life. I'd like to share it with you." The book was Rainer Maria Rilke's *Letters to a Young Poet*.

Born in the Czech city of Prague, Rilke was a poet as restless as he was brilliant. He traveled extensively, but Paris was his base during an especially productive period from 1901 to 1910. It was also during these years that Rilke received his first letter from a young man named Franz Kappus. Studying in an Austrian military academy in the late autumn of 1902—Rilke's upbringing, incidentally, had included a similar interlude—Kappus was not yet 20. Like so many contemporary students, he wondered what profession he should pursue. He loved poetry—Rilke's in particular. He wanted to write, but found himself "close on the threshold of a profession which I felt to be entirely contrary to my inclinations." Feeling in need of help to decide what his future should be, Kappus one day decided to send some of his poetry to Rilke. He would see if the master found anything in it. Accompanying the poetry, Kappus sent a covering letter "in which," he later observed, "I unreservedly laid bare my heart as never before and never since to any second human being."[13]

Many weeks later Kappus received Rilke's reply. The exchange of occasional letters that continued from 1903 to 1908 became the slim volume, *Letters to a Young Poet*, which the Pitzer College student sent to me. While we do not know exactly what Kappus's first letter asked, Rilke's response indicates that the young poet wanted an evaluation of his poetry, so he could know whether he should try to become a writer. Teaching life, Rilke counseled Kappus not to imagine that such an evaluation is easily made. "Things are not all so comprehensible and expressible as one would mostly have us believe," wrote Rilke. Then he added, "Most events are inexpressible, taking place in a realm which no word has ever entered."[14]

Rilke's point was that the opinion of others is not ultimate: "You are looking outward, and that above all you should not do now," he insisted. "Nobody can counsel and help you, nobody. There is only one single way. Go into yourself."[15] By saying this, of course, Rilke was not denying the fatal interdependence of all human actions. In fact, his teaching life was counseling Kappus, relating with him, and trying to help him. But Rilke's insight was that he could do so best by pressing Kappus, as he put it, to "acknowledge to yourself whether you would have to die if it were denied you to write." Consider what is truly most important to you as you face a decision, Rilke urged, and then "build your life according to this necessity."[16]

If he followed this advice, Rilke contended, Kappus might find himself called to be an artist. On the other hand, he might not. The finding would be in the searching, and the guide for the search would be the question—one that

Harry Cargas holds dear—"What is truly most important to me?" Responding to that question, cautioned Rilke, neither is nor should be easy. Responding well requires "growing quietly and seriously throughout your whole development." Answering quickly, once-and-for-all, is not a good substitute. "Seek the depth of things," Rilke urged, and note that care is necessary in the process: "*Everything*," he insisted, "is gestation and then bringing forth."[17]

Learning such a lesson is easier said than done, as Rilke himself could attest. At the end of one of his longer letters to Kappus, this one sent from Sweden in August 1904, he counseled the young man not to think Rilke himself had found it simple to live the advice he gave. To the contrary, said Rilke, his own life had tasted difficulty and sadness. Had it been otherwise, he told Kappus, he would not have been able to write the words that might help his friend.

From such remarks one can surmise that Rilke was not always a patient man, for his advice to Kappus comes back again and again to the need for patience. "I learn it daily, learn it with pain to which I am grateful," says Rilke, "*patience* is everything."[18] Granted, not all decisions can be made patiently. Some have to be made quickly; others are demanded before we are ready. Rilke was aware of such constraints, and that recognition is one reason why he urged patience nonetheless. For life is a series of decisions, and the significance of any one of them is not restricted to a single moment. Life takes time. If some decisions must be made instantly, others need not, and the latter provide occasions that may enable us to bring things together and make them whole. In that vein, Rilke advanced the proposition that forms the most memorable portion of his *Letters to a Young Poet*:

> . . . Be patient toward all that is unsolved in your heart and . . . try to love the *questions themselves* like locked rooms and like books that are written in a very foreign tongue. Do not now seek the answers, which cannot be given you because you would not be able to live them. And the point is, to live everything. *Live* the questions now. Perhaps you will then gradually, without noticing it, live along some distant day into the answer.[19]

Romantic though he may have been, Rilke did not play down the difficulty of this advice, either. We all want answers, not more questions. But that impatience, as Harry Cargas understands, is precisely what Rilke urged Kappus to guard against, lest he decide prematurely and rashly. Decision must come, and Rilke knows it will, but he counsels that haste makes waste. Decisions that emerge from loving and living questions about what is good, right, and beautiful have a better chance of leading us to what we ought to do.

Several things happened during the teaching-life correspondence that brought Kappus and Rilke together. Kappus wrote better poetry, but he came to see what a challenging path awaited him. Rilke kept encouraging the young man, partly by urging him to "hold to what is difficult" and even to consider that, if something is difficult, that may be "a reason the more for us to do it." To illustrate what he meant, Rilke chose his example carefully: "For one human being to love another," he told Kappus, "that is perhaps the most difficult of all our tasks, the ultimate, the last test and proof, the work for which all other work is but preparation."[20] The right decisions—like the right questions—Rilke seems to be saying, are those difficult ones that teach us what love involves and how to live what love requires. The voice—the life—of Harry James Cargas embodies those lessons, too.

Related themes about life and love were beginning to form a continent and an ocean away from Rilke's Europe in 1945. Best known for his classic, *Invisible Man*, American novelist Ralph Ellison was working on a different narrative when what he identifies as "blue-toned laughter" began to dominate his imagination.[21] Eventually that laughter compelled him to give full expression to its voice, which belonged to an invisible man "who had been forged," the author noted, "in the underground of American experience and yet managed to emerge less angry than ironic."[22] That irony would lead Ellison's invisible man to remark—and he speaks for more than himself—that "I'd like to hear five recordings of Louis Armstrong, playing and singing all at the same time":

> Cold empty bed; springs hard as lead; pains in my head; / Feel like old Ned— What did I do to be so Black and Blue? / No joys for me; no company; even the mouse ran from my house. / All my life thru I've been so Black and Blue. / I'm white inside—it don't help my case. / Cause I can't hide what is on my face. I'm so forlorn; / Life's just a thorn, my heart is torn. Why was I born? / What did I do to be so Black and Blue?[23]

Ellison's postponed story was to be about an American pilot. Downed by the *Luftwaffe* and interned in a Nazi POW camp, he was the highest-ranking officer there and, thus, owing to war's conventions, the spokesman for his fellow-prisoners. Ellison's pilot, like the author who created him, was an African-American. Prisoner of racists and also the "leader" of prisoners who in normal American circumstances would not see him as their equal, let alone as their superior, the pilot would have to navigate his way between the democratic ideals he affirmed and "the prevailing mystique of race and color." This dilemma, Ellison adds, was to be "given a further twist of the screw by [the African-American pilot's] awareness that once the peace was signed, the German camp commander would immigrate to the United States and immediately take advantage of freedoms that were denied the most heroic of Negro servicemen."[24]

The voice of Ellison's pilot, like that of *Invisible Man*, would seem to echo another African-American writer, the poet Langston Hughes, whose 1938 poem, "Let America Be America Again," insists: "Oh yes, / I say it plain, / America never was America to me, / And yet I swear this oath— / America will be! / An ever-living seed, / Its dream / Lies deep in the heart of me."[25] For

Invisible Man ends where it begins: Ellison's character is in the underground hideout where American life has driven him. He is awakening from a state of hibernation, as he calls it, and his awakening entails writing. Thus, in the novel's epilogue—making poetry out of invisibility, it is, in my judgment, one of the most insightful writings produced by an American author—Ellison expresses his character's outlook as follows:

> So why do I write, torturing myself to put it down? Because in spite of myself
> I've learned some things. Without the possibility of action, all knowledge
> comes to one labeled "file and forget," and I can neither file nor forget. Nor
> will certain ideas forget me; they keep filing away at my lethargy, my
> complacency. . . . So it is that now I denounce and defend, or feel prepared to
> defend. I condemn and affirm, say no and say yes, say yes and say no. I
> denounce because though implicated and partially responsible, I have been
> hurt to the point of abysmal pain, hurt to the point of invisibility. And I defend
> because in spite of all I find that I love. In order to get some of it down I have
> to love. I sell you no phony forgiveness, I'm a desperate man—but too much
> of your life will be lost, its meaning lost, unless you approach it as much
> through love as through hate. So I approach it through division. So I denounce
> and I defend and I hate and I love.[26]

In the wake of the Great Depression, another American writer, poet Archibald MacLeish, worked with a set of photographs that documented devastation of American ground in the 1930's. "The original purpose," explained MacLeish, "had been to write some sort of text to which these photographs might serve as commentary." Finding in them vividly what he named a "stubborn inward livingness," MacLeish reversed that plan and produced not "a book of poems illustrated by photographs" but "a book of photographs illustrated by a poem."[27]

MacLeish called the book *Land of the Free*. Its final page pictures a wizened, old man. Hat torn, his soiled suit worn, he does not have it made. And yet he's looking squarely at the camera, jaw set, unsmiling, eyes glinting. Apparently he's asking questions, too. They are not without discouragement, but no one would confuse his expression with despair. It's got too much insistence, too much resistance, too much wonder and determination for that.

"The Sound Track"—that's what MacLeish called his poetic accompaniment to *Land of the Free*. Like features of that old man's face, some of its closing lines—they are among my favorites—sound like this:

> We wonder whether the great American dream
> Was the singing of locusts out of the grass to the west and the
> West is behind us now:
>
> The West wind's away from us

We wonder if the liberty is done:
The dreaming is finished . . .

We wonder

We don't know

We're asking[28]

Wondering, not knowing, asking—teaching life involves all three and more. Thus, I find myself listening to another poetic American. This voice differs, however, from MacLeish's masculinity. Feminist instead, it belongs to Adrienne Rich. The title she gave to her 1991 book of poems was what attracted me to read them. She calls it *An Atlas of the Difficult World*. That title, and the poems within Rich's book, are well worth thinking about.

Consider, for instance, that in the mythology of the ancient Greeks, Atlas was a Titan. He challenged Zeus and paid a price. His punishment was to hold up the sky, although he is sometimes pictured as the one who must hold up the earth. In any case, Atlas can make us think of strength.

Most often, however, the word 'atlas' makes us think of something else. It suggests a book of maps. In this sense, an atlas does not hold up the earth, much less the sky, and yet it does suggest strength of another kind. A good atlas can help us to know where in the world we are, where the earth has been, and what has been happening in it. These days, of course, most atlases have gone out of date. The map-drawing and map-revising businesses are thriving with the many political and geographical upheavals that the world has witnessed in recent months. Good maps, carefully drawn, are needed for teaching life to help us see where we have been and where we are going.

As the title for a book of poetry, *An Atlas of the Difficult World* suggests a variety of themes: poems as maps, for example, or the poet as Atlas (in this case in feminine or even feminist form). Rich's poems are indeed about a difficult world, one that she tries to map and perhaps to hold in ways that keep the skies from falling or the earth from going completely out of orbit.

Adrienne Rich's *Atlas of the Difficult World* maps poisoned environments. It explores issues of race, class, and gender. It tracks the Holocaust and its legacy. Rich protests against the waste that forgets, ignores, or marginalizes "those who could bind, join, reweave, cohere, replenish . . . those needed to teach, advise, persuade, weigh arguments . . . those urgently needed for the work of perception."[29] This is the work that Harry James Cargas does. He is an Atlas for a difficult world.

No tribute to Harry Cargas could be complete without the voice of Elie Wiesel, for his voice and Cargas' have long been linked. So it is worth noting that some time ago Wiesel, survivor of Auschwitz and recipient of the 1986

Nobel Peace Prize, convened a meeting of seventy-four Nobel laureates in France. Among other things, that conference produced a list of 16 conclusions. One of them states: "Mankind's wealth...stems from its diversity. This diversity must be protected in all its aspects—cultural, biological, philosophical, spiritual. To this end, the virtues of tolerance, listening to others, and refusing ultimate truths must be unendingly reiterated."

Such a statement is not free of problems, but it strikes some important notes for reasons that another Holocaust survivor, Primo Levi, puts forth powerfully in his book, *Survival in Auschwitz*. Early on, Levi describes his camp initiation. Once he reached out a window to quench his painful thirst with an icicle. An SS guard immediately snatched it away from him. "*Warum?*" Levi asked him, only to be told with a shove, "*Hier ist kein warum.*"[30] Levi's "why?" sought explanation. He got none, because questions of life and death were already settled there. No asking was permitted the likes of Levi. In Auschwitz no "why?" existed—not as question and certainly not as satisfying explanation, either.

Auschwitz raises every "why?" but it did not tolerate the kind Levi posed. Paradoxically the Holocaust was beyond "why?" because the minds that produced it were convinced they "understood" why. They "recognized" that one religion had superseded another. They "comprehended" that one race was superior to every other. They "saw," what nature's laws decreed, namely, that there was what they deemed "life unworthy of life." Thus, they "realized" who deserved to live and who deserved to die.

Hitler and his followers were beyond "why?" because they "knew" why. Knowing they were "right" their "knowing" made them killers. One can argue, of course, that such "knowing" perverted rationality and mocked morality. It did. And yet to say that much is too little, for one must ask about the sources of such perversion. When that asking occurs, part of its trail leads to the tendency of human reason to presume that indeed it can, at least in principle, figure everything out and understand why.

People are less likely to savage and annihilate each other, they are less likely to create or legitimate boots stamping on human laces forever, when they ask "why?" instead of "knowing" why, when their minds are less made up than opened up through questioning. There may be no voice more important to hear about the fatal interdependence of all human actions than that one.

At the beginning of his classic memoir, *Night*, which details his experiences in Auschwitz when he was 15, Elie Wiesel introduces one of his teachers. His name was Moshe, and the year was 1941. Although the Holocaust was under way, it had not yet reached Wiesel's hometown. One day the 12-year-old Wiesel asked his teacher, "And why do you pray, Moshe?" The reply Wiesel heard said, "I pray to the God within me that He will give me the strength to ask Him the right questions." Wiesel adds, "We talked like this nearly every evening."[31]

Few, if any, have asked more of the right questions than Harry James Cargas. Hearing and living them is unlikely to put Borges's "Book of books" into our hands, but there may be no better way to find our way in life's labyrinth. And so in a spirit akin to that which lives in Harry James Cargas' voice, as well as in the exchange between Elie Wiesel and his teacher, Moshe— a spirit that seeks to nourish the strength that is needed to keep asking the right questions so that they can be heard and lived—let these reflections conclude with words from sixteenth-century England. Their voice is a hymn that asks:

> God be in my head,
> And in my understanding;
> God be in mine eyes,
> And in my looking.
> God be in my mouth,
> And in my speaking.
> God be in my heart,
> And in my thinking.
> God be at mine end,
> And at my departing.
> Amen.

1. Annie Dillard, *The Writing Life* (New York: HarperCollins, 1990), p. 3.

2. Ibid., p. 3.

3. Ibid., p. 68.

4. Eudora Welty, *One Writer's Beginnings* (New York: Warner Books, 1985), pp. 12-13.

5. Harry Cargas' life and my own share more than a little in common. In addition to being Christians who have devoted much of our teaching and scholarship to Holocaust studies, we also share concerns about American culture, literature, philosophy, and religious thought.

6. Ibid., p. 51.

7. Ibid., p. 56.

8. Ibid., p. 55.

9. George Orwell, *1984* (New York: Signet Books, 1983), p. 220.

10. Gitta Sereny, *Into That Darkness: An Examination of Conscience* (New York: Vintage Books, 1983), p. 23.

11. Ibid., pp. 367, 15.

12. Robert McAfee Brown, ed., *The Essential Reinhold Niebuhr: Selected Essays and Addresses* (New Haven: Yale University Press, 1986), xxiv.

13. Rainer Maria Rilke, *Letters to a Young Poet*, trans. M. D. Herter Norton (New York: W.W. Norton, 1954), p. 12.

14. Ibid., p. 17.

15. Ibid., p. 18.

16. Ibid., pp. 18-19.

17. Ibid., p. 24, 29.

18. Ibid., p. 30.

19. Ibid., p. 35.

20. Ibid., pp. 53-54.

21. Ralph Ellison, *Invisible Man* (New York: Vintage Books, 1982), xiii.

22. Ibid., xv.

23. Ibid., pp. 7-8.

24. Ibid., x.

25. Quoted from Robert H. Fossum and John K. Roth, eds. *American Ground: Vistas, Visions and Revisions* (New York: Paragon House, 1988), p. 350.

26. Ellison, *Invisible Man*, pp. 566-67.

27. Archibald MacLeish, *Land of the Free* (New York: Da Capo Press, 1977), p. 89. Harry Cargas has done something similar in *Shadows of the Holocaust: A Christian Response to the Holocaust* (New York: Crossroad, 1990), which creates a kind of "sound track" for Holocaust photographs. This book, incidentally, also contains a statement that has become especially important to me. Once again Harry Cargas drew out the thought from another, for this passage comes from Elie Wiesel's foreword: "The Holocaust demands interrogation and calls everything into question. Traditional ideas and acquired values, philosophical systems and social theories—all must be revised in the shadow of Birkenau" (ix).

28. Ibid., pp. 83-84, 88.

29. Adrienne Rich, *An Atlas of the Difficult World: Poems 1988-1991* (New York: W.W. Norton, 1991), p. 11.

30. Primo Levi, *Survival in Auschwitz*, trans. Stuart Woolf (New York: Collier Books, 1976), p. 25.

31. Elie Wiesel, *Night*, trans. Stella Rodway (New York: Bantam Books, 1986), p. 3.

IN MEMORY AND HOPE
Six Poems for Harry James Cargas
William Heyen

Candy

"All we could do was to remember it, to continue to deal in our memories, to create out of them poems and stories, history and reminiscences. It was the only way through which that irrevocably destroyed past could survive. Vilna had once been a red giant star in the firmament and had once illuminated the Jewish universe. It had now been extinguished. It had become a white dwarf star, emitting a feeble light visible only to those who knew of its existence." Lucy S. Dawidowicz

I dreamed I worked in a shop in old Vilna,
there again this dim morning for the thousandth time.
First the boiling of sugar and milk in a large cauldron
over an open fire, then the stirring in of fruit syrups
with a wooden paddle. Was it you who helped me
carry the cauldron to a trough, and pour?

We kneaded the smoky mixture with our smoking hands,
then pushed it into a metal roller. Then the cutter.
That's all I remember, except for a huge map hanging
in the heavens, festooned with hundreds of tiny bulbs
where Jews had lived for centuries. The bulbs blinked
on and off for a while, then one by one blinked off....

We taste them, we taste them again, we taste them,
we taste them again, we cannot taste them but
for how long O are we among the last we
taste them we cannot taste them their
living sweetness in this air with our tongues we
taste them in this dreamed dim light of old Vilna....

You had left me. Where were you? Were you there?
I woke with the taste of red and green candies
in my mind, and in my chest a loss of light
sweet beyond redeeming – all that was left, for now,
of that city, until our next passage over cobblestones
through the feeble starlight of old Vilna.

Kristallmusik

A Lepzig street.
Here, brownshirts
bust their way

to the third floor,
fling open balcony doors,
shout something about

blessings from above.
Several wheel out
an upright piano,

& batter it
through the balustrade.
It falls, it

is still falling
to the street this day
of *Kristallmusik*.

Here, inevitably,
its wooden case
breaks open,

revealing what looks like
a glass harp,
unplaying.

Parity

It is, apparently, a fact,
that at Auschwitz in its season
occurred at least one soccer game
between the *SS* who, of course,
administered all deathcamps,
& the *SK*, the *Sonderkommando*,
the Special Squad, mainly Jews
whose daily survival depended
on beating order into arrivals,
on shorning, sorting clothes,
keeping the ovens operating,
pulling corpses from the gas,
removing gold teeth, checking
orifices for coins & gems,
disposing of ashes....

In *The Drowned and the Saved*,
Primo Levi says that the *SS*
could not conceivably
have played against others
than these "crematorium ravens"
of their own creation. Forced
to help kill their own people,
embraced & corrupted
by the satanic Aryan engine—
with these existed parity,
a logical opposition &
the conjoining of spirit
for mutual health & benefit:
Come, said the *SS*,
we will play.

"Christmas Celebration of *SS* Guards in Neuengamme"

On page 1058 of *The Encyclopedia of the Holocaust*,
at the center table, fourth down on the left side,
artless face resigned to the camera,
myself of a sudden & back in my previous life.

I now know that I knew: my camp is poised
for large transports, Jews from Hungary & Poland.
Mein Leben ist vorbei. Of dozens, at this instant,
no one is smiling. Thus I hate our prisoners,

even the dead & dead-to-come, hate us all
& myself seeing myself here, a Heyen head....

But this is Christmas; candles set in tall tapered
ceramic canisters incised with hearts;

a bottle of wine in front of each of us; & what seems
an angel in a burst of glare against the back wall O
I know how long I've lasted, wandering spirit,
& will. I would get drunk that evening, &,

in barracks, remove my boots as though they were
a mummy's leather skin, & sleep, & wake,
disgusted, sick of the wine, *und* cake, *und* cameraderie,
und schnaps, *und* work, but then get on with it.

The Bear

Was alone, was carrying her bear with her.
Was alone, was carrying her bear with her.
Was alone, was carrying her bear with her,
bear to counsel, comfort, & protect her.

Arrived with a thousand other children
carrying toys to keep them quiet.
Was alone, was carrying her bear with her.
Was alone, was carrying her bear with her.

In the gas, her bear clawed free of her.
In the gas, her bear clawed free of her.
She held her bear as tightly as she could,
but in the gas her bear clawed free of her.

The mind & heart of her bear are wool.
The mind & heart of her bear are wool.
Its eyes black & shiny as tiny mirrors,
her bear is stuffed with wool.

Was alone, was carrying her bear with her,
its eyes black & shiny as tiny mirrors,
its heart wool, its mind wool,
Was alone, was carrying her bear with her.

The Others

Anne Roiphe tells of living in Munich in 1957,
in an elegant apartment over a field
where masses of Nazis had rallied.
Each day on the cold windowpane she wrote her name.
She was there, her name said, & all of them were gone.

One day her landlady invited her for tea – patterns
of edelweis on cups, of buttercups in napkins
over meadows of memory. Then Anne noticed,
above a sideboard, two framed photographs,
bordered in black, the woman's two sons,

each wearing the uniform of the *SS*.... Anne writes,
I am a Jewish woman, I said to her,
and stood up to go. I thought so, she said,
and passed me my tea, and that was all that happened....
I could find no pity for her,...

& at the instant Anne said this, I was riven by light,
& had no pity for her, who I was,
or for the woman who had lost her sons, who I was,
or for the *SS*, who I was, or for Anne's murdered family,
who I was, or for myself, who at that instant I was,

& I hated us all, & the mute God we call
out of our graves in sky on earth it is not time,
is it, as Anne concludes, *It's time to forgive God,*
to take up the covenant again, I say, stand up
and sit down with theothers. But I don't, and I do.

CONTRIBUTORS

ALAN L. BERGER is Raddock Eminent Scholar Chair of Holocaust Studies and Director of Judaic Studies, Florida Atlantic University. His publications include *Methodology in the Academic Teaching of the Holocaust, Crisis and Covenant: The Holocaust in American Jewish Fiction* and *Children of Job: American Second-Generation Witnesses to the Holocaust.*

RACHEL FELDHAY BRENNER teaches at the University of Wisconsin – Madison. She has written extensively on Canadian literature, her publications including *Assimilation and Assertion: The Response to the Holocaust in Mordecai Richler's Writing* and *A.M. Klein, The Father of Canadian Jewish Literature.*

EUGENE J. FISHER is Executive Secretary of the Secretariat for Catholic-Jewish Relations of the National Conference of Catholic Bishops. Included among his many publications are *On Jews and Judaism: 1979-1986* and *Spiritual Pilgrimage: Texts on Jews and Judaism: 1979-1995* (both with Leon Klenicki) and *Interwoven Distances: Jews and Christians through the Ages.*

ZEV GARBER, Co-Editor of this volume, is Professor and Chair of Jewish Studies, Los Angeles Valley College and served as Visiting Professor in Religious Studies at the University of California at Riverside. A Past President of the National Association of Professors of Hebrew and Editor-in-Chief of Studies in the Shoah series (UPA), his publications include *Methodology in the Academic Teaching of the Holocaust, Shoah: The Paradigmatic Genocide,* and *What Kind of God?*

WILLIAM HEYEN, an American poet of German heritage, is the author of *Erika, The Swastika Poems* and many other volumes.

RICHARD LIBOWITZ, Co-Editor of this volume, is on the faculties of Temple and Saint Joseph's Universities. A Vice President of the Philadelphia Center on the Holocaust, Genocide and Human Rights, he is a member of the Program and Publications Committees of the Annual Scholars' Conference and the editorial board of Studies in Shoah. His own writings include *Methodology in the Academic Teaching of the Holocaust, Faith and Freedom* and *The Holocaust: Lessons for the Third Generation.*

FRANKLIN H. LITTELL, Emeritus Professor, Temple University, and Ida E. King Distinguished Visiting Professor at Richard Stockton College of New Jersey, is the father of Holocaust education in the United States. His many publications include *The German Phoenix* and *The Crucifixion of the Jews.* He is co-founder of the Annual Scholars' Conference on the Holocaust and the German Church Struggle.

MARCIA SACHS LITTELL is Director of the National Academy for Holocaust and Genocide Teacher Training at the Richard Stockton College of New Jersey and Executive Director of the Annual Scholars' Conference on the Holocaust and the German Church Struggle. Her most recent publication is *Confronting the Holocaust: A Mandate for the 21st Century.*

HUBERT LOCKE is John and Marguerite Corbally Professor of Public Service, Dean Emeritus, Graduate School of Public Affairs, University of Washington and Director of the William O. Douglas Institute. Co-founder of the Annual Scholars' Conference on the Holocaust and the German Church Struggle, his writings include *The German Church Struggle and the Holocaust, Letters from Moabite Prison* and *Remembrance and Reconciliation.*

JAMES MOORE is Associate Professor of Theology at Valparaiso University (Indiana). He is on the editorial board of Studies in Shoah, an educational consultant to the Philadelphia Center for the Holocaust, Genocide and Human Rights and the author of *Christian Theology after the Shoah.*

JACOB NEUSNER, prolific scholar, author and lecturer, teaches at the University of South Florida (Tampa), where he is Graduate Research Professor of Religious Studies, and Bard College. He is the author of more than six hundred volumes, including *Stranger at Home, A Short History of Judaism: Three Meals, Three Epochs* and *Death and Birth of Judaism: The Impact of Christianity, Secularism and the Holocaust on Jewish Faith.*

DAVID PATTERSON is Dean of the University Honors Program at the University of Memphis. His publications include *The Shriek of Silence: A Phenomenology of the Holocaust Novel* and *In Dialogue and Dilemma with Elie Wiesel.*

JOHN T. PAWLIKOWSKI, O.S.M., is Professor of Social Ethics at Catholic Theological Union in Chicago. His books include *The Challenge of the Holocaust for Christians, Christ in the Light of the Christian-Jewish Dialogue* and *Jesus and the Theology of Israel.*

CAROL RITTNER, R.S.M., is Distinguished Professor of Religion at The Richard Stockton College of New Jersey. She is the author of numerous articles on the Holocaust and the editor of several books, including, *Elie Wiesel: Between Memory and Hope* and *Different Voices: Women and the Holocaust* (with John Roth).

JOHN ROTH is Pitzer Professor of Philosophy, Claremont McKenna College. His books include *A Consuming Fire: Encounters with Elie Wiesel and the Holocaust* and *Holocaust: Religious & Philosophical Implications* (with Michael Berenbaum). In 1988, he was named "Professor of the Year" by the Council for the Advancement and Support of Education.

PIERRE SAUVAGE, a filmmaker, is best known for "Triumph of the Spirit", a tribute to the residents of the village of Le Chambon-sur-Lignon. He is President of the Friends of Le Chambon.

ANDRÉ STEIN, a survivor of the Holocaust, is a psychotherapist in Toronto and Professor Emeritus, Department of Sociology, University of Toronto. His current manuscript is entitled "God and His Children—A Joint Venture."

NECHAMA TEC recounted the means of her survival in *Dry Tears* and *When Light Pierced the Darkness.* She is Professor of Sociology at the University of Connecticut, Stamford.

KURT VONNEGUT, the author of *Cat's Cradle*, *Slaughterhouse Five* and many other popular works is a veteran of the Second World War.

ELIE WIESEL, Andrew Mellon Professor in the Humanities at Boston University, received the 1986 Nobel Peace Prize. *Night* is perhaps the best known of his more than two dozen books.

LEON WELLS, a survivor, was appointed to the United States Holocaust Memorial Council by President Jimmy Carter. His writings include *Janowska Road* and *Who Speaks for the Vanquished? American Jewish Leaders and the Holocaust*.

INDEX

Source Index

South Florida Studies in the History of Judaism

| 240187 | Jewish Law from Moses to the Mishnah | Neusner |
| 240188 | The Language and the Law of God | Calabi |

South Florida Academic Commentary Series

243001	The Talmud of Babylonia, An Academic Commentary, Volume XI, Bavli Tractate Moed Qatan	Neusner
243002	The Talmud of Babylonia, An Academic Commentary, Volume XXXIV, Bavli Tractate Keritot	Neusner
243003	The Talmud of Babylonia, An Academic Commentary, Volume XVII, Bavli Tractate Sotah	Neusner
243004	The Talmud of Babylonia, An Academic Commentary, Volume XXIV, Bavli Tractate Makkot	Neusner
243005	The Talmud of Babylonia, An Academic Commentary, Volume XXXII, Bavli Tractate Arakhin	Neusner
243006	The Talmud of Babylonia, An Academic Commentary, Volume VI, Bavli Tractate Sukkah	Neusner
243007	The Talmud of Babylonia, An Academic Commentary, Volume XII, Bavli Tractate Hagigah	Neusner
243008	The Talmud of Babylonia, An Academic Commentary, Volume XXVI, Bavli Tractate Horayot	Neusner
243009	The Talmud of Babylonia, An Academic Commentary, Volume XXVII, Bavli Tractate Shebuot	Neusner
243010	The Talmud of Babylonia, An Academic Commentary, Volume XXXIII, Bavli Tractate Temurah	Neusner
243011	The Talmud of Babylonia, An Academic Commentary, Volume XXXV, Bavli Tractates Meilah and Tamid	Neusner
243012	The Talmud of Babylonia, An Academic Commentary, Volume VIII, Bavli Tractate Rosh Hashanah	Neusner
243013	The Talmud of Babylonia, An Academic Commentary, Volume V, Bavli Tractate Yoma	Neusner
243014	The Talmud of Babylonia, An Academic Commentary, Volume XXXVI, Bavli Tractate Niddah	Neusner
243015	The Talmud of Babylonia, An Academic Commentary, Volume XX, Bavli Tractate Baba Qamma	Neusner
243016	The Talmud of Babylonia, An Academic Commentary, Volume XXXI, Bavli Tractate Bekhorot	Neusner
243017	The Talmud of Babylonia, An Academic Commentary, Volume XXX, Bavli Tractate Hullin	Neusner
243018	The Talmud of Babylonia, An Academic Commentary, Volume VII, Bavli Tractate Besah	Neusner
243019	The Talmud of Babylonia, An Academic Commentary, Volume X, Bavli Tractate Megillah	Neusner
243020	The Talmud of Babylonia, An Academic Commentary, Volume XXVIII, Bavli Tractate Zebahim A. Chapters I through VII	Neusner
243021	The Talmud of Babylonia, An Academic Commentary, Volume XXI, Bavli Tractate Baba Mesia, A. Chapters I through VI	Neusner

243112	The Talmud of the Land of Israel: An Academic Commentary of the Second, Third, and Fourth Divisions, IV. Yerushalmi Tractate Yoma	Neusner
243113	The Talmud of the Land of Israel: An Academic Commentary of the Second, Third, and Fourth Divisions, V. Yerushalmi Tractate Pesahim A. Chapters One through Six, Based on the English Translation of Baruch M. Bokser with Lawrence Schiffman	Neusner
243114	The Talmud of the Land of Israel: An Academic Commentary of the Second, Third, and Fourth Divisions, V. Yerushalmi Tractate Pesahim B. Chapters Seven through Ten and The Structure of Yerushalmi Pesahim, Based on the English Translation of Baruch M. Bokser with Lawrence Schiffman	Neusner
243115	The Talmud of the Land of Israel: An Academic Commentary of the Second, Third, and Fourth Divisions, VI. Yerushalmi Tractate Sukkah	Neusner
243116	The Talmud of the Land of Israel: An Academic Commentary of the Second, Third, and Fourth Divisions, VII. Yerushalmi Tractate Besah	Neusner
243117	The Talmud of the Land of Israel: An Academic Commentary of the Second, Third, and Fourth Divisions, VIII. Yerushalmi Tractate Taanit	Neusner
243118	The Talmud of the Land of Israel: An Academic Commentary of the Second, Third, and Fourth Divisions, IX. Yerushalmi Tractate Megillah	Neusner

South Florida-Rochester-Saint Louis
Studies on Religion and the Social Order

245001	Faith and Context, Volume 1	Ong
245002	Faith and Context, Volume 2	Ong
245003	Judaism and Civil Religion	Breslauer
245004	The Sociology of Andrew M. Greeley	Greeley
245005	Faith and Context, Volume 3	Ong
245006	The Christ of Michelangelo	Dixon
245007	From Hermeneutics to Ethical Consensus Among Cultures	Bori
245008	Mordecai Kaplan's Thought in a Postmodern Age	Breslauer
245009	No Longer Aliens, No Longer Strangers	Eckardt
245010	Between Tradition and Culture	Ellenson
245011	Religion and the Social Order	Neusner
245012	Christianity and the Stranger	Nichols
245013	The Polish Challenge	Czosnyka
245014	Islam and the Question of Minorities	Sonn
245015	Religion and the Political Order	Neusner
245016	The Ecology of Religion	Neusner
245017	The Shaping of an American Islamic Discourse	Waugh/Denny
245018	The Muslim Brotherhood and the Kings of Jordan, 1945–1993	Boulby
245019	Muslims on the Americanization Path	Esposito/Haddad

South Florida International Studies in Formative Christianity and Judaism